# Lecture Notes in Computer Sci

*Commenced Publication in 1973*
Founding and Former Series Editors:
Gerhard Goos, Juris Hartmanis, and Jan van Leeuw..

T0238062

## Editorial Board

Arosha K. Bandara   Mark Burgess (Eds.)

# Inter-Domain Management

First International Conference on Autonomous
Infrastructure, Management and Security, AIMS 2007
Oslo, Norway, June 21-22, 2007
Proceedings

 Springer

Volume Editors

Arosha K. Bandara
The Open University
Wlton Hall Campus, Milton Keynes, MK 76AA, UK
E-mail: a.k.bandara@open.ac.uk

Mark Burgess
Oslo University College
PO Box 4, St Olavs Plass, 0130 Oslo Norway
E-mail: mark@iu.hio.no

Library of Congress Control Number: 2007928329

CR Subject Classification (1998): C.2, D.4.4, H.3, H.4

LNCS Sublibrary: SL 5 – Computer Communication Networks
and Telecommunications

ISSN        0302-9743
ISBN-10     3-540-72985-2 Springer Berlin Heidelberg New York
ISBN-13     978-3-540-72985-3 Springer Berlin Heidelberg New York

Springer is a part of Springer Science+Business Media

springer.com

© Springer-Verlag Berlin Heidelberg 2007
Printed in Germany

Typesetting: Camera-ready by author, data conversion by Scientific Publishing Services, Chennai, India
Printed on acid-free paper      SPIN: 12074792      06/3180      5 4 3 2 1 0

# Preface

Research needs ideas, discourse and experimentation in order to thrive, but more than ever we are expected to make research immediately 'relevant' and available to society and the world of commerce. Of these three poles (ideas, discourse and experimentation), ideas lie farthest from a finished product, and it is therefore ideas that are most easily left behind in the rush to catch the gravy train. The pressure to prioritize applications rather than understanding hinders researchers from thinking deeply about problems, and in the worst case prevents us from truly understanding and innovating.

The first Autonomous Infrastructure Management and Security conference (AIMS 2007) was proposed as an act of optimism by the leaders of the EMANICS Network of Excellence in Network and Service Management. It was a proposal aimed at avoiding the tar-pit of "apply existing knowledge only, " to reach out for new ideas that might expand our network of concepts and solutions.

There are already many excellent conferences in the field of Network of System Management : LISA, IM, NOMS, DSOM, Policy Workshop, etc. Although there is an overlap, both in attendance and ideas, AIMS does not compete with any of these. Rather we have sought a strong cross-disciplinary forum, in which novelty and discussion are made paramount. An additional objective of AIMS is to provide a forum for doctoral students, the future leaders of our research, to discuss their research with a wider audience and receive training to help make their research careers successful. To this end, AIMS incorporates a European PhD Student Symposium and a tutorial programme that covers a broad range of topics.

We have sought sometimes bold or ambitious ideas, even those that are unfinished, and this naturally invites controversy. We have ensured nevertheless the highest standard, and each paper in this volume has received not merely acceptance, but at least one enthusiastic endorsement from a referee. For the main track, 58 submissions were received and 14 were accepted. For the European PhD symposium, 31 submissions were received and 18 accepted. Of the 15 tutorials proposed, ten were provided.

The AIMS conference was arranged and sponsored by the IST EMANICS Network of Excellence (#26854), in cooperation with the ACM. This yielded an established network of experts in the field of network and service management. Networks are not static of course, they grow as meaningful dialogue pushes at the borders of the established connections, spreading into other fields. Where should one draw the borders of a network? This is a question that some of our contributors have asked in their work. Canright and Engø-Monsen tell us that the natural borders in a network can be defined where dialogue stops, and one-way communication begins. So we have fashioned the AIMS conference around dialogue, not just presentation. With short presentations and extensive, guided discussion of each paper, it is our goal to capture the spirit of scientific discourse, and to inspire and propel the PhD students to be the next generation of experts in our field.

We would like to thank everyone who gave their time to the project, either as a contributor or as an organizer. We are grateful to the Programme Committee, reviewers and to the organizers of students symposium and tutorial tracks for their efforts. Most of all we thank the authors of the papers for allowing us to realize the goal of our conference.

During the conference, we also benefited from student volunteers and behind-the-scenes administrators who mobilized the conference smoothly and seamlessly. The conference was supported by the EMANICS Network of Excellence (http://www.emanics.org).

June 2007                                                    Arosha Bandara
                                                             Mark Burgess

# Organization

AIMS 2007 was organized by the EC IST-EMANICS Network of Excellence (#26854) in cooperation with ACM SIGAPP, SIGMIS and Oslo University College.

## Main Conference Chairs

Arosha Bandara      Open University, UK
Mark Burgess      Oslo University College, Norway

## Student Symposium Chair

Rolf Stadler      Royal Institute of Technology, Sweden

## Tutorial Coordinators

Isabelle Chrisment      LORIA, France
David Hausheer      University of Zurich, Switzerland

## Student Symposium Technical Programme Committee

Rolf Stadler      Royal Institute of Technology, Sweden
Gyorgy Dan      Royal Institute of Technology, Sweden
Emil Lupu      Imperial College London, UK
Joan Serrat      Universitat Politècnica de Catalunya, Spain
Burkhard Stiller      University of Zurich, Switzerland
Felix Wu      University of California Davis, USA

## Local Arrangements

Conference Coordinator      Mark Burgess
Finance Coordinator      Marianne Kjær Bakke
Travel and Finance Coordinator      Gro Birgitte Ruste
Marketing Liason      Kjersti Hilden Smørvik
Conference Registration      Jon Ørstavik
Conference Design      Mark Burgess

## Technical Programme Committee

| | |
|---|---|
| Arosha Bandara | The Open University, UK |
| Jan Bergstra | University of Amsterdam, The Netherlands |
| Claudio Bartolini | HP Labs, USA |
| Artur Binczewski | Poznan Supercomputing and Networking Center, Poland |
| Mark Burgess | Oslo University College, Norway |
| Geoffrey Canright | Telenor Research, Norway |
| Isabelle Chrisment | LORIA, Nancy University, France |
| Alva Couch | Tufts University, USA |
| Gabi Dreo | University of Federal Armed Forces Munich, Germany |
| Olivier Festor | INRIA, France |
| David Hausheer | University of Zurich, Switzerland |
| Heinz-Gerd Hegering | Leibniz Supercomputing Center, Germany |
| Alexander Keller | IBM, USA |
| Karst Koymans | University of Amsterdam, The Netherlands |
| Jorge Lobo | IBM Research, USA |
| Emil Lupu | Imperial College London, UK |
| Hanan Lutfiyya | University of Western Ontario, Canada |
| George Pavlou | University of Surrey, UK |
| Aiko Pras | University of Twente, The Netherlands |
| Helmut Reiser | Leibniz Supercomputing Center, Germany |
| Frode Eika Sandnes | Oslo University College, Norway |
| Jacques Sauve | UFCG, Brazil |
| Jürgen Schönwälder | Jacobs University Bremen, Germany |
| Joan Serrat | Universitat Politècnica de Catalunya, Spain |
| Morris Sloman | Imperial College London, UK |
| Rolf Stadler | Royal Institute of Technology, Sweden |
| Burkhard Stiller | University of Zurich, Switzerland |
| John Strassner | Motorola Inc., USA |

## Additional Reviewers

| | |
|---|---|
| Cristian Morariu | University of Zurich, Switzerland |
| Edgar Magana | Cisco Systems, USA |
| Ha Manh Tran | Jacobs University Bremen, Germany |
| Helmut Reiser | Leibniz-Supercomputing Centre, Germany |
| Isabelle Chrisment | LORIA - University of Nancy, France |
| Marco Aurlio Spohn | Universidade Federal de Campina Grande, Brazil |
| Siri Fagernes | Oslo University College, Norway |
| Thomas Bocek | University of Zurich, Switzerland |
| Tiago Fioreze | University of Twente, The Netherlands |

# Table of Contents

## Autonomous Infrastructure and Security

## Management Models

## Policy Interactions

## Security Management

# On the Impact of Management Instrumentation Models on Web Server Performance: A JMX Case Study⋆

Abdelkader Lahmadi, Anca Ghitescu, Laurent Andrey, and Olivier Festor

LORIA - INRIA Lorraine - Université de Nancy 2
615 rue du Jardin Botanique
F-54602 Villers-lès-Nancy, France
{Abdelkader.Lahmadi,Anca.Ghitescu,Laurent.Andrey,Olivier.Festor}@loria.fr

**Abstract.** JMX (Java Management eXtension) is a Java framework that allows any Java technology-based application or accessible resource to become easily manageable. This standard begins to be widely used within different managed systems which vary from large mainframes to small mobile devices, limited in both resource and computing capacity. Today, little is known about the costs associated with the manageability of a system. In this paper, we analyse the impact of various instrumentation models on the behavior of both the functional and the management plane. We show on a JMX instrumented web server that the service is highly affected by the management activity in driver and component models while a daemon approach limits the management impact on the functional service.

**Keywords:** JMX, Agent, Daemon, Driver, Component, Benchmarking, Management Performance.

## 1 Introduction

The Java technology deployment varies from small devices to huge data centers with a considerable number of servers. The functionality that controls these applications work is split into two main planes:(i) a value-added plane or *functional plane* that handles the users data ; (ii) the management plane that monitors and configures the functional plane. While the original functional plane was designed to be independent from the management plane, today's applications and services are far more integrated and more complex than before. The functional plane needs to expose both client's services and management interfaces.

Another important trend over the past couple of years is the emergence of the JMX standard for managing Java based applications, mainly the J2EE applications [3]. This standard aims to provide a management architecture and an

---

⋆ Some of the authors of this paper are supported in part by the IST-EMANICS Network of Excellence project.

API set that allows any Java technology-based or accessible resource to be inherently manageable. As the number of resources being managed grows and the systems become more distributed and more dynamic, the behavior of application management technologies such as JMX needs to be studied. The overhead of management activities could be important on the user perceived performance of a JMX based managed applications such as a web server where delays and throughput are the key performance metrics for quality of service guarantee [11].

In the past few years, several works [11,1,5] have looked at the performance of multi-tier Internet services which are the base of many businesses, such as retailers, auctioneers and banks. Most of them focus on studying their performance independently from the existence of the management tier. Therefore there is a need to study the performance of such Internet applications accounting for the behavior of the management tier.

Little is known about the cost associated with JMX based management activities. To assess these costs, it is necessary to collect data about the performance and operations of this management system. Furthermore, it is important to collect this data under various configurations and management assumptions. One aspect of these management configurations is the integration model of a JMX agent within a managed system. In the literature, three integrations models are proposed: *daemon*, *driver* and *component* [8]. Overhead associated with management activities of those three models on a managed system performance is unavoidable apart from switching off any instrumentation. However, basic questions we are trying to answer arise: *Does the three models impact differently a managed system performance ? Does it also impact the management part's performance ? Which model is more appropriate and in which context ?*

The main contribution of this paper is to present an experience report on the design and implementation of a simple benchmark to evaluate the three integration models and their impact on the user perceived delays and throughput of the managed web server. In complement to the work in [9], we compared the three models against the same managed application which is a small Java based web server (Tiny Java Web Server[1]) to derive credible performance assessment within comparable experimental environment. This could be helpful for JMX based management systems designers to select one of them regarding performance metrics guarantee. The remainder of this paper is organized as follows. Section 2 gives an overview of the three integration models of a JMX agent. Section 3 describes our benchmarking methodology to assess the impact of the three models. Section 4 analyses the obtained empirical results. Section 5 presents concluding remarks.

## 2   JMX Agent Integration Models

A common paradigm for traditional management systems and even for the autonomic management framework [7] is the manager-agent model [8]. The JMX management framework [10] is based on this model. In this model, agents mediate between managed devices or services, and managers. An agent is responsible

---

[1] see: http://sourceforge.net/projects/tjws/

for processing requests from managers, gathering responses, returning them to the requester and issuing notifications when registered events occur. The JMX agent, or MBean server, satisfies the definition and requirements of a management agent. Its functionality is to control the resources and make them available to remote management applications. According to the JMX specification, the JMX agent is composed of the MBean server, MBeans mapped on managed resources, agent services and adaptors or connectors. Basically the MBean server is a registry of objects that provide to the managers the attributes and operations through which the resources are monitored. On the other side, the manager is responsible for collecting management information from the agents using one of the two modes: polling or notification, and then takes any defined automated actions or solicits a human decision. The JMX API does not provide a specification for a manager, but it supplies all necessary requirements to design and develop a full management system. We are mostly interested in the deployment of the management agent in the managed resource. The main question here is: *how can a new or an existing application be designed in order to become manageable.* Therefore we implemented the three agent integration models identified by the authors of [8]: *daemon, driver* and *component.*

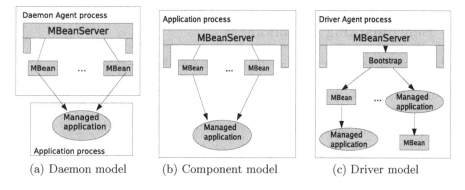

(a) Daemon model        (b) Component model        (c) Driver model

**Fig. 1.** JMX agent integration models

## 2.1   Daemon Model

In the daemon model as depicted in figure 1(a), the JMX agent and the managed application are running in two separate processes. The managed application is not influenced by the overhead imposed by the JMX implementation. Therefore in case of low utilization by the JMX agent, the performance of default functionality should not be affected. One advantage of using the daemon model is that the system can have a single MBean server available for multiple applications. Due to its existence outside the scope of managed applications, the MBean server can be used to control the life-cycle of the application or possibly many applications. On the other hand, problems may arise when the applications try to find or use the MBean server.

## 2.2   Component Model

As it can be observed on figure 1(b), in the component model, the agent is embedded into the managed application. They are both running in the same process and sharing the same resources. The application is responsible for creating and starting the JMX component, therefore it can rely on the MBean server's availability. But we expect that the managed resources will be affected by the overhead imposed by the agent integration.

## 2.3   Driver Model

The driver model is opposite to the component model (see figure 1(c)). In this case the agent becomes the core of the system, and the managed application runs within the scope of the agent. The JMX agent is responsible for creating the managed application and the MBeans. Either it loads the MBeans that then load the applications, or it creates the applications that in turn load the MBeans. Although it is a reliable strategy, this model has a disadvantage when it is used for instrumenting existing applications, because the latter one needs to be redesigned in order to respect the model style. According to [9] this model affects severely the performance of a managed application.

# 3   Benchmarking Methodology

In this section we discuss our benchmarking methodology underlying the agent integration model experiments. We address two separate issues: how to make the measurements, and how to analyze them.

## 3.1   Benchmarking Platform

We have developed a benchmarking platform for JMX based management applications, with a goal of devising a highly modular and flexible measurement platform. It achieves flexibility by varying the number of management nodes, management rates, the agent integration model within the managed application and the web client loads. The platform is based on a *manager-agent-managed application* pattern using a polling interaction mode. Despite that the polling model is inefficient from a scalability perspective [2], it is simple to implement for monitoring a single web server.

Figure 2 depicts the overall architecture of the benchmarking platform. Three important software elements appear: (1) The managed application, represented by the Tiny Java Web Server $(TJWS)^2$ has four different implementations: a simple one, without any JMX instrumentation, and the implementations of the three JMX integration models (*daemon, driver, component*), described in section 2. (2) The JMX client emulates a manager with a monitoring task sending a set of *getAttribute*() requests per unit of time. (3) The web client represents an

---

2 see: http://tjws.sourceforge.net

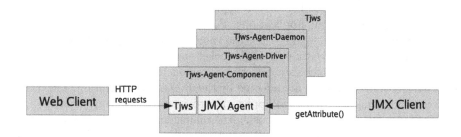

**Fig. 2.** JMX integration models benchmarking platform

application designed to model web user's functional behavior and sends HTTP requests to the managed application.

*Manager description.* The JMX client behaves like a multi-threaded fake manager. It implements a specific number of threads, each of them issuing a management request per time unit to retrieve the value of a specific attribute from the agent using the *getAttribute*() method. This method is a synchronized one and does a remote call on the MBean Server implemented within the agent. Thus, each time a thread issues a request, it should wait for the response, before starting a new request. The triggered requests and their respective responses are carried with an underlying connector. The manager mainly implements the RMI/JRMP (Remote Method Invocation/Java Remote Method Protocol) connector to interact with the agent. Though RMI is known to be heavy, with a significant impact on the performance, it is more reliable and performant than other distributed object protocols [6].

*Managed application description.* We chose $TJWS$ as an implementation of a web server because it has a small java code, as well as a small compiled byte code and might be hosted on light devices such as PDA, handhelds, mobile phones. Thus, the performance and the impact of monitoring tasks on such kind of devices is crucial. The web server is instrumented with *dynamic MBeans* that expose their management interfaces (attributes and operations) at runtime. We identified a set of components as being part of $TJWS$ and we created for each of them a corresponding MBean. *ThreadPool* or *HTTPSession* are such types of components. When created, the corresponding MBeans receive a reference to these components through their constructor. For each component we chose a set of significant attributes to be monitored. The instrumentation attributes are divided into three categories: statistical attributes (e.g. number of TCP connections, size of pool of threads) that change over the life cycle of the managed application; configuration attributes (e.g. TCP port number, the name of the server) that have quite constant values; and attributes retrieved from the server logs. The two first categories are accessed *internally* by the agent on the web server. On the opposite, logged attributes are accessed *externally* by the agent.

*Daemon implementation.* The $TJWS$ application and the JMX agent are implemented as two different applications. For the communication of the agent daemon with the web server to retrieve the values of the management attributes, we investigated two alternatives: a single socket connection and a fixed size pool of sockets. The pool of sockets connections are concurrent and persistent. The processing of web requests is not affected by the JMX implementation. The complexity of adapting the managed application to new requirements is low, as it needs only to provide a form of exposing the management attributes and operations to the agent. In our case a TCP server waits for simplified JMX forwarded requests, either *getAttribute()* or calling of an operation, performs them and sends the responses back to the agent.

*Component implementation.* The start-up process of the $TJWS$ is adjusted in order to enable the creation of the JMX agent. The complexity of the implementation increases, due to the integration of the agent into the main application. The JMX agent component and the web server share the same thread. Nevertheless, the TJWS is a multi-threaded web server that creates a separate pool of threads to serve web connections.

*Driver implementation.* According to the description of this model from section 2.3, we decided to chose the second method of implementation: Bootstrap $\rightarrow$ Application $\rightarrow$ MBean. The agent owns the main thread and is in charge of creating and starting the web server within the same thread, that in turn registers the MBeans. After that, the web server creates its pool of HTTP connections threads when starting.

*Web (HTTP) injector description.* Web users are emulated using the JMeter tool[3]. JMeter models a heavy load and uses a thread group in order to simulate concurrent users. The thinking time is simulated by a uniform random timer with a mean of 7 seconds and range of 10 seconds. The timer will cause JMeter to delay a certain amount of time between each request that a thread makes.

### 3.2   Test Scenarios and Metrics

We have defined 10 test scenarios as shown in Table 1 to evaluate the three integration models and their impact on the performance of the JMX protocol and the web server. The first scenario represents a web server without any JMX instrumentation, where we exercised a steady-state generated web workload; therefore it is our reference scenario. Within each of the other three scenarios that represent the three integration models, we varied either separately or concurrently the number of web users and JMX requests from 20 to 1000 by a step of 20 to see the impact of each of them on the management and the web server planes. For the concurrent JMX and web loads test, the two loads are proportional, i.e, when 20 web users exercise their workload on the web server, the JMX manager injects 20 requests/second. Each experiment lasts 20 minutes, after a ramp-up duration of 1 minute. The ramp-up period represents the amount of time for

---
[3] http://jakarta.apache.org/jmeter

**Table 1.** Benchmarking scenarios

| Scenario / Workload | No agent | Daemon | Component | Driver |
|---|---|---|---|---|
| Web load only | X | X | X | X |
| JMX load only | - | X | X | X |
| Concurrent JMX and Web loads | - | X | X | X |

creating the total number of threads. Measurement data sets used to assess performance metrics for each scenario are recorded at the application level. For each JMX request, we recorded timestamps via the *System.currentTimeMillis* method form the Java SDK before and after calling remotely the *getAttribute* function provided by the MBean server. We collected the same measurement data for each HTTP pair request-response played against the web server. Our performance metrics of interest are delays that experience both JMX and HTTP requests and the number of HTTP responses per second (throughput) for the web part and the number of collected attributes per second for the JMX part. In the following sections, *JMX (attribute) delay* stands for *round-trip delay for a manager to read an attribute*.

### 3.3   Experimental Environment

Each experimental software element is running on a dedicated host. Thus, we used 4 hosts: one for launching and deploying experiments (the test console), one for running the JMeter tool, one for running the managed application (the web server) and the last one for the JMX manager. All machines are hosted within an isolated cluster located in Grenoble that belongs to the Grid5000 project[4]. Machines are connected via a gigabyte Ethernet without any significant background traffic. We used a BEA WebLogic JRockit JVM from a JDK 1.5 running on an Itanium 2 with 2x900MHZ CPU and 3GB memory. We kept the default options values of all running JVMs on nodes. By default, Java provides a garbage collection (GC) mechanism which automatically destroys objects which are not referenced by the application when the GC is launched. We activate GC by default on order to evaluate the common use of Java-based managed applications. The used JMX implementation is the one bundled in the JDK.

### 3.4   Analysis Methodology

Benchmarking various agent's integration models requires to collect and analyze a large amount of measures due to the determination of the offered load to execute against the server part and the JMX part. We attempt to isolate the impact of the offered load (web or monitoring) on the server performance within a specific integration model by charging either the web part or the JMX part. We

---

[4] http://www.grid5000.fr

vary the two loads according to the used scenario to assess the impact of each of them. Currently we use text files for collecting measures and a set of Perl scripts for analyzing them. The analysis scripts infer monitoring round-trip delays from JMX traces collected on the manager side. Both monitoring and web delays are computed by the difference between response timestamp and request timestamp. In order to calculate the number of responses, we count the number of entries in the log file for each second. For both of them, we calculated the mean and standard deviation and some robust statistics like median and quartiles.

## 4   Empirical Results and Analysis

This section presents some empirical results comparing the performance of the various agent integration models that we have defined in the previous section. The main objective of the measurement results is to show the impact of each model on the web and JMX performances.

### 4.1   Throughput Analysis

Figure 3(a) shows the number of collected monitoring attributes per second measured on the JMX manager side without any web load exercised on the managed web server. The objective of this benchmark is to assess the proper monitoring capacity of a JMX agent in terms of the number of collected attributes from an unloaded monitored web server. Under monitoring rates up to 200 requests/second, the three models have similar throughput. Beyond this point, their throughput becomes lightly different, especially for the daemon model which is penalized by the TCP local communication overhead between the agent and the managed web server. The two other models (driver and component) respond more correctly even if monitoring rates become higher. In these two later cases the knee capacity (as defined in [4]) of the agent is close to 1000 monitored attributes per second. This is not a surprise because these later models have no communication overhead to access monitoring attributes on the monitored web server.

When web users start to inject a steady state web load (figure 3(b)) on the web server and the JMX manager injects monitoring requests against the agent, the JMX throughput decreases significantly for the three models. Regarding the daemon model only, the JMX throughput decreases of about 50% when a web load is exercised against the web server and monitoring rates are beyond 100 requests/second. Thus, we could conclude that **the daemon model is less efficient from a monitoring perspective, than the component and the driver models**. This is mainly due to the communication overhead between the agent and the monitored web server. The two other agent models have a more important throughput and their knee monitoring capacity is close to 300 requests/second. From a web performance perspective, as depicted in figure 4(a), the number of HTTP responses per second received by web users is not affected by using one of the three models without any JMX load against the web server. The web server has a maximum achievable throughput close to 35 HTTP transactions per second. However, when we start injecting the JMX load, the HTTP

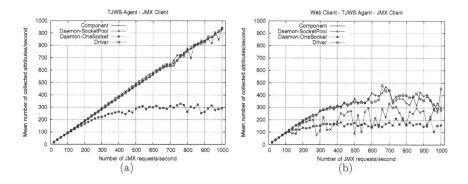

**Fig. 3.** JMX mean throughput in terms of the number of collected attributes per second for the three different integration models under (a) JMX load only and (b) concurrent JMX and Web loads

throughput decreases for all three models. But, we observe that **the driver and the component models have more impact on the web throughput than the daemon model**. This is again because the latter runs on a separate process and affects less the functional plane of the web server. The daemon model divides by a factor of 1.5 the web server maximum achievable throughput. In other hand, the factor is about 2.3 for the driver and the component models.

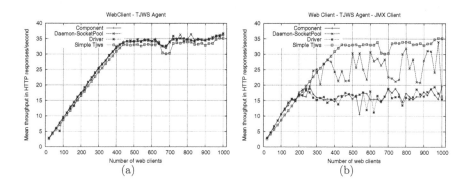

**Fig. 4.** Web mean throughput in terms of number of HTTP responses per second for the three different integration models under (a) Web load only and (b) concurrent JMX and Web loads

### 4.2 Delays Analysis

Regarding JMX delays as shown on figure 5(a), the attribute delays for the three models with unloaded web server remain less than 1 second regardless that we varied monitoring rates up to 1000 requests/second. However, the daemon model attribute delays are greater than the two other models. This is mainly due,

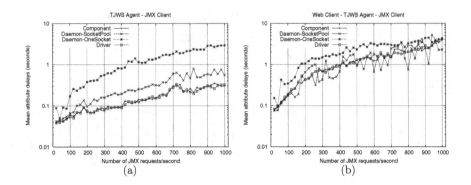

**Fig. 5.** JMX attribute mean delays measured at the manager side for the three different integration models under (a) JMX load only and (b) JMX and Web loads scenarios. The $y - axis$ is in $log_1 0$ scale

as stated in the throughput analysis, to the communication overhead between the daemon and the web server processes. Obviously, when the monitored web server experiences a web load, the JMX attribute delays for the three models are affected as depicted in figure 5(b). The more integrated models (driver and components) become less performant and the monitoring attributes experiences more delays that become greater than 1 second when monitoring rates are greater than 400 requests/second. The attribute delays of the daemon model fluctuate more than the two other and their corresponding curve exhibit more spikes.

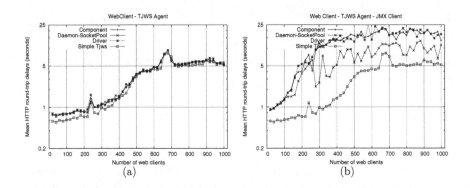

**Fig. 6.** Web mean HTTP transactions round trip delays for the three different integration models under (a) Web load only and (b) JMX and Web loads scenarios. The $y - axis$ is in $log_5$ scale

Figure 6(a) shows that the HTTP transactions delays are closely the same for the three models without any JMX load exercised on the agent. The few spikes on the plots are due to the lack of measurement series repetitions. With a number of web users less than 300, the HTTP transactions delays are less than 1 second. The HTTP transactions delays become more important beyond this point. However, when the web server is both confronted to web and monitoring loads, the HTTP transactions delays fluctuate much more and become more significant. The component and the driver models affect severely the web plane. HTTP transactions round-trip delays are from 2 (best case) to 3.5 (worst case) much higher than a web server without any JMX load when the number of Web users increases from 20 to 1000. Nevertheless, when using a daemon model, web delays are only affected with a factor of 2 times under the same monitoring and web loads. This is due to the fact that the component and driver models run on the same process as the web server and they are in resource consumption contention with it.

## 5   Conclusion

Nowadays, built-in management frameworks like the JMX model promote a novel model to design inherently manageable applications and integrate their management part automatically within the application primary functions which are designed to support the user requirements. In this context, the impact of the integration models of an agent within a managed application is very crucial in order to be able to compare them and select the right one according to performance requirements both for management and managed applications.

The main contribution of this paper was to present an experience report on the design and the implementation of a managed web server with three integration models (*daemon*, *driver* and *component*) of an agent, and to evaluate their impact on the performance of management and managed applications parts. Regarding to our objectives, the following concluding remarks could be expressed:

- Comparing various integration models has shown that the daemon model is less performant on the monitoring part than the driver and component models. This is due to the communication overhead between the daemon agent and the managed application. However, it has a lower impact on the user perceived performance of the managed web server.
- Under monitoring activities the number of HTTP transactions per second is decreased by a factor of 1.5 to 2.3 and the HTTP round-trip delays are increased by a factor of 2 to 3.5, rather than those of a web server without any monitoring load against it.

Despite the impact of management activities, we find that under low monitoring rates close to 100 requests/second, the web server users perceived performance metrics are still acceptable. To optimize this impact and better understanding of its sources, especially within the driver and component model, we need to profile both the server and the agent to find the performance bottlenecks within them.

# References

1. Cecchet, E., Marguerite, J., Zwaenepoel, W.: Performance and scalability of ejb applications. In: OOPSLA '02: Proceedings of the 17th ACM SIGPLAN conference on Object-oriented programming, systems, languages, and applications, pp. 246–261. ACM Press, New York, USA (2002)
2. Chen, T.M., S. S. liu.: A model and evaluation of distributed network management approaches. IEEE journal on selected areas in communications, 20(4), (May 2002)
3. Fleury, M., Lindfors, J.: JMX: Managing J2EE Applications with Java Management Extensions. Sams, Indianapolis, IN, USA (2001)
4. Jain, R.: The art of Computer Systems Performance Analysis. John Wiley & Sons, Inc, ISBN: 0-471-50336-3 (1991)
5. Jenq, B.-C., Kohler, W.H., Towsley, D.: A queueing network model for a distributed database testbed system. IEEE Trans. Softw. Eng. 14(7), 908–921 (1988)
6. Juric, M.B., Rozman, I., Nash, S.: Java 2 distributed object middleware performance analysis and optimization. SIGPLAN Not. 35(8), 31–40 (2000)
7. Kephart, J.O., Chess, D.M.: The vision of autonomic computing. IEEE Computer 1(36), 41–50 (January 2003)
8. Kreger, H.: Java management extension for application management. IBM systems Journal 40(1), 104–129 (2001)
9. Lahmadi, A., Andrey, L., Festor, O.: On the impact of management on the performance of a managed system: A jmx-based management case study. In: DSOM 2005. LNCS, vol. 3775, pp. 24–35. Springer, Heidelberg (2005)
10. Sullins, B.G., Whipple, M.B.: JMX in Action. Manning Publications, Greenwich, UK (October 2002)
11. Urgaonkar, B., Pacifici, G., Shenoy, P., Spreitzer, M., Tantawi, A.: An analytical model for multi-tier internet services and its applications. In: SIGMETRICS '05: Proceedings of the 2005 ACM SIGMETRICS international conference on Measurement and modeling of computer systems, pp. 291–302. ACM Press, New York, USA (2005)

# RAQNet: A Topology-Aware Overlay Network

Seyed Iman Mirrezaei[1], Javad Shahparian[1], and Mohammad Ghodsi[1,2,*]

[1] Computer Engineering Department, Sharif University of Technology, Tehran, Iran
[2] IPM School of Computer Science,Tehran, Iran
{mirrezaei,shahparian}@ce.sharif.edu, ghodsi@sharif.edu

**Abstract.** Peer-to-peer overlay networks provide a useful infrastructure for building distributed applications. These networks provide efficient and fault-tolerant routing and object locating within a self-organizing overlay network. This paper presents a multi-dimensional overlay network called RAQNet which is based on RAQ[1]. RAQ supports exact match queries and range queries over multi-dimensional data efficiently. Moreover, its routing cost does not depend on the dimension of the search space. In RAQNet, we have improved its original routing algorithms and extended it to have topology awareness property. In RAQNet, nodes are connected to each other if their labels are "close" to each other with respect to the topology of its underlying network. A topology match between the overlay and underlying network results in reduced routing delay and network link traffic. In comparison with RAQ, we will describe different node-join algorithms and routing table maintenance in order to provide the topology awareness. We present the experimental results through a prototype implementation of two emulated networks.

**Keywords:** Overlay Network, Topology Awareness, Proximity Metric.

## 1 Introduction

A peer-to-peer (P2P) overlay network is a logical network on the top of its physical layer. The overlay organizes the computers in a network in a logical way so that each node connects to the overlay network through its neighbors.

Several recent systems (CAN [10], Coral [12], Chord [11], Pastry [6] and Tapestry [4]) have recently appeared as flexible infrastructure for building large P2P applications. A DHT can be built using these networks, which allows data to be uniformly distributed among all the participants in such systems.

In these overlays, any item can be found within a bounded number of routing hops, using a small per-node routing table. While there are algorithmic similarities among these overlays, one significant difference lies in the approach they take to consider topology awareness in the underlying network. Chord, for instance, does not consider topology that it rides. As a result, its protocol for maintaining

---

* This work has been partially supported by IPM School of CS (contract: CS1385-2-01) and Iran Telecommunication Research Center (ITRC).
[1] A Range-Queriable Distributed Data Structure [1].

A.K. Bandara and M. Burgess (Eds.): AIMS 2007, LNCS 4543, pp. 13–24, 2007.
© Springer-Verlag Berlin Heidelberg 2007

the overlay network is very light weight, but queries may travel arbitrarily long distances in the underlying network in each routing hop.

Content Addressable Network (CAN) is another overlay network which assumes the attendance of a set of nodes that act as landmarks on the Internet, in order to optimize distances among nodes. Each CAN nodes measure their relative distances from this set of landmarks and measures its round-trip time to each of these landmarks and orders these values in order of increasing RTT. According to these values, topologically close nodes are likely to have the same ordering and so neighbors in the overlay are likely to be topologically close on the Internet [10].

Coral is a P2P content distribution system which is based on a distributed sloppy hash table (DSHT) [12]. In order to restrict queries to close nodes, Coral gathers nodes in groups called clusters. The diameter of a cluster is the maximum desired round-trip time (RTT) between any two nodes that it contains. So, Coral uses round-trip time as distance metric obtained from the underlying topology to obtain better performance [12].

We see that the mentioned overlays use underlying topological information to improve their communication performance. These overlays are aware of their underlying network and use this to improve their performance.

A mathematical model for topology awareness of P2P overlay networks has been introduced by Rostami et al [3]. They constructed their model based on an optimization problem called IP labeling. They also proved that IP labeling optimization is an NP-hard problem. So, it is impossible to build a perfect topology aware overlay network, but it can be solved in certain situations.

Based on RAQ [1], we present a new multi-dimensional overlay network, called RAQNet, with the topology awareness and improve its routing algorithms. RAQ supports exact match queries and range queries over multi-dimensional data efficiently. The routing cost in RAQ does not depend on the dimension of search space. In RAQNet overlay, nodes are connected to each other if they have the same labels and also are close to each other with respect to the topology of the underlying network. A topological match between overlay and underlying network resulted in reduced routing delays and network link traffic. We will describe a refined protocol for joining nodes and failure recovery in order to provide a topology-aware overlay network.

The rest of this paper is organized as follows. In Section 2, we provide a brief overview of the RAQ. Design of RAQNet and the new protocols for joining a node and failure recovery are presented in Section 3. Section 4 presents experimental results. We will conclude the paper in Section 5.

## 2   Basic RAQNet Structure

In this section, we introduce the basic design of RAQ and present a brief overview of its data structure.

## 2.1  Overview of RAQ Data Structure

In RAQ, the search space is $d$-dimensional Cartesian coordinate space which is partitioned among $n$ nodes of the overlay network by a partition tree. Each node has $O(\log n)$ links to other nodes. Each single point query can be routed via $O(\log n)$ message passing. In addition, RAQ supports range queries as well as single point query through $O(\log n)$ communication steps. Each node is corresponded to a region and it is responsible for the queries targeting any point in its region. Furthermore, out-degree of a node and routing cost in RAQ is not dependent on the dimension of the search space. The partition tree splits the search space with no attention to the dimension of the search space.

## 2.2  Space Partitioning

The partition tree is the main data structure in RAQ which partitions the search space into $n$ regions corresponding to $n$ nodes. Assuming $r$ is the root of partition tree and representing the whole search space, each internal node divides its region into two smaller regions using a hyperplane equation. Although only leaves in the partition tree represent actual network nodes, each node in this tree has a corresponding region in the search space. Every network node $x$ which corresponds to a leaf in the partition tree assigned a *Plane Equation* or PE to specify its region in the whole space. Each PE consists of some paired labels which is defined as $X_{PE} = ((p_1, d_1), (p_2, d_2), \cdots, (p_{r(x)}, d_{r(x)}))$. In each label, $r(x)$ presents the distance of $x$ from the root of the tree and $p_i$ shows the plane equation that partitions the $i$th region into two regions and $d_i$ determines one side of the plane $p_i$ (left or right). Every leaf node in the RAQ stores its own PE as well as the PE of its links. Using theses information, every node like $x$ can locally recognize whether a requested query belongs to a node to the left or the right of $x$ or to the left or right of any of its links in the partition tree. Figure 1 (right) portrays partitioning of 2-dimension search space. In figure 1 (left), the PE of node $c$ is $[(x = 4, -), (y = 2, +), (x = 2, +), (y = 1, -)]$. We use "+" and "-" in the PE of nodes to determine one side of the plane (left or right).

## 2.3  Network Links in RAQ

Every node has some links to other nodes of the network. Each link is the addressing information of the target node which can be its IP address and its PE. Connection rule in RAQ is based on partition tree. Consider the node $x$ and its PE, $x$ has link to one of node in each of these sets: $[((p_1, \bar{d}_1))], [((p_1, d_1), (p_2, \bar{d}_2))], \cdots, [((p_1, d_1), (p_2, d_2), \cdots, (p_{r(x)}, \bar{d}_{r(x)}))]$, where $\bar{d}_i$ is the opposite side of $d_i$. It is easy to show that each node has links to $O(\log n)$ nodes in RAQ.

## 2.4  Query Routing in RAQ

Whenever a node in the network receives a single point query, it must route the query to the node which is responsible for the region containing the point. Once the query $Q$ is received by a node $z$, if destination point matched with PE of node $z$ completely, then routing is finished. Otherwise, node $z$ sends the query via a network link to a node $y$ with a PE that matches the destination point at a higher level. This will go on further until the query reaches the destination node.

## 3    Design of RAQNet

In this section we modify RAQ to build a topology aware overlay network. We select node's link based on RAQ data structure and also based on topology of underlying network. Additionally, we hold more node pointers in routing tables in comparison to the basic data structure. A new routing table is also added. We thus propose different procedures for join, departure, and maintenance of RAQNet overlay in order to provide topology awareness.

Each RAQNet node has a fairly random point in a $d$-dimensional Cartesian search space. As in RAQ, search space is a logical space that is divided among network nodes and each node is responsible for responding to the queries matching with its PE. We suppose that PE of nodes are strings and contains some paired label as we mentioned before. We enforces some constraints on the plane equations that a node may choose when it joins the network and splits another region node. These constraints cause the PE of nodes remain simple after node's join or departure. The constraints that we enforce are the following:

- Each plane should be perpendicular to a principal axis. Hence, in a $d$-dimensional space of $(x_1, x_2, \cdots, x_d)$ each plane takes the form of $x_i = c$ for some $1 \leq i \leq d$ and some value of $c$. This effectively means that each plane equation partitions the regions in the space based on the value of $x_i$ for some $i$.
- If the search space is $d$-dimensional, we define the form of the plane equation that may be assigned to an internal node depending on the depth of that node. If $A$ is an internal node, the plane equation assigned to $A$ must be of the form $x_i = c$ for an arbitrary value of $c$, that is for any given $i$, all of the nodes whose depth numbers are $i$ are assigned plane equations of the form $x_i = c$, so that regions can be re-merged when node leaves the overlay. For a 2-d search space, All the internal nodes which are in depth $i$ split the search space along dimension $X$.

This implies that whenever a new node joins the RAQNet and divides the region of another node which leads to a new internal node, the plane equation of that internal node must obey the above constraints.

### 3.1    Routing Tables in RAQNet

The routing state maintained by each node consists of a *routing table* and a *hop table*. Each entry in the routing tables contains the PE and IP address of a node.

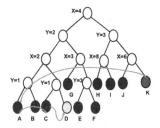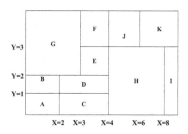

**Fig. 1.** Left: Routing a query from node whose PE is $[(x = 4, +), (y = 3, +), (x = 6, +)]$ to destination point $(2.5, 1.5)$, Right:2-dimension search space

**Routing Table.** The routing table is organized with $O(\log n)$ rows and $2^t$ columns, where $t$ is a configuration parameter with typical value of 2. The entry in $r$th row and $n$th column of the routing table refers to a node whose PE that shares the first $r$ labels with the local node's PE, and its $(r + 1)$th label of node's PE, corresponds to plane like $x_{r+1} = c$. All entries in row $r$ were sorted increasingly according to values of $(r + 1)$th label of PE. Figure 2 depicts a sample routing table. This routing table is similar to those used by Tapestry[4] and RRR[5].

Each entry in the routing table contains the IP address of one of potentially many nodes whose PE have the appropriate prefix; in practice, a node is chosen that is close to the local node, according to the topology of underlying networks. We will show in 3.3.

**Hop Table.** The hop table is the set of H nodes with half of label's of their PE that are shared with the present node's PE's. All nodes in hop table are sorted increasingly according to $\left| \frac{present\ node_{PE}}{2} \right| + 1$th label of their PE. A typical value for H is approximately $2^t$ or $2 * 2^t$. Figure 2 shows a routing table and hop table of node $c$ whose PE is $(X = 4, -), (Y = 2, -), (X = 2, +), (Y = 1, -)$.

## 3.2 Query Routing

At each routing step, the current node usually sends the query to a node whose PE shares at least one label longer with the destination point than the prefix with the local node's PE. If no such node is known, the query is sent to a node whose PE is closer to the destination point and shares a prefix with the destination point having the same length. If there is no such node, the query is delivered to the local node because it is closest node to the destination point. Before sending a query to the one of the nodes in $r$th row , we search for the proper node whose $(r + 1)$th label of its PE is also matched with the destination point.

## 3.3 Neighbor Selection Based on Topology Awareness

This section focuses on topology aware property. RAQNet seeks to exploit topology awareness from the underlying network in order to fill its routing table rows

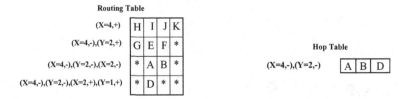

**Fig. 2.** Left: Routing table of node $c$, Right: hop table of node $C$. The associated IP addresses are not shown. If no node was known with a suitable PE, then the routing table entry is filled with "*".

```
1.  if ( z.isInPlaneEquationof HopTable(l)
2.      //Use the hop table
3.      forward to H_i such that H_i is closer to z than   other nodes in H table
4.  else
5.      //Use the routing table
6.      Let r = PlaneEquationMatch(z, l)
7.      Let c = FindingProperColumn(z, r)
8.      if (R_r^c exists)
9.          Forward to R_r^c
10.     else
11.         //Rare case
12.         forward to t ∈ H ∪ R such that
13.             PlaneEquationMatch(z, l) ≥ r
```

**Fig. 3.** RAQNet Routing procedure, when a query with destination point $z$ arrives at a node whose PE is $l$. $R_r^c$ is the entry in the routing table $R$ at $c$th column and $r$th row.

effectively. Hence, any node with the required prefix in PE can be used to fill an entry, topology aware neighbor selection selects the closest node in the underlying network among nodes whose PE have the required prefix. Topology awareness relies on a proximity metric that indicates the "distance" between any given pair of nodes. The choice of a proximity metric depends on the desired quality of the resulting overlay (e.g., low delay, high bandwidth). Our proximity metric in RAQNet overlay network is round trip time.

Topology aware neighbor selection was first proposed in PRR [5] and pastry [6]. In RAQNet, the expected distance traveled in the beginning routing hop is small and it increases at each successive routing step. Because the number of nodes decreases with the increasing length of the prefix match between their PE and the destination point.

### 3.4   Node Join

When a new node ,$x$ , joins the overlay, it chooses a fairly random point $X$ in the search space and contacts an existing close node $e$ sending its join request. The close node $e$ can be found using IP multi-cast in some applications or the algorithm described in Section 3.7. RAQNet uses the join mechanism similar to pastry [6] as follows.

Node $e$ routes join request using $X$ as the query, and $x$ gets the first row of its routing table and first label of its PE from the node $e$. Then $e$ forwards the join request to the second node which sends second row of its routing table and second label of its PE to $x$ and so forth. We will show that $x$'s resulting routing table is filled with close nodes if node $e$ is close to $x$, according to the proximity metric.

We assume that triangle inequality holds in the proximity space and entries of each node's routing table refers to overlay nodes close to itself according to proximity metric.

$x$ is close to $e$ because we search for a close node to send join request. Also, the nodes in the first row of $e$'s routing table are close to $e$. Due to triangle inequality, these nodes are also close to $x$. This holds for the next rows in the same way.

It is also important to update other node's routing tables to ensure that they are filled with close nodes after new nodes join the overlay network. Once $x$ has initialized its own routing table, it sends the each row of its routing table to each node that appears as an entry in that row. This causes both to announce its attendance and to spread information about new nodes that joined before. Each node receives a row then checks the nodes in the row to measure if $x$ or one of the entries is closer than the corresponding entry in its own routing table, and updates its routing table properly. This procedure ensures that routing tables filled with close nodes. Additionally, $x$ and the nodes that appear in $n$th row of $x$'s routing table form a group of $2^t$ close nodes whose PEs share in the first $n$ labels. It is clear that these nodes need to know of $x$'s entrance since $x$ may displace a more distant node in one of the node's routing tables. In an opposite way, a node with same prefix in the first $n$ labels of its PE that is not a member of this group is more distant from the members of the group, and therefore from $x$. Thus, $x$'s entrance is not likely to affect its routing table and it does not need to be informed of $x$'s entrance.

### 3.5   Node Departure

According to RAQ [1], each node has departure links to the nodes which have links to it. When a node decides to leave overlay, it informs their neighbors by departure links. All nodes that receive this message, mark their corresponding entry in the routing table. Instead of using a marked entry to route a query, RAQNet routes the query to another node in the same row whose PE also matches the destination point. If the next node has a proper entry that matches the next label of the destination point, it automatically informs the previous node of that entry. The next node is usually an entry in the same row as the failed node. If that node provides an alternative entry for the failed node, its expected distance from the local node is low since all three nodes were member of the same group of close nodes with same PE prefix. If no replacement node is supplied by the next node, a replacement is found by triggering the routing table maintenance task, which is described next.

## 3.6   Routing Table Maintenance

Whenever an overlay node could not find an alternative entry for its failed entry, it triggers the maintenance procedure to handle this problem.

Another concern is that deviations could cascade and lead to a slow deterioration of the topology aware properties gradually. To prevent a deterioration of the route quality, each node runs a periodic routing table maintenance task (e.g., every 20 minutes). The maintenance task performs the following procedure for each row of the local node's routing table. It selects a random entry in the row, and requests a copy of associated node's row. Each entry in that row is compared to the corresponding entry in the local routing table. If they differ, the node probes the distance to both entries and puts the closest node in its own routing table.

## 3.7   Locating a Nearby Node

When a new node $x$ want to join to overlay, it should contact the close node $e$ around itself to fill its routing table with close nodes properly. Karger et al [8] proposed an algorithm to find close node but this would require maintaining additional information. In Figure 4 we describe an algorithm to find a close overlay node to $x$. This algorithm is interesting because it does not need any other information beyond the routing table and hop table that are already preserved by RAQNet nodes.

```
1.  discover (anyNode)
2.      nodes = getHopTable (anyNode)
3.      nearNode = pickClosest(nodes)
4.      depth = getMaxRoutingTableLevel(nearNode)
5.      closest = nil
6.      while (closest ! = nearNode)
7.          closest = nearNode
8.          nodes = getRoutingTable(nearNode,depth)
9.          nearNode = pickClosest(nodes)
10.         if (depth > 0 ) depth = depth −1
11.     end
12.     return closest
```

**Fig. 4.** Finding near node

This algorithm exploits position of node in the network. In each step, distance of all nodes in the same row is checked in order to find closer node from joining node. This is achieved bottom up by picking the closest node at each level and getting the next level from it. This performs a constant number of probes at each level but the probed nodes get closer at each step. The last phase repeats the process for the top level until there is no more progress. As it was showed in RAQ, routing tables have $\log n$ rows. Hence, the complexity of this algorithm is $O(\log n)$ too ($n$ is number of nodes in the overlay network).

# 4   Experimental Results

In this section, we present experimental results quantifying the performance of topology aware neighbor selection in RAQNet under realistic conditions. The results were obtained using a RAQNet implementation running on top of a network simulator, using Internet topology models. The RAQNet parameter was set to $d = 2$. Higher dimensions can be used without imposing extra over-head because routing mechanism of RAQNet does not depend on the dimension of the search space. Our results obtained with a simulated RAQNet overlay network of 10,000 nodes.

## 4.1   Network Topologies

Two simulated network topologies were used in the experiments. In the "Sphere" topology nodes are placed at uniformly random locations on the surface of a sphere with radius 1000. The distance metric is based on the topological distance between two nodes on the sphere's surface. However, the sphere topology is not realistic, because it assumes a uniform random distribution of nodes on the Sphere's surface, and its proximity metric satisfies the triangulation inequality. A second topology was generated by the Georgia Tech transit-stub network topology model[9]. The round trip delay (RTT) between two nodes, as provided by the topology graph generator, is used as the proximity metric with this topology. As in the real Internet, the triangle inequality does not hold for RTTs among nodes in the this topology. Our experimental results are significantly good for both topologies although our assumption of triangle inequality does not hold for the second topology.

## 4.2   Routing Hops and Distance Ratio

In the first experiment, 200 lookup queries are routed using RAQNet from randomly chosen nodes, using a random point. Figure 5 (left) shows the number of RAQNet routing hops and the distance ratio for the sphere topology. Distance ratio is defined as the ratio of the distance traveled by a RAQNet query to the distance between its source and destination nodes, measured in terms of the proximity metric. The distance ratio can be interpreted as the penalty, expressed in terms of the proximity metric, associated with routing a query through RAQNet instead of sending the query directly in the Internet.

Two sets of results are shown. "RAQ" shows the corresponding experimental results with RAQ. "RAQNet" shows results of experiments in RAQNet overlay network. According to analysis in RAQ [1], the expected number of routing hops is slightly below $\frac{\log 10000}{2} = 6.64$ and the distance ratio is small. The reported hop counts are independent of the network topology, therefore we present them just for the sphere topology.

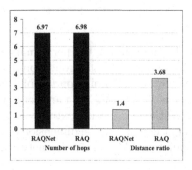 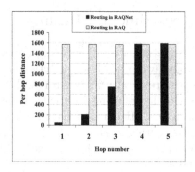

Fig. 5. Left: Number of routing hops and distance ratio in the sphere topology, Right: Distance traversed per hop in the sphere topology

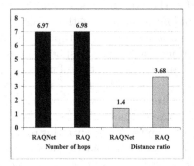 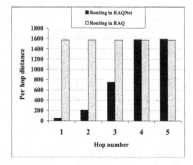

Fig. 6. Left: Distance traversed per hop in the GT-ITM topology, Right: Number of routing hops and distance ratio in the sphere topology

### 4.3   Routing Distance in RAQNet

Figure 5 (right) shows the distance messages travel in each following routing hops. The results confirm the increase in the expected distance of following hops up to the fourth hops. Moreover, in the absence of the topology awareness, the average distance traveled in each hop is constant and corresponds to the average distance between nodes which are placed on the surface of a sphere $1571 = \frac{\pi * r}{2}$ (where $r$ is the radius of the sphere).

Figures 6 (left) shows the same results for the GT-ITM topology respectively. Due to the nonuniform distribution of nodes and the more complex proximity space in this topology, the expected distance in each following routing step still increases monotonically. However, the node join algorithm continues to produce routing tables that refer to close nodes, as indicated by the modest difference in hop distance to the routing tables in the first three hops.

Figures 6 (right), and 7 (left) show raster plots of the distance query travel in RAQNet, as a function of the distance between the source and destination nodes, for each of the two topologies. Queries were sent from 50 randomly chosen source nodes to random destination points in this experiment. The mean distance ratio

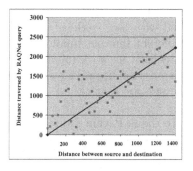 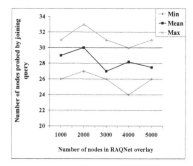

**Fig. 7.** Left: Number of routing hops and distance ratio in the GT-ITM topology, Right: number of probes by a newly joining node

is shown in each graph as a solid line. The results show that the distribution of the distance ratio is relatively firm around the mean. Not surprisingly, the sphere topology produces the best results, because of its uniform distribution of nodes and the geometry of its proximity space. However, the far more realistic GT-ITM topology produces still good results, with a mean distance ratio of 1.63, a maximal distance ratio of about 8.3, and distribution that is fairly firm around the mean.

### 4.4   Overhead of Node Join Protocol

In this section, we measure the overhead incurred by the node join protocol to preserve topology awareness in the routing tables. We measure this overhead in terms of the number of probes, where each probe corresponds to the communication required to measure the distance according to the proximity metric between two nodes. Of course, in our simulated network, a probe simply involves looking up the corresponding distance according to the topology model. However, in a real network, probing would likely require at least two message exchanges. The number of probes is therefore a meaningful measure of the overhead required to maintain the topology awareness. Figure 7 (right) shows the maximum, mean and minimum number of probes performed by a node joining the RAQNet overlay network. This overhead is independent of number of nodes which we varied from 1,000 to 5,000 nodes. In each case, the probes performed by the last ten nodes that joined the RAQNet overlay network were recorded. It is assumed here that once a node has probed another node, it stores the result and does not probe again.

## 5   Conclusion

This paper presented a new multi-dimensional topology aware overlay network and analysis as well as an experimental evaluation of the RAQNet. A refined protocol for node joining and node failure recovery achieves in order to provide topology awareness in RAQNet overlay network. Experimental results showed that topology aware properties can be achieved with low overhead in network topologies. Additionally, simulations on two different Internet topology models show that these properties can hold in more realistic network topologies. The results also show that considering topology awareness can be provide a significant performance improvement relative to topology unaware routing.

**Acknowledgments.** The authors would like to thank Payam Bahreini, Hesam Chiniforoushan and Hojatollah Vaheb for their reviews and supports.

# References

1. Nazerzadeh, H., Ghodsi, M.: RAQ: A range queriable distributed data structure (extended version). In: Vojtáš, P., Bieliková, M., Charron-Bost, B., Sýkora, O. (eds.) SOFSEM 2005. LNCS, vol. 3381, pp. 264–272. Springer, Heidelberg (February 2005)
2. Alaei, S., Toossi, M., Ghodsi, M.: SkipTree: A Scalable Range-Queryable Distributed Data Structure for Multidimensional Data. In: Deng, X., Du, D.-Z. (eds.) ISAAC 2005. LNCS, vol. 3827, pp. 298–307. Springer, Heidelberg (2005)
3. Rostami, H., Habibi, J.: A Mathematical Foundation for Topology Awareness of P2P Overlay Networks. In: Zhuge, H., Fox, G.C. (eds.) GCC 2005. LNCS, vol. 3795, pp. 906–918. Springer, Heidelberg (2005)
4. Zhao, B.Y., Kubiatowicz, J.D., Joseph, A.D.: Tapestry: An infrastructure for fault-resilient wide-area location and routing, Tech. Rep. UCB//CSD-01-1141, U.C. Berkeley (April 2001)
5. Plaxton, C.G., Rajaraman, R., Richa, A.W.: Accessing nearby copies of replicated objects in a distributed environment. In: Proc. 9th ACM Symp. on Parallel Algorithms and Architectures, June 1997, Newport, Rhode Island, USA, pp. 311–320 (1997)
6. Rowstron, A., Druschel, P.: Pastry: Scalable,distributed object location and routing for large-scale peer-to-peer systems. In: Proc. IFIP/ACM Middleware 2001, Heidelberg, Germany (November 2001)
7. Costa, M., Castro, M., Rowstron, A., Key, P.: PIC: Practical Internet Coordinates for Distance Estimation. In: 24th IEEE International Conference on Distributed Computing Systems (ICDCS' 04), Tokyo, Japan (March 2004)
8. Karger, D.R., Ruhl, M.: Finding nearest neighbors in growth-restricted metrics. In: STOC'02 (July 2002)
9. Zegura, E., Calvert, K., Bhattacharjee, S.: How to model an internetwork. In: INFOCOM96 (1996)
10. Ratnasamy, S., Francis, P., Handley, M., Karp, R., Shenker, S.: A Scalable Content-Addressable Network. In: Proc. of ACM SIGCOMM (August 2001)
11. Stoica, I., Morris, R., Karger, D., Kaashoek, M.F., Balakrishnan, H.: Chord: A scalable peer-to-peer lookup service for internet applications. In: Proceedings of the ACM SIGCOMM '01 Conference, San Diego, California (August 2001)
12. Freedman, M., Mazieres, D.: Sloppy hashing and self-organizing clusters. In: Proc. 2nd International Workshop on Peer-to-Peer Systems (IPTPS03) (2003)

# IBGP Confederation Provisioning

M. Nassar, R. State, and O. Festor

LORIA - INRIA Lorraine
615, rue du jardin botanique
54602 Villers-les-Nancy, France
{nassar,state,festor}@loria.fr

**Abstract.** This paper proposes an optimization method for the design of large scale confederation based BGP networks. We propose a graph based model and an associated metric to evaluate the reliability of large scale autonomous systems. We propose and validate an effective methodology to find the optimal design for a given physical topology. According to our experiments, we consider that replacing the traditional IBGP topology by an appropriate confederation design could increase at the same time the scalability and the reliability into the domain. Our work might be a step further towards a large scale confederation deployment.

## 1  Introduction

The confederation topology is one solution to control IBGP scalability into a large Autonomous System. Although, some general guidelines propose to follow the physical topology and use a hub-and-spoke architecture [9], a dedicated analytical design methodology has not yet been developed. This issue is of extreme importance for large networks and complex topologies. Questions such as "how many sub-AS do we need?" and "where is the border of each sub-AS?", do not have answers based on a theoretical approach.

The paper is organized as follows: Section 2 introduces the BGP protocol and highlights the scalability problem and the current approaches to deal with. Section 3 presents the requirements of confederation reliability and gives hints for optimal confederation design. Section 4 presents a network model and proposes metrics and constraints to create a confederation framework. Solving of the reliability-aware design problem together with implementation and experimental results are in section 4 as well. Section 5 concludes the paper.

## 2  BGP Protocol and Scaling Large ASs

Today's Internet is structured according to separate administrative domains, called *autonomous systems* ASs, where each has its own independent routing policies. *The Internal Gateway Protocol* IGP is responsible for packets forwarding within a domain. *The Border gateway protocol* BGP is currently the de facto standard protocol for inter domain routing in the Internet. The routers

A.K. Bandara and M. Burgess (Eds.): AIMS 2007, LNCS 4543, pp. 25–34, 2007.
© Springer-Verlag Berlin Heidelberg 2007

running BGP are called *speakers*, and a *neighbor connection* (also referred as *peer connection*) can be established between two speakers over TCP. If the two speakers are within the same AS, BGP is called *internal BGP* (IBGP), while two speakers residing in two different ASs and directly attached by a physical segment can established a BGP session and in this case we have an *external BGP* session (EBGP). The speakers using EBGP are called *border routers*.

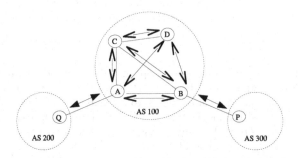

**Fig. 1.** IBGP and EBGP

Figure 1 shows an example of three ASs, the nodes represent BGP speakers and the solid lines represent physical links. We have two EBGP sessions between A and Q and between B and P, which are border routers, and six IBGP sessions forming a logical full mesh. The border routers A and B inform all the speakers within the domain (by IBGP) about the reachable network addresses outside the domain (learned by EBGP).

EBGP speakers can detect routing loops by the AS-path BGP attribute. But inside the AS, a full mesh of IBGP sessions between speakers is required. The problem with the IBGP mesh is that it is not scalable. If a mesh between $n$ routers has to be deployed, each router handles concurrently $n-1$ sessions. As n grows, routers with higher CPU power and larger memory are required to process and maintain routing information. To solve the IBGP scalability problem, the network community has proposed two practical approaches: Route Reflection and confederation [3].

The route reflection method elects some routers to be route reflectors, and then clusters are formed by assigning clients to each route reflector. The full mesh is only required between reflectors and each client only communicates with its reflector. This method has advantages such as low migration complexity because there is no need to reconfigure all the routers, and it supports hierarchical structures.

The underlying idea of the confederation is to divide a large AS into a number of smaller autonomous systems, called *member AS* or *sub-AS*. Each sub-AS will have a different AS number. The direct consequence is that External BGP sessions must be deployed between them. This sessions are called *intra confederation* EBGP sessions, because they are slightly different of the regular EBGP sessions. Inside each sub-AS, a full IBGP mesh is required, but we can also deploy a route reflection architecture.

From the outside, a confederation looks like a single AS, because it doesn't expose its internal topology when advertising routes to EBGP neighbors. An exterior AS, basing its routing policy on AS path length, will count a confederation like one hop while the traffic may pass through multiple sub-ASs. Since there may be a shorter path that doesn't include the confederation, this will cause suboptimal routing. Moreover, in standard BGP, sub-ASs do not alter the overall AS-path length, which causes sub-optimal routing inside the confederation.

The advantage of the confederation design with respect to the route reflectors design is its scaling potential for the IGP protocol. An IGP protocol can be run on one sub-AS totally independent from running other IGPs on other sub-ASs, which helps to control the instability of IGP in a large autonomous system. For more details on BGP, route reflection and confederation issues, the reader is invited to consult the excellent BGP overview in [3].

# 3   Guidelines for Optimizing Confederation Networks

A good BGP network design must satisfy the following requirements: reduced complexity, simple routing procedure and in the same time high reliability.

The *hub-and-Spoke architecture* is advised in the literature([9],[3]). One sub-AS forms a backbone and play the role of a transit center. All other members connect exclusively with it. The goal of such design is to reduce the number of intra-confederation EBGP sessions, because if a sub-AS has multiple EBGP sessions, it will receive multiple copies of the same routes, which means redundant traffic and processing. The other benefit is the consistency and the predictability of the routing. Uniformly, a traffic entering the confederation from one sub-AS will take two hops to get out by another sub-AS.

But in term of network resilience, a reduced number of intra confederation sessions may be a bad design in case of component failures: for example if one sub-AS is connected to the backbone sub-AS via one session carried by one physical link, the failure of this link or one of the two end routers causes the complete isolation of this sub-AS from the rest of the confederation. A second example is when multiple sub-ASs are connected to the backbone sub-AS and all the sessions are initiated exclusively with the same router. The failure of this transit router transforms the confederation into islands. In backbone networks, there is a small probability that two components fail in the same time, or that the second component fails before we recover the first one. Under this assumption, a topology where there are two independent sessions formed by independent physical components (router, physical-link, router) between every sub-AS and the transit sub-AS, prevents the isolation between sub-ASs.

The authors in [8] propose an IBGP route reflection optimization algorithm, based on the expected session loss metric. This work is focused on optimizing route reflection architectures. The damage caused by a BGP session failure is: 1) the invalidation of routing entries, which are directly or indirectly related to this session, 2) the consequent route flaps, 3) the unreachable network addresses, or 4) the potential isolation of two parts of the network. Inside each sub-AS, an

IBGP mesh must be deployed. When two routers don't have a direct physical link to build a peer session, they use IGP routing tables to make a multi-hop TCP connection and establish an IBGP session. The result is that some physical links will support multiple sessions, and some routers may be also in the path of sessions that it doesn't initiate. When a component (router or link) fails, the overlying sessions may break down.

The session failure is of probabilistic nature [4]. If a router fails, all the initiated sessions will break down, and with certain probability the sessions which pass through it will also fail. If a physical link fails, then each of its overlying sessions may break down with certain probability.

A good sub-AS design should prevent a high expected session loss. The guideline is to follow the logical topology by the physical topology [9]. A sub-AS structure with a physical segment for every two of its IBGP speakers, limits the loss to probably one session per link failure, and certainly all the initiated sessions per router failure.

## 4   Reliable Confederation Topology Design

### 4.1   Network Models

We represent the physical network in the AS as a graph $\mathcal{G}(\mathcal{V}, \mathcal{E})$, where $\mathcal{V}$ represent the set of routers and $\mathcal{E}$ represent the set of physical links. We denote $(i, j) \in \mathcal{E}$ the edge between node $i \in \mathcal{V}$ and node $j \in \mathcal{V}$. Typically, there are some routers that don't run BGP, we denote $\mathcal{V}_r$ the set of routers running BGP, $\mathcal{V}_r \subseteq \mathcal{V}$, and we define $n = |\mathcal{V}_r|$ as the number of BGP speakers. We focus on a transit domain where $\mathcal{V} = \mathcal{V}_r$, and we consider that our model can be simply extended to be applicable on a general case. A reliability model is inherently bounded to the reliability of single components like routers and physical links. The reliability of a router is strongly related to its resource consumption (CPU for route processing, and memory for routing table). When the number of sessions handled concurrently increases over a certain threshold, the router can no longer maintain an up-to-date map. In a confederation topology, except border routers, a router must manage sessions just with the speakers of its sub-AS rather than all the speakers of the AS. The scalability problem is solved this way. Let $v_i$ be the proportion of time where router $i$ has a healthy status. $v_i$ can be assigned based on monitoring history or estimated basing on CPU performance and memory capacity. Likewise, we represent the reliability of a link $(i, j)$ by a value $w_{ij}$, which is the proportion of time where the link works properly. If no physical link between i and j, $w_{ij} = 0$.

In a logical topology formed by $k$ sub-ASs, each sub-AS is represented by a sub-graph and assigned a number SAS, $1 \leq SAS \leq k$. The logical model $G(\mathcal{V}, \mathcal{E}, f)$ is obtained by characterizing the physical model by a function $f$ : $\mathcal{V} \mapsto [1, k]$. $f$ assigns for each node the sub-graph that contains it. The main property of $f$ is that it divides the graph into connected sub-graphs. Basing on $f$, we can calculate the number of nodes of a sub graph by the formula: $y(SAS) = card(\{i \in \mathcal{V}; f(i) = SAS\})$. The number of edges between the nodes of the same sub-graph can be also calculated: $m(SAS) = card(\{(i,j) \in \mathcal{E}; f(i) = f(j) = SAS\})$. We can denote the border routers by a function $b$: $b(i) = 1$ if $\exists j \in \mathcal{V}; (i,j) \in \mathcal{E} \wedge f(i) \neq f(j)$. So $b(i) = 1$ if $i$ is a border router and 0 else. To build an EBGP session, two border routers must be in different sub-ASs. We use a function $s$ to detect this property, $i, j \in \mathcal{V} : s(i,j) = 1$ if $f(i) \neq f(j)$ and 0 otherwise.

## 4.2 Problem Statement

Given the physical network topology $\mathcal{G}(\mathcal{V}, \mathcal{E})$ of an autonomous system, find among all the possible logical confederation topologies, the one having the best reliability.

For example, we give the physical topology in figure 2. We suppose that one or more of the seven routers don't have the necessary performances to handle six sessions concurrently. The problem is to divide the routers in a number of sub-ASs and to optimize the reliability of the routing protocol.

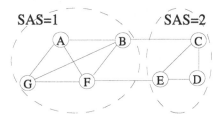

| $i$ | $A$ | $G$ | $B$ | $F$ | $D$ | $C$ | $E$ |
|------|-----|-----|-----|-----|-----|-----|-----|
| $f(i)$ | 1 | 1 | 1 | 1 | 2 | 2 | 2 |
| $b(i)$ | 0 | 0 | 1 | 1 | 0 | 1 | 1 |

**Fig. 2.** Physical topology and associated solution-logical topology

The solution for this topology is depicted in the table of figure 2. A theoretical justification of this choice can't be completed without a study of the factors that influence either IBGP or EBGP reliabilities. We will model these factors by a suitable metric accompanied by three essential constraints.

## 4.3 Density Metric and Accompanying Constraints

We define a metric capable to evaluate the difference between the physical topology of a sub-graph and a Clique [2] of the same size. The motivation for our approach is that a Clique has the weakest expected session loss and the highest edge connectivity [1] (for a Clique of size n nodes the edge connectivity is n-1). Our approach is to cut the network into a small number of dense sub-ASs. The density notion was used in [7] to characterize the Internet hierarchy. We define the Density of a sub-graph as the ratio of the number of its edges $m$ to the number of edges required to accomplish a Clique between its nodes. For n nodes, we need $\frac{n \times (n-1)}{2}$ edges to make a Clique.

$$D(SAS) = \frac{m}{\frac{y(SAS) \times (y(SAS)-1)}{2}}$$

We define the density of a graph k-cut (i.e. the graph is cut into k connected sub-graphs) as the average of densities of its sub-graphs.

$$D = \frac{\sum_{SAS=1}^{k} D(SAS)}{k}$$

A logical topology which concentrates the edges in the sub-graphs reduces in the same time the number of edges between the sub-graphs, and that the number of EBGP sessions is minimized.

To address the EBGP resilience, we introduce here the cut reliability constraint. We define the reliability of intra-confederation EBGP as the sum of reliabilities of the underlying network components (border routers and physical links) and we denote it by R. R indicates approximately how many components deploy EBGP and how much these components are reliable.

$$R = \sum_{i \in \mathcal{V}} v_i \times b(i) + \sum_{(i,j) \in \mathcal{E}} w_{ij} \times b(i) \times b(j) \times s(i,j)$$

Our constraint requires that R should be greater than a certain threshold weighted by a fraction $\alpha$ to the sum of reliabilities of the components of all the network.

$$R_T = \sum_{i \in \mathcal{V}} v_i + \sum_{(i,j) \in \mathcal{E}} w_{ij}$$

The second constraint that we have used is limiting the number of sub-ASs. The intra-confederation EBGP routing is not optimal without manually setting BGP policies. When the number of sub-ASs increases, the IGP advantages become non relevant. Thus, we choose not to exceed a certain threshold of number of sub-ASs, otherwise we need much administration effort to save the stability and the efficiency on the routing plan.

Finally, it is important to uniformly distribute the routers among the sub-ASs. We balance between the numbers of IBGP sessions that a router will handle concurrently, what protects certain routers from unsupportable resource consumption, and we balance between the different IGP's working in the sub-ASs. The third constraint is so called the load balancing constraint.

## 4.4   Reliable Confederation-Density (RC-D) Problem

Given a graph $\mathcal{G}(\mathcal{V}, \mathcal{E})$, $\{v_i\}$ and $\{w_{ij}\}$ reliability values of nodes and edges, the RC-D problem aims to find k and the k-cut of the graph which maximize the density metric while respecting the three constraints formulated below:

1. The cut reliability constraint: $R > \alpha \times R_T$;
2. The number of sub-AS constraint: $2 \leq k < \lceil \ln(n) \rceil$;
3. The load balancing constraint: $\forall SAS; \beta \times \frac{n}{k} < y(SAS) < \frac{(2-\beta) \times n}{k}$ where we choose $\beta$ from $[0.5, 0.9]$.

We can choose $\alpha$ and $\beta$ and change the threshold of $k$ to strengthen or relax the constraints. A good choice requires practical experience and studying BGP confederation history examples.

## 4.5   Heuristic Solution for Reliable Confederation Topology Design

If k is fixed and the graph will be divided on exactly k sub-graphs, then we get the k-RC-D problem. Solutions of the k-RC-D problem for k going from 2 to $\lceil \ln(n) \rceil$ can be compared to elect the optimum design. In this paper, we apply a technique similar to one of the Min k-cut problem solving methods [6].

Our solution HS fixes k first and uses a randomized procedure called *contract* next to divide the graph into k connected sub-graphs. the Contract procedure chooses an edge from $\mathcal{E}$ randomly (the same probability for all the edges). The chosen edge is erased and its two extremities are joined in one meta node. The edges of each of the two extremities belong now to the new meta node. This contraction is repeated iteratively and stops when we reach k meta nodes. The nodes compacted on each meta node are returned as a connected sub-graph. The output of this procedure is a logical topology and the associated function f is represented by a list that assigns for every node in $\mathcal{V}$ the $SAS$ of the sub-graph containing it.

Next, HS calculates the cut reliability R, and the number of routers for each sub-graph y(SAS). If the topology exceeds the reliability constraint or the load balancing one, HS gives it a null density. Otherwise, HS calculates the density of each sub-graph and then the average density. HS repeats this work (*contract+metric calculation*) for $n^2 \times \log n$ iterations like in the algorithm of the Min k-cut to increase the chance to be close to the optimal solution. At the end of this loop, HS picks the maximum density and the associated list representing f as the response to the k-RC-D problem. To respond to the RC-D problem, HS assigns to k all the integer values between 2 and $\lceil \ln(n) \rceil$, solves each of the k-RC-D problems, and finally returns among all the k-RC-D solutions the one having the maximum density. Thus, the complexity of our solution is $O(n^4(\ln(n))^2)$ because the complexity of *contract* procedure is $O(n^2)$. The pseudo-code of HS is depicted below:

```
for k = 2 to ⌈ln(n)⌉
        for topology= 1 to n² × log n
                f[topology]=contract(G);
                if (f[topology] satisfies constraints):
                        D_top[topology] = calculate_D(f[topology])
                else:
                        D_top[topology]=0
        D_k[k]= max(D_top)
D_opt=max(D_k)
return(D_opt,k_opt,f_opt)
```

## 4.6   Experimental Results

We have implemented a brute force algorithm (ET) which works in exponential time ($k^n$), tries all combinations, generates all possible logical topologies and returns exactly the maximum possible density. Our objective is to compare the results of HS and those of ET.

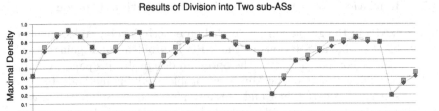

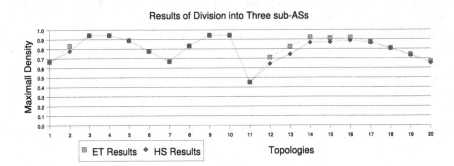

**Fig. 3.** experimental results(1)

Physical network topologies are generated using the BRITE network topology generator [5]. We have chosen BRITE because it is one of the generators commonly used in the networks and Internet research community. We have chosen to use the Heavy-tailed distribution to place the nodes and the Waxman model to interconnect them. The reliabilities of physical links, $w_{ij}$, are generated randomly from the interval $[0, 1.9]$ and the reliabilities of routers, $v_i$, from $[0, 0.99]$. We choose $\alpha = \frac{1}{n}$ for the cut reliability constraint and $\beta = 0.5$ for the load balancing constraint. We have generated 33 physical topologies: 10 for every network size of 10, 15 and 20 nodes, and 3 for the size of 25 nodes. For each topology, we decided to cut the graph into two sub-graphs, so we fixed k at 2, and we executed the two algorithms. Because it's much harder for ET to cut the graph into 3 sub-graphs for topologies of twenty nodes and more, we did the comparison only for the first twenty topologies of sizes 10 and 15 nodes. The two diagrams in figure 3 show the difference between the two algorithms.

For a given topology, the density of the optimal confederation design returned by the ET algorithm is noted $D_{ET}$ and the density of the one returned by the HS algorithm is noted $D_{HS}$, thus the relative error for a given topology is:

$$e_r = \frac{D_{ET} - D_{HS}}{D_{ET}} \times 100.$$

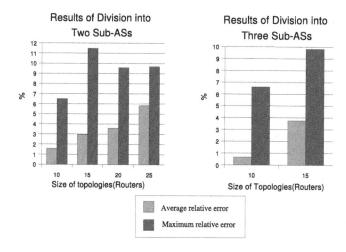

**Fig. 4.** experimental results(2)

For each set of topologies of the same size, we have compared the average relative error and the maximum relative error. The results are shown in the two diagrams of figure 4. After interpreting these diagrams, we have concluded that the HS algorithm could be a good solution to solve the RC-D problem.

## 5    Conclusion

We have proposed in this paper a new method for optimizing BGP confederation networks. Our approach consists on determining a criteria for the sub-AS IBGP resilience, as well as its integration in the global EBGP resilience model. We have adopted a randomized algorithm to optimize the confederation design with respect to our defined resilience, and we have experimentally evaluated its performance.

**Acknowledgment.** This paper was supported in part by the EC IST-EMANICS Network of Excellence (#26854).

## References

1. Cole, R., Hariharan, R.: A fast algorithm for computing steiner edge connectivity. In: STOC 03: Proceedings of the thirty-fifth annual ACM symposium on Theory of computing, ACM Press, New York (2003)
2. Cormen, T. H., Stein, C., Rivest, R.L., Leiserson, C E.: Introduction to Algorithms. McGraw-Hill, New York (2001)
3. Halabi, S., McPherson, D.: The definitive BGP resource: Internet Routing Architectures Second Edition. Cisco Press (2000)
4. Xiao, L. L., Nahrstedt, K.: Reliability models and evaluation of internal bgp networks. In: IEEE INFOCOM 2004, Hong Kong, China, (March 2004)

5. Medina, A., Lakhina, A., Matta, I., Byers, J.: Brite: Universal topology generation from a user's perspective (user manual). Technical report, Boston University (2001)
6. Motwani, R., Raghavan, P.: Randomized algorithms. SIGACT News, vol. 26(3) (1995)
7. Subramanian, L., Agarwal, S., Rexford, J., Katz, R.: Characterizing the internet hierarchy from multiple vantage points. Technical report, University of California at Berkeley (2001)
8. Xiao, L., Wang, J., Nahrstedt, K.: Reliability-aware ibgp route reflection topology design. Technical report, Department of Computer Science University of Illinois at Urbana-Champaign, (August 2003)
9. Zhang, R., Bartell, M.: BGP Design and Implementation: Practical guidelines for designing and deploying a scalable BGP routing architecture. Cisco Press (2004)

# Ontology-Based Management for Context Integration in Pervasive Services Operations

J. Martín Serrano[1], Joan Serrat[1], Sven van der Meer[2], and Mícheál Ó Foghlú[2]

[1] Universitat Politècnica de Catalunya. Barcelona, Spain
{jmserrano,serrat}@tsc.upc.edu
[2] Telecommunications Software & Systems Group,
Waterford Institute of Technology. Waterford, Ireland
{vdmeer,mofoghlu@tssg.org}

**Abstract.** Next generation networks require information and communications systems able to support pervasive services and especially context-aware applications. This paper presents research challenges in self-management, autonomic communications and integration requirements of context information for supporting management operations of such services in next generation networks. The research focuses on a framework of information systems and their interoperability. Management techniques using information and data models for context information are discussed and studied and then the novel system architecture for context handling and delivery using ontology-based models is presented. In this paper, ontology-based management and modelling techniques are used and referenced in the framework of a distributed context handling and delivery system. Following this, the representative ontology-based information management system within an application scenario is presented. The flexibility of the introduced approach allows for end-user scenarios, which are briefly described at the end of the paper.

**Keywords:** Autonomic Systems, Self-Management Infrastructure, Information Data Models, Ontology-Based Models, Policy-Based Service Management, Context Information, Next Generation Services, Context-Aware Framework.

## 1 Introduction

Pervasive Computing impacts the communications field offering the users various tools and possibilities for creating and supporting better and more efficient communications services. Pervasive computing applications are offered as tools for communication networks and computer systems allowing them to be extended to new services and scaled for more and diverse users. It is known that pervasive applications are characterized by their self-responding capability or autonomy to cope with highly dynamic environments [1]. When we refer to pervasive services we are describing services available to any user anywhere, anytime [2], thus describing the mobility and context-awareness panorama in the services.

Pervasive Computing brings with it the concept of context-awareness and as a consequence context-aware services are understood as applications that take advantage

A.K. Bandara and M. Burgess (Eds.): AIMS 2007, LNCS 4543, pp. 35–48, 2007.

of their surrounding environment for improving the performance or developing new services or applications for the benefit of the end users and/or network operators [2]. The advantages that context aware services can bring are rather obvious but at the same time it is also clear that the complexity of designing, deploying and managing their support systems is also high and requires appropriate tools and management mechanisms.

Traditionally, the management of communications systems (services, computing components and network infrastructures) has been done by humans. Currently those actions are becoming so complex that the human operators need to be assisted by appropriate computing systems capable of supporting the complexity of current communications systems. Autonomic systems emerge to solve this management complexity and technologically are the result of mobile computing technologies and information technologies interacting and cooperating together to support the creation, authoring, customisation, deployment and execution, i.e. the management and operation, of communication services [3][4]. This interaction is supported by the high semantic levels embedded in the context information by means of ontologies and other specific technologies such as policies languages.

This paper partially addresses the areas above mentioned focusing on an approach consisting of the integration of context information and network management operations for autonomic network infrastructure devices. Specifically, we present a system architecture for integrating and gathering context information to support network management operations of pervasive services lifecycles using ontology-based management and modelling techniques. As depicted in Figure 1, all the context information contained in the networks and devices can be used for multiple operations in other abstraction layers and then give support for customization, definition and deployment and even more, the maintenance of the services. In the depicted autonomic environments the possibility of upload the context information from source levels to overlay networks is increasing the pervasive level of the applications and as consequence, the services using such information (to see left side in figure 1). Our aim is to satisfy the need for making context network information available to service abstraction layers for triggering management operations in autonomic systems.

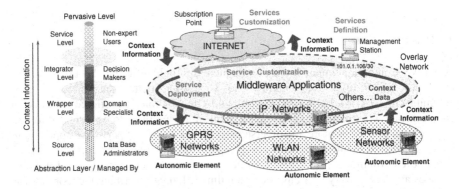

**Fig. 1.** Context Information Role in Pervasive Computing Environments

The remainder of the paper is structured as follows. Section 2 presents fundamental differences for management operations when using traditional information models and ontology-based models. Section 3 present results from ongoing research activity on the Ontology-bAsed Semantic Integrator System (OASIS), which is intended for integrating and gathering context information to support the management operations of pervasive services lifecycle. This section makes reference to the shared-Ontology for Support and Management of pervasive services (OSM) approach. Section 4 describes a service application scenario to show the flexibility and adaptability of the ontology-based framework using ontology-based information models. Section 5 presents the related work on ontology-based integration and information models and Section 6 is devoted to concluding remarks.

## 2   Management Using Information Models vs. Ontology-Based Models

Due to the complexity of modern communication systems, the integration of the context information in the network and services management operations constitutes a real challenge. It is highly desirable that the context information and operands can be distributed all over the networks or inclusive to services and users in a cross-layered panorama, from their corresponding context information sources in a most simply possible way. This highly complex and distributed scenario poses considerable problems to the interoperability of all this information in a consistent, coherent and formal way. In particular, one of the most difficult aspects is gathering the context information, e.g. people, applications, networks or any other study object, and its post processing so that the system can react in real time. Another one is the problem related to modelling and structuring of the context information. Finally without a model, applications wouldn't be able to use such information. The models must be semantically rich and extensible enough to accommodate not only the current but also future aspects of context information [5].

A data or information model represents the structure and organization of the data elements. In principle it is also specific to the application(s) for which it has been used or created. Therefore, the conceptualisation and the vocabulary of a data model are not intended a priori nor considered to be shared by other applications [6]. Data models, such as databases or XML-schemas, typically specify the structure and the integrity of data sets in certain types of data bases. Thus, building data models depends on the type of language, platform, and protocol to satisfy specific needs and tasks that have to be performed within an enterprise. The semantics of data models often constitute an informal agreement between the developers and the users of such data and that finds its way only in applications that use the data model. According to what is considered in the area of knowledge engineering [7][8][9], an based on these descriptions an ontology is *an agreement about a shared, formal, explicit and partial conceptualization that contains the vocabulary (terms or labels) and the definition of the concepts and their relationships for a given domain, including the instances of the domain as well as domain rules that are implied by the intended meanings of the concepts.* Ontologies represent knowledge that formally specifies agreed logical theories for an application domain. Additionally ontologies specify domain rules that represent the intended meaning of a conceptualisation. However, both Ontologies and data models, are partial representations of concepts that consider the structure and the rules of the domain, but unlike specific and implementation-oriented data models, ontologies in principle should be as generic and task-independent as possible.

Having in mind the requirements dictated by the pervasive services regarding information interoperability requirements and the different types of models that have been proposed for modelling context information (Key-Value, Mark-Up Scheme, Graphical, Object-Oriented, Logic based and Ontology-Based), and that have been described in [10]. The table 1 shows a ranking with a qualification based on three levels, and relate those levels to the context information modelling approaches with the objective of establish an analysis of the more suitable solution for modelling the context information according the information requirements and the level of how much they contribute to the requirements. e.g. the fact that Ontology-Oriented approach is ranked "Y" in "Formality" requirement indicates that approaches in this category fully support such property for information interoperability purposes.

**Table 1.** Information Interoperability Requirements Vs. Information Modelling Approaches

| Information Requirement Type | | Information/Data Model Approach | Key-Value * | Mark-Up Scheme * | Graphical * | Object-Oriented * | Logic-Based * | Ontology-Based * |
|---|---|---|---|---|---|---|---|---|
| Service Level | Nature-Associated | Composition | Z | Z | X | Y | Y | Y |
| | | Validation | X | Y | X | Z | X | Y |
| | | Quality | X | X | Z | Z | X | Z |
| | | Ambiguity | X | X | X | Z | X | Y |
| | | Formality | X | Z | Z | Z | Y | Y |
| | Operations-Associated | Extensibility | Z | Y | Z | X | Y | Y |
| | | Scalability | X | Z | X | Z | Y | Y |
| | | Automation | X | Z | X | Z | Z | Y |
| | | Flexibility | Z | Z | X | Z | Y | Y |
| | | Management | X | X | X | Y | Z | Y |
| | | Independence | X | X | X | Y | Z | Y |
| | | Integration | X | X | Z | Z | Z | Y |
| Schema Level | Entity Identifier | | Z | Y | X | Y | Z | Y |
| | Scheme Isomorphism | | X | Z | Z | Y | Z | Y |
| | Generalization | | X | Y | X | Y | Y | Y |
| | Aggregation | | Z | Y | Z | Y | Y | Y |
| | Naming | Atribute Synonymus | X | Y | Y | Y | Y | Y |
| | | Atribute Homonyms | X | Z | Z | Z | Y | Y |
| | | Entity Synonyms | X | Y | Y | Y | Y | Y |
| | | Entity Homonoyms | X | Z | X | Z | Y | Y |
| | | Data Value-Attribute | X | Z | X | X | Y | Y |
| | | Atribute-Entity | X | Y | Y | Y | Y | Y |
| | | Entity-Data Value | X | Z | X | Z | Y | Y |
| Data Level | Value | | Z | Z | X | Z | Y | Z |
| | Representation | | Z | Y | X | X | Y | Y |
| | Unit | | X | Z | X | Z | Y | Z |
| | Precision | Granularity | X | Z | X | X | Y | Y |
| | | Spatial Resolution | X | Z | X | X | Y | Y |
| | Data Value Reliability | | X | X | X | X | Z | Z |
| | Spatial Domain | | X | X | X | X | Z | Z |

\* See [10] for detailed description and examples.      Representation:   Z - Partially Support  Y- Full Support  X - No support

According to this ranking we can see that the ontology-based approaches offer more capabilities for satisfying the information requirements at schema and service levels. It is true that these approaches have shortages at data level due to the necessary logic operations, however for service-oriented applications in pervasive environments and furthermore support autonomic communications the ontologies seemingly offer upper and broadly support for the information requirements.

## 3 Ontology-Based System Architecture

OASIS (Ontology-bAsed Semantic Integrator System) is an ongoing research project that is working on integrating and gathering context information to support the management operations of pervasive services lifecycle. OASIS uses a global domain ontology that captures the knowledge around context information and includes a vocabulary of terms with a precise and formal specification of their associated meanings. We call this global domain ontology OSM (Ontology for Support and Management of pervasive services). OSM makes use of OWL. OASIS is inspired by HandS (Context Information Handler System) presented in [4] and based on the conceptual architecture mediation studied in [11]. OSM is essentially a language for semantic representations and reasoning that enables easy access to heterogeneous information systems.

From a functional point of view OASIS can be seen as an information system in four levels as follows. The *Service level* provides the data in the format that applications and users understand for executing network management operations (data type, structure, and language). Users do not have to know the query language syntax nor the ontology concepts at networks or operating levels. The *Integrator level* provides a unified view of the data, independent of which data source was used, masking their heterogeneity. The global ontology (OSM) and the local ones are provided at this level. We recall that the user's query is expressed in terms of the global ontology. In order to be executed by the local sources, the query has to be rewritten and expressed using concepts present in the local ontologies. This process is achieved using the mapping between the global ontology and the local ones. The Integrator also contains a reasoning engine that allows reasoning during the ontology mapping. The *Wrapper level* adapts the query to the source query language syntax before sending it to the source. After getting the results from the local source, it presents them in the global language in XML format before forwarding them to the Integrator. The *Source level* contains a set of autonomous sources in different formats: relational databases, XML repositories, text documents etc. These represent data that may be turned into context data, depending on their relevance. The wrapper level translates between each of their specific formats to a common format and back.

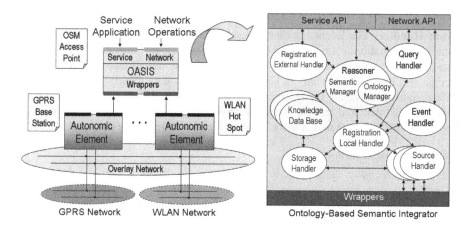

**Fig. 2.** Simplified Scenario and OASIS Architecture - Functional Components

Figure 2 gives high level view of the OASIS role through an example with two wireless access technologies, GPRS and WLAN. OASIS is the semantic integrator and therefore constitutes a unique access point for both, applications and network operations regardless of the access technology.

### 3.1 OASIS Detailed Functionality

The functionality of OASIS architecture (Ontology-bAsed Semantic Integrator System) can be understood through the functions of the elementary components shown in Figure 2 – right side, as described hereafter:

**Query Handler:** The Query Handler is responsible for resolving "pull" context requests issued for the application of the service logic. This component translates the"pull" into queries supported by the repositories. Once the Query Handler receives a context request, it contacts the Source and Storage Handlers through the Registration Handler to know if there is some context associated to the "pull".

**Registration Handler:** The Registration Handler enables the context handlers (Source and Storage Handlers) to publish their context information by providing a registration system of the context information, together with the interface to acquire it. If the requested context information is not registered previously, the Reasoner is triggered to initiate the mechanism for starting the search (we are referring to semantic forms) and provide the context information, contacting the Source Handler(s) and the Knowledge Data Base.

The *Local Context Handler* collects local context information from the Storage Handler. The interfaces to interact with these components are provided by the Registration Handler. When a request for context information is issued, Local Context Handler obtains the corresponding interfaces and acquires the requested context.

The *External Context Handler* is entrusted to feed the distributed context provisioning mechanism to retrieve context from remote sources. Searching will be performed taking into account that a set of candidate nodes for each type of Source and Storage Handlers is known a priori. If this is not the case, then a flooding approach will be adopted. Alternatively, the option where a Context Broker periodically receives context from other Context Brokers without explicit requests could be cost-effective.

**Event Handler:** The Event Handler is responsible for resolving "push" requests for context information exclusively that trigger management operations. The Event Handler allows the service to subscribe, through the use of appropriate APIs, to receive specific context events to acquire the relevant data. Note that context is not differentiated (events for management operations and raw context) at this level, the context is just gathered from sources and stored having a registration mark from the Registration Handler, then it is work for Reasoner for taking those decisions.

**Source Context Handlers:**

The *Source Handler* deals directly with context producers to retrieve the context information from remote sources, previously identified as context sources. This information arrives in raw formats -text line descriptions- that are parsed, using the concepts and relationships from the ontology language (OWL) to the common information data model in form of object classes that can be managed by the system.

The *Storage Handler* deals directly with the data bases and once it is activated it assumes responsibility for updating and storing the information. If the data base needs to be updated the storage handler can directly deal with the context sources, ensuring the context updating, and publishing through the Registration Handler.

**Reasoner:** The Reasoner is the engine that takes decisions during the ontology mapping between general ontology terms contained in the information model and local context terms coming from the context sensors. The enrichment of this component is supported in two ways, by one side the ontology-based information model defined by the language and concepts generated in the shared-ontology and by second one the ontology language itself (OSM for this application purposes). The reasoning process is done looking for semantic similarities between the data information model and the concepts parsed to the ontology language from raw sensor's context . This activity is supported by the relationships contained in the ontology structure, and then two concepts are correctly matched. The objective of generating an ontology is to create an ontology-based, extensible context information model supported by a formal language that provides information interoperability towards the semantic web for giving semantic support to web services and integrate additional information coming from business rules. The ontology is built using OWL Ontology Language [12] represented in XML [13] and edited with Protégé [14]. We have chosen Protégé as editing tool, first because it is an open source ontology editor, second and principally because of its ability to edit, capture, represent and showing in graph form the concepts and relationships between them, and finally, for the extensibility to use standard formats such as RDF-Schemas, HTML, etc.

The *Onto-Manager* is in charge for managing the entire context related to service provisioning activity and contained in the ontology. The management is performed by means of service policies for adapting the behaviour of the source context handler containing conditions that the services will require. The use of policy rules is a pre-condition that relates the context information with the management operations. Note that the service policies are not rules for relate the concepts contained in the ontology with the service policies, service policies are only the mechanism for managing the operations that the language define, and then the context is the knowledge content in the language that we use for trigger, deploy and execute also maintain the services operating normally. The adaptability of the behaviour of a context handler makes that the ontology-based manager needs to take into consideration the goals and requirements of the user's services through the context information model.

The *Semantic Context Manager* is in charge for managing the integrity of the context information and keeps it updated, in knowledge data bases, regarding the surrounding of the context handler. This component also modifies the ontology when it is updated. In contrast of previous applications that use completely centralized context data bases and are complex and difficult to access, this component will contain a distributed data-base containing the terms from the general ontology and the logic sentences in order to relate concepts and find semantic equivalences following rule-based queries becoming a knowledge tool for integration of semantic platforms.

## 3.2   Ontology for Support and Management of Pervasive Services - OSM

We propose the use of an ontology for integrated management covering service management operations such as creation, delivery and management of pervasive services, and also for integration of user's context information in service management operations OSM like. OSM is driven by a set of use cases on pervasive service management using policy-based architecture [15]. OSM is inspired from the integrated management needs in the autonomic management area [16]. The synergy obtained between context-awareness, ontologies and policy-driven services promotes the definition of a new, extensible, and scalable knowledge platform for the integration of context information and services support in autonomic networking.

OSM defines a set of dialects following a formal relationships defined in the ontology web language (OWL); this can be used to support the integration of context information in service and network management operations, policy-based systems and promote the integrated management in autonomic communications. This is an innovative aspect of our research work and part of our contributions in the information technologies (IT) area.

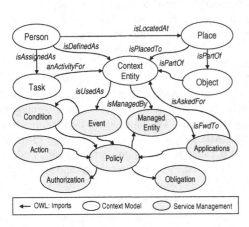

**Fig. 3.** OSM Upper Ontology

Figure 3 is a graphical representation of the highest level ontology for services support and management using context (OSM representation). Part of the constituting entities, concepts and their mutual relationships are also represented. For instance a ContextEntity is part of Events defined as Condition in a Policy and the Policy takes effect directly over Managed Entity and the effect *isFwdTo* Applications using the context information from ContextEntity. OSM aims to solve one of the main problems in the management of services and networks, the integration of the context information in tasks for managing the networks service operations, to achieve it, OSM use the policy-based paradigm.

Figure 4 shows part of the links as definitions and properties of upper classes. It shows the Policy class as part of a Policy-driven set of classes for managing services and how Policy is composed of Condition plus Action. OSM integrate the class ContextEntity as Event for triggering the management operations. Note that with the use of an upper ontology can be related concepts to create new concepts that are used by other applications into a specific-domain.

For instance Router is part of Resource and this concept is defined as an Object in ContextEntity with relationships to IP class, which is a type of Network. In consequence for a specific Application using ManagedEntity, a Router is the part of the Condition contained as Event that comes from ContextEntity and that triggers the Action of a Policy for a User in a specific Service. Note that User002 is a User contained in Person with a Task related to ManagedEntity. The example, on left side, shows how the OSM ontology describes an event consisting of the disconnection of an AccessPoint on February 05 2005 at 00:00:00 in a WiFi network.

**Knowledge Data-Base:** The associated Data Base is in charge of storing the global ontology and the ontextual information following the ontology-based, contextual information data model. The local ontology (e.g. WordNet) is stored in this data base. Then a user's query expressed in terms of the global ontology (OSM in this case) is rewriten in terms of the local ontology for the semantic-similarity purposes.

## 4 ServiceApplication Scenario

Assume large quantity of users that subscribe to a video conference service with quality of image guarantee, called CACTUS (Context-Aware Conference To You Service). This application scenario, depicted in the figure 5, uses OASIS system for taking advantage of networks and users

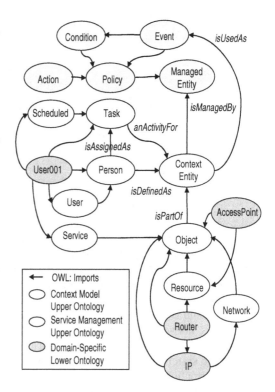

**Fig. 4.** OSM Ontology representation

```
<owl:Class rdf:ID="APDisconnected">
  <rdfs:subClassOf
   rdf:resource="&eve;TempSpatEvent"/>
</owl:Class>

<owl:ObjectProperty rdf:ID="RouterOff">
  <rdfs:domain
   rdf:resource="#APDisconneted"/>
</owl:ObjectProperty>

<APDisconnected>
  <spt:hasNetwork>
    <loc:TypeNetwork rdf:datatype>
      WiFi
    </loc:TypeNetwork>
  </spt:hasNetwork>

<RouterOff rdf:resource="UrlSomeResource"/>
  <tmp:atTime>
    <tmp:Time>
      <tmp:atTime
       rdf:datatype="xsd;dateTime">
       2005/02/05 Time 00:00:00
      </tmp:atTime>
    </tmp:Time>
  </tmp:atTime>
</APDisconnected>

</APDisconnected>
```

environment information and then provides a better and advanced 3G/4G service to its users. CACTUS is responsible for providing the QoS guarantees for a specific time period, in order to hold a video conference session among the members of a group. CACTUS upgrades the services as result of the information interoperability involved in all information handling and dissemination system and the service life-cycle; in other words this service is better than conventional ones without using context information to configure its service logic. The code of the service will be referred as Service Logic Object (SLO).

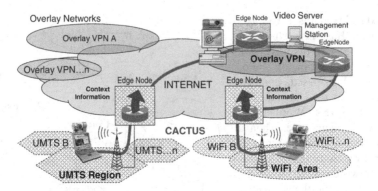

**Fig. 5.** CACTUS Testbed Architecture

The organizer of the conference specifies the participants of the conference and its duration, and then user profiles and personalized services are generated. All the conference participants should have already registered to the service utilizing the conference setup service web interface. When a user registers to this service, he enters: a) personal information (name, address etc) and b) information about the network cards he/she owns and is able to use, in order to connect to the network: MAC addresses for WLAN/LAN network cards and MSISDN numbers for UMTS/GPRS cards and c) service level, i.e. user chooses among service levels which correspond to different policies. The system uses this information for future services deployment and distributes the information to be stored in the knowledge data-bases.

The conference session is scheduled by a registered user (consumer) who utilizes the conference setup service web interface to input the information for the conference session. Specifically, he enters the conference start time, duration and the participants' names. This information is used to customize personalized communication services. Once the service's consumer schedules a conference session, a customized SLO is created and the service management policies are generated and loaded in the policy-based management system. Then, SLOs are distributed and stored in appropriate storage points depending on the nearest nodes and their characteristics as candidates to execute the service. Node proximity is measured in respect to user's location. Moreover, a service invocation sensor is launched to produce a "Start Time" event when the right moment for the service execution comes (usually when the participants connect/logon to the system). This event causes the invocation of the SLO by evaluating the context information, comparing with the information in the knowledge data-bases stored. The SLO is deployed and then the service is monitored with the network information monitor to guarantee the QoS.

## 4.1 OASIS Support of the Application Scenario

To support the information interoperability system, we use principles and components from the Context Architecture [17]. The system is directly supported by the ontology-based context information model based on OSM and OASIS. As a testbed intended for behavioural simulation of all the above concepts. A precondition is that a programmable platform (e.g. Context Platform [17]) is installed in the appropriate network nodes constituting an overlay network (in fact an overlay programmable network [17]) and that the user terminal is a mobile device that can access multiple wireless technologies, in particular IEEE 802.11a,b or IEEE 802.11g, as well as GPRS and Ethernet. Specific events are forced in the testbed to trigger the evaluation of certain conditions and test the context integrator system (OASIS), according to the corresponding variations of the context information. For instance, a network node disconnection is always a context variation. Then when an adjacent node update its context (surrounding information) this node disconnection is sent as a context variation, which triggers an event that OASIS evaluates and send information, updating connections conditions, and as consequence new SLOs are deployed according new user profiles to satisfy the QoS requested or necessary.

The information can be categorized in four groups containing the relevant context to our scenario: resource, network, application, and service context. This four context categories are part of the information model and they are contained in the ontology and modelled as object classes containing the information that is used for supporting the network service life-cycle and the management operations.

- Resource Object: This relates to the performance information about the network elements and also parameters that can modify the operation and dynamics of the network such as network addresses, bandwidth, network capacity, traffic levels, routing information, and network type in this scenario.
- Network Object: This relates to information about the network (UMTS network, WLAN network, IP network, and VPN network nodes). Specifically we refer to the physical aspects like servers, switches, routers, access points, edge nodes in the VPNs, and even user's gadgets of the CACTUS, i.e. PDAs. Smart Phones, laptops.
- Application Object: This context includes the description of the network services and its components. The discovering of such services is responsibility of the applications and then for instance a video server will public its usable services by other applications. Specifically in this scenario the application object includes descriptions like if it is part of a UMTS coverage area or from a WiFi hotspot for customizing and personalizing the services with this information.
- Service Object: This context relates the end user network services to the applications supported; for instance if they are using HTTP, FTP, or other protocols for supporting a VPN, amount of traffic produced, and bandwidth consumption to build new routing tables when a edge node is down, etc.

For the above described scenario, in both WLAN and UMTS domains, organizer's network and the interoperability Information system are linked via Internet. The scenario consists of the following components:

- VPN server and Edge Node: Those routers are the endpoint of the VPNs from participant laptop. It simulates any network provider server.
- Three Edge Routers: These host the OASIS platform. The routers closest to the WLAN and UMTS also host a network provider wrapper for the appropriate network access which constitute Source and Storage Handlers in this scenario.
- WLAN and/or UMTS access points: A WiFi complaint access point and UMTS base station respectively.

- Participant laptops: These are the mobile terminals, which connect to the participant with organizer's network VPN router and transfer the information. This user's terminal acts also as the source handlers for position of the terminal.
- Management Station: It simulates the pervasive service provider and contains the policies and all information as well management applications for the entire system.

## 5  Related Work

We have proposed to integrate the context information as part of the service lifecycle operations, we modelling the context information and take advantage of the formal languages for using the context information in such management operations and then make the management systems more pervasive and offer more service functionalities behind autonomic communications. The work above presented is based on an extensive search on several projects and initiatives briefly described in this section. In particular FOAF Ontology [18] allows the expression of personal information and relationships and it is a useful building block for creating information systems that support online communities. SOUPA [19], a standard ontology for ubiquitous and pervasive applications, includes modular components with vocabularies to represent intelligent agents with associated beliefs, desires, and intentions. COBra-ONT & MoGATU BDI ontologies are aimed to support knowledge representation and ontology reasoning in pervasive computing environments, each one in specific tasks. While COBra-ONT [20] focuses on modelling context in smart meeting rooms, MoGATU BDI [21] focuses on modelling the belief, desire and intention of human users and software agents. We had detected how in the majority of works on the integration of context using ontologies in pervasive applications the importance of context-awareness for management operations is marginal and leaved by side then we work in this way towards promote and support autonomic systems.

## 6  Conclusions

We have presented OASIS architecture for integrate the context information in pervasive environments and satisfy part of the information interoperability needs in service management operations in autonomic environments. Our efforts have been conducted towards providing an information system using an ontology-based information model for the contextual information and take advantage of the formal language description of context for the service lifecycle management operations.

OASIS framework aims to demonstrate that using ontology-based information model we can provides a functional support for managing context information and support pervasive services, OASIS framework increase the pervasiveness of the services and improving the cross-layer dissemination and information interoperability in autonomic communications towards the integrated management. OASIS provides the context information as service's event, and we work on enhance the architecture to integrate context information from multiple sources with multiple formats directly.

## Acknowledgments

This research activity is partially funded by the Ministerio de Educación y Ciencia under the project TSI2005-06413.

## References

[1] Gray, P.D., Salber, D.: Modelling and Using Sensed Context Information in the Design of Interactive Applications. In: Proceedings of 8th IFIP Working Conference on Engineering for Human-Computer Interaction, Toronto, Canada (2001)

[2] Henricksen, K., et al.: Modelling Context Information in Pervasive Computing System. In: Mattern, F., Naghshineh, M. (eds.) Pervasive Computing. LNCS, vol. 2414, pp. 160–167. Springer, Heidelberg (2002)

[3] Kephart, J.O., Chess, D.M.: The Vision of Autonomic Computing, IEEE Computer (January 2003) http://research.ibm.com/autonomic/research/papers/

[4] Serrano, J.M., Serrat, J., O'Sullivan, D.: Onto-Context Manager Elements Supporting Autonomic Systems: Basis & Approach. In: IEEE 1st International Workshop on Modelling Autonomic Communications Environments - MACE 2006. Manweek 2006, Dublin, Ireland, October 23-27, 2006, pp. 23–27 (2006)

[5] Dey, A.K.: Understanding and using context. Journal of Personal and Ubiquitous Computing 5(1), 4–7 (2001)

[6] Sheth, A., Kashyap, V.: So far (schematically) yet so near (semantically). In: Hsiao, D., Neuhold, E., Sacks-Davis, R. (eds.) Proc. of the IFIP WG2.6 Database Semantics Conf. on Interoperable Database Systems (DS-5), Lorne, Victoria, Australis, pp. 283–312. North-Holland, Amsterdam (1992)

[7] Ushold, M., Gruninger, M.: Ontologies: Principles, methods and applications. In: The. Knowledge Engineering Review 11(2), 93–155 (1996)

[8] Guarino, N., Giaretta, P.: Ontologies and Knowledge Bases: Towards a Terminological Clarification. In: Mars, N. (ed.) Towards Very Large Knowledge Bases: Knowledge Building and Knowledge Sharing, pp. 25–32. IOS Press, Amsterdam (1995)

[9] Gruber, T.: Towards Principles for the Design of Ontologies Used for Knowledge Sharing. International Journal of Human-Computer studies 43(5/6), 907–928 (1995)

[10] Serrano, J.M., Serrat, J.: Context Modelling and Handling In Context-Aware Multimedia Applications. In: IEEE Wireless Magazine, Multimedia in Wireless/Mobile Ad-hoc Networks (2006)

[11] Wiederhold, G.: Mediators in the Architecture of Future Information Systems. In: IEEE Computer Conference (1992)

[12] De Bruijn, J., Fensel, D., Lara, R., Polleres, A.: OWL DL vs. OWL Flight: Conceptual Modelling and Reasoning for the Semantic Web (November 2004)

[13] Boag, S., Chamberlin, D., Fernandez, M.F., et al.: XQuery 1.0: An XML query language ( 2002) http://www.w3.org/TR/xquery/

[14] http://protege.stanford.edu/plugins.html

[15] Serrano, J.M., Serrat, J., Strassner, J., Carroll, R.: Policy-Based Management and Context Modelling Contributions for Supporting Autonomic Systems. In: IFIP/TC6 Autonomic Networking. France Télécom, Paris, France (2006)

[16] Strassner, J., Kephart, J.: Autonomic Networks and Systems: Theory and Practice. In: NOMS 2006 Tutorial (April 2006)

[17] IST-CONTEXT project, Active Creation, Delivery and Management of Context-Aware Services http://context.upc.es

[18] Brickely, D., Miller, L.: FOAF vocabulary specification. In: RDFWeb Namespace Document. RDFWeb, xmlns.com (2003)

[19] Chen, H., Perich, F., Finin, T.W., Joshi, A.: SOUPA: standard ontology for ubiquitous and pervasive applications. In: Proc. of the First Int. Conf. on Mobile and Ubiquitous Systems: Networking and Services. (MobiQuitous'04), Boston, MA, August 22–26, 2004, pp. 258–267 (2004)

[20] Chen, H., Finin, T., Joshi, A.: An Ontology for context-aware pervasive computing environments. Special issue on Ontologies for Distributed Systems, Knowledge Engineering review (2003)

[21] Perich, F.: MoGATU BDI Ontology, University of Maryland, Baltimore County (2004)

# A Terminology for Control Models at Optical Exchanges

Freek Dijkstra[1], Bas van Oudenaarde[2], Bert Andree[1], Leon Gommans[1],
Paola Grosso[1], Jeroen van der Ham[1,3], Karst Koymans[1], and Cees de Laat[1]

[1] Universiteit van Amsterdam, Kruislaan 403, Amsterdam, The Netherlands
**fdijkstr@science.uva.nl**
[2] Finalist IT Group, Postbus 1354, Rotterdam, The Netherlands
[3] TNO Defense, Security and Safety, The Hague, the Netherlands

**Abstract.** Optical or lambda exchanges have emerged to interconnect
networks, providing dynamic switching capabilities on OSI layer 1 and
layer 2. So far, the only inter-domain dynamics have occurred on layer 3,
the IP layer. This new functionality in the data plane has consequences
on the control plane. We explain this by comparing optical exchanges
with current Internet exchanges.

Descriptions of optical exchanges have appeared in the literature,
but discussions about these exchanges have been hampered by a lack
of common terminology. This paper defines a common terminology for
exchanges. Discussion in the community revealed four different meaning
for the term "open exchange". We list them in this paper.

We classify the different kind of exchanges based on the interactions
between the domains at the control plane. We use these control models
to distinguish between different types of interconnection points.

## 1 Introduction

### 1.1 Overview

The main function of Interconnection points, such as exchanges, is to facilitate
traffic flows between the connected domains. Besides regular Internet-based exchanges, new types of exchanges are emerging. A wide variety of names has
been proposed for these new exchanges, including optical exchange, transport
exchange, grid exchange, GLIF open lambda exchange (GOLE), optical interconnection point and lightpath exchange.

The goal of this paper is to create a generally usable terminology for exchanges, both optical and Internet exchanges. The novelty in our work comes
from the fact that we do so by looking at the control plane rather than the
data plane, we identified conflicting definitions, and we are the first to compare
optical and internet exchanges in detail.

Section 2 gives a classification of existing and new exchanges, and defines our
terminology. Where possible, existing terminology is re-used. Other terminology,

A.K. Bandara and M. Burgess (Eds.): AIMS 2007, LNCS 4543, pp. 49–60, 2007.

in particular the term open exchange, draws upon discussions in the GLIF community [1,2][1].

A distinguishing factor for exchanges is the ability or inability of connected domains to influence the state of the core network. To this end, we define a total of three control models for exchanges in Sect. 3. This categorization will aid the discussion about the design of new exchanges. Section 4 maps these control models to each type of exchange.

The paper concludes with future trends and conclusions.

We refer to the extended version of this paper for a discussion about advanced network services on the data plane, like the conversion of data between different formats (interworking) and layers (elevator services), or on the control plane, like automated provisioning of network elements, policy based authorization, broker services, and index servers [3,4].

### 1.2  Related Work

This work builds on experience and discussions in the GLIF community, a collaboration of mostly National Research and Education Networks (NRENs). Here the need for high bandwidth circuits led to hybrid networks offering both routed and circuit switched network connections. Interconnections between NRENs are often made at new optical exchanges, like NetherLight, StarLight, ManLan, T-Lex, HK Light, UKLight and NorthernLight.

We rely as much as possible on exisiting terminology. In particular, the ownership terminology in Sect. 2.3 builds upon the management layers in Telecommunication Management Network (TMN) [5] and current practice in economic and legal communities [6].

This paper deals with the network node interface (NNI) of networks connected to an exchange, and is by no means the first to discuss this interface. The Optical Interworking Forum specified the network to network interface between domains (E-NNI) based on RSVP messaging [7]. Recent work comes from the L1VPN [8] workgroup in the IETF, which deals with the NNI for GMPLS [9].

The work provided in this paper is complimentary because it specifically deals with the network interface for an exchange rather than a transit network. This paper deals with a high level overview of the relation between the different actors, rather than specifying a practical signaling protocol.

## 2  Terminology

In this section we introduce a concise definition of terms like *domain, administrative control*, as well as *open* and *automated*.

---

[1] The only exception is that we use the term "optical exchange". The GLIF community currently uses the term "GOLE", and the authors personally prefer the term "transport exchange", but we felt that "optical exchange" was most widely recognized in all communities.

## 2.1    Peering

Traffic between separate networks is often exchanged at geographically clustered locations, called *interconnection points* or *peering points* [10,11]. For the regular Internet, the Internet service providers (ISPs), can interconnect using either *transit* or *peering* [12]. Peering, in most literature, is limited to providing connectivity to each others networks and to the customers of the other network, but not to other destinations. Transit on the other hand implies that traffic for any destination can be handled by the party providing the connectivity, usually for a fee.

In this paper we do not distinguish between peering and transit. In our terminology **peers** are network owners who connect to an interconnection point and **peering** is the concept of exchanging traffic between peers, regardless of the economic model.

## 2.2    Types of Interconnection Points

The most trivial interconnection point is a co-location that only provides rack space and power. This already gives the ability to initiate bilateral peerings between peers at the same facility. We are interested in exchanges, which are interconnection points with one or more core networks in place, dedicated to the exchange of traffic between peers.

**Classification.** We currently observe four types of interconnection points, based on the function, rather than the technical implementation:

– Internet exchanges
– mobile roaming exchanges
– optical exchanges
– points of presence

**Internet exchanges**, also known as Internet exchange points (IXP) or Network access points (NAP), serve as an interconnection points to exchange packet data between individual peers. The peers have one or a few physical connections to a central core infrastructure. The core network can be Ethernet LAN, ATM, or MPLS-based. The first variant is stateless, while the other two are stateful and require that the individual peers set up a path between them. Such a path is a channel in the physical connection.

**Mobile roaming exchanges**, such as GPRS roaming exchanges (GRX) [13] and UMTS exchanges, exchange packet data for respectively 2.5th and 3rd (3G) generation mobile telephony. In telecommunications, however, the term "exchange" is different from our usage and refers to a transit provider rather than an interconnection point. An exchange point between mobile roaming exchanges is technically not different from a packet-based[2] Internet exchange.

---

[2] GPRS and UMTS are packet based. The older CSD system is circuit switched.

**Optical exchanges**[3], also known as lambda exchanges, grid exchange points, transport exchanges or GLIF open lambda exchanges, are interconnection points where peers exchange traffic at OSI layer 1 or layer 2 [3]. GMPLS Internet exchanges as defined by Tomic and Jukan [14] share the concept of circuit-switched interconnection points, but have not been implemented yet.

We use the term **Transport Exchange** to refer to circuit-switched exchanges, like current-day optical exchanges.

Unlike exchanges, **points of presence** (POP) are interconnection points where the peers are unequal. Access networks connect with an upstream network provider at a POP. In this case, the peers are unequal since the upstream provider accepts transit traffic from the customer, but the reverse is not true.

**Internet versus Optical Exchanges.** Table 1 highlights the differences between Internet exchanges and optical exchanges. Peers at an Internet exchange interconnect to exchange IP traffic. The core of an Internet exchange contains exactly one circuit per peering relation. In contrast, an optical network supports circuits between end-users, so at an optical exchange there is a circuit between peers for each end-to-end connection that goes through the exchange. The table further emphasizes that for an optical exchange these circuits can carry any layer 1 or layer 2 traffic. Differences in function and purpose lead to different choices in technology between Internet exchanges and optical exchanges. Finally, the table highlights that an optical exchange may offer more advanced services than an Internet exchange.

There is no clear boundary between the different interconnection points since each interconnection point may take multiple roles. We expect that the differences listed in Table 1 will change over time, as new technologies become

**Table 1.** Functional differences between Internet exchanges and current optical exchanges

|  | Internet Exchange | Optical Exchange |
|---|---|---|
| **OSI Layer** | Transports traffic at layer 2, peers connect with layer 3 devices | Transports traffic at layer 1 or layer 2, peers connect at that same layer. |
| **Traffic type** | IP traffic only | Any packet data or any data at a specific framing or bit rate |
| **End-points** | Connection between two peering networks | Connections are part of a larger circuit between two end-hosts |
| **Dynamics** | Stateless, or state changes only when peering relations change | State changes for each data transport |
| **Technology** | Often packet switched, sometimes label-switched (with virtual circuits like MPLS and ATM) | Circuit or virtual-circuit switched (e.g. using SONET or VLANs) |
| **Services** | Only data transport | Data transport and other services, like the conversion of data between different formats and layers |

---

[3] Optical does not imply that the exchange itself is purely photonic.

available and are implemented. For example, customers at a POP may also directly peer with each other, a function typically seen at exchanges. Circuit switching is typically associated with optical exchanges, but not a technical necessity: ATM- and MPLS-based Internet exchanges are also circuit switched and it might be possible to create a non-circuit switched optical exchange using optical burst switching (OBS) [15].

## 2.3   Ownership

**Owner, Administrator and Users.** We distinguish between legal owner, economic owner, administrator and user(s) for each network element[4]. The **legal owner** of a network element is the entity that purchased the device and the **economic owner** is the entity that acquired the usage rights from the legal owner. We base these terms on current practice in economic and legal communities [6].

The **economic owner** determines its policy of the network. This entity carries the responsibility for the behavior of a device and has the final responsibility in case of hazards and abuse. In addition, each network element can also have a separate **administrator**, the person, organization, or software component that configures and administers the device on behalf of the economic owner. The economic owner determines the policy for a network element; the administrator enforces this policy. Finally, the **users** may use or invoke an element, if their request is in compliance with the active policy.

We assume that each network element has exactly one legal owner, one economic owner, and one administrator, but may have multiple users over time (though typically only one at a specific time).

**Domains.** We define a **domain** as a set of network elements[5]. An **administrative domain** is a set of network elements with the same administrator. An **owner domain** is a set of network elements with the same economic owner.

A **core network** is an administrative domain within an interconnection point that is able to exchange traffic between at least three peers. Core networks are of special interest throughout this paper and we use the term **core** to refer to a core network and its administrator.

**Examples.** Often the legal owner, economic owner, and administrator of a network element are the same entity. For example, in the Internet, a transit provider is typically owner and administrator of its network. But this is not always the case.

An organization leases a trans-oceanic fiber from a carrier for a year, the carrier is the legal owner, while the other organization is the economic owner.

If an organization outsources the maintenance of its network, the economic owner and administrator of this network are different entities.

---

[4] Network element is a generic term to include network devices, links, interfaces and hosts.

[5] Including non-disjoint sets. Note that a domain does not necessarily have to be an AS-domain.

In the next subsection we explain the concept of open control, where the exchange is both the legal owner as well as the administrator of a specific interface, while the peer is the economic owner of this interface.

## 2.4 Open Exchanges

We found that in the the GLIF community, the use of "open" in "open exchanges" was ambiguous. It could refer to at least four different meanings, as described below. We recommend that it is only used in the now prevalent meaning of *open control*. For other meanings, we suggest alternative wording.

**Open Control Model.** In a **closed** interconnection point, the economic owner domain is equal to the administrative domain: everyone both decides upon and enforces the policy of their network elements. In particular, the core ultimately decides on the policy for each interface in the core network.

In the open control model, the core of an open exchange delegates the policy decision of each external interface to the peer that connects to that interface. Therefore, peers of an open exchange have the ability to configure "their" interfaces in the core network and thus can decide who connects to their networks.

Figure 1 shows an optical exchange consisting of an optical cross connect at the core. The exchange has three peers: Anet, Bnet and Cnet. If Anet wants to connect to Cnet, it signals that request to the exchange. A closed exchange would autonomously decide to grant or deny that request, and choose interface 4 or 5. An open exchange outsources this policy decision to Cnet which has policy control over interface 4 and 5, even though this policy is enforced in the optical cross connect which is legally owned and administrated by the exchange.

In the open control model, the core does not define an acceptable use policy (AUP) for its peers, and is thus *AUP free*.

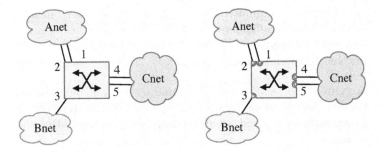

**Fig. 1.** Example of an optical exchange. On the left the administrative domains are shown, which are equal to the owner domains for the closed control model. On the right, the owner domains for the open control model are shown.

**Business Model.** We use the word **"public"** or **"neutral"** to refer to an interconnection point with an open business model. An open business model requires that an interconnection point must have a published, clear policy for new peers to join, and has a reasonable and non-discriminatory (RAND) policy[6] towards its peers.

A non-public interconnection point is called "**private**" or "**non-neutral**". An open exchange can still be non-neutral. For example, an exchange economic owner may decide to only connect business partners as peers, but not others, and have the partners then decide on the policy for connections. Similarly, a neutral exchange may not be open. Hypothetically, an exchange may decide to allow every peer to connect to the core network, but grant path setup requests depending on an arbitrary decision.

**Service Exposure.** The term "**service exposure**" can be used to refer to the ability by peers to look in the inner workings of the exchange. The opposite of service exposure is "**service overlay**". An exchange with a service overlay would behave like a black box. While peers can make requests to a black box, they do not know what exact devices, interfaces or other equipment are used to fulfill the request.

**Automated Exchange.** An exchange is called "**automated**" if peers are able to set up circuits between each other and invoke other services from the exchange without manual intervention from the economic owner of the core network.

# 3    Control Models

In this section, we define three different control models for interconnection points: the autonomous, federated and distributed control models. The autonomous control model is the simplest model. The federated and the distributed control model respectively extend the autonomous and the federated control models.

These models make a clear distinction between administrative control (policy enforcement) and owner control (policy decision) of the network elements. We consider a few administrative domains on the transport plane, each operated by a specific administrator. For each model, we explain how owner domains control network elements, and in particular how peers decide on the business policy for some network elements in the core network.

It is only possible to control network elements in another administrative domain if the administrators work together by sending messages to each other. It should be noted that we do not assume that these messages are automated.

## 3.1    Autonomous Control Model

In the autonomous control model, there is exactly one core network, which is owned and administrated by a single entity. Peers can connect their network to the interconnection point, but there is no interaction between the peers and the

---

[6] This may seem to imply equal access rights to all peers. However, a distinction can be made based on the service level, as long as the service level is achievable by all peers on non-discriminatory conditions. E.g., if they pay a certain fee.

core network on the control plane. Peers may interact with each other, but that is not relevant to this model.

Figure 2 shows an example of the autonomous control model. In this figure, the transport plane shows five distinct administrative domains: core, A, B, C and D, each operated by a administrator on the control plane. On the transport plane, each box represents an administrative domain, interconnected by links. On the control plane, each square represents a separate controller. There is no communication between the peers and the core on the control plane.

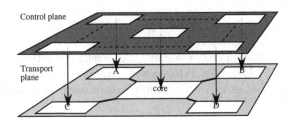

**Fig. 2.** Example of the autonomous control model. Squares represent administrative domains.

The economic owner of a core network determines a limited number of policies. Peers either accept the policies or take their business elsewhere.

The peers of a LAN-based Internet exchanges exchange control messages using an external routing protocol, but not with the exchange itself. So these exchanges are examples of the autonomous control model.

The autonomous control model is always closed.

## 3.2   Federated Control Model

In the federated control model, the interconnection point has exactly one core network. The core offers services to each peer, including the ability to interconnect with other peers.

The inner workings of the core network may be unknown to the peers (making it a black box), but peers can still check information about the state of some resources. For example, a peer can still inquire about the availability of a certain resource or get the status of a circuit it established earlier.

Figure 3 shows an example of the federated control model. The transport plane is the same as in Fig. 2, but the control plane is different: here the controller of each peer exchanges messages with the controller of the core network.

When a peer wants to use a certain service, it invokes the administrator of the core network, which may delegate parts of the request to other parties. For example, if peer D sends a request to set up a circuit from B to D, the core economic owner checks if the requested resources in the core itself are available and contacts the economic owner(s) of the resources involved. In the case of open control, the core asks peer B if this request must be honored. If that is true, the core administrator then creates the requested circuit.

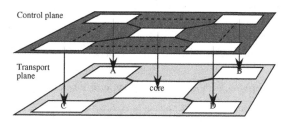

**Fig. 3.** Example of the federated control model

## 3.3   Distributed Control Model

In the distributed control model there can be multiple federations, each controlling a different core network. Every party can bring in its own equipment, e.g. fibers, and most important: its own services (and control software). Each peer exposes its own services to the rest of the community, possibly without revealing the inner details. A broker may combine multiple services and expose this combination as a single service.

The idea is that each peer still administratively controls its own network elements, but interacts with other administrators, or partially delegates its policy control, forming collaborations. Each peer can partner in multiple collaborations.

It is possible to regard one instance of the distributed control model as multiple interconnected instances of the federated control model. However, the distributed control model highlights the intelligence that is required to make all parts work together. This intelligence is not always necessary in the federated model.

Figure 4 shows an example of the distributed control model. The figure shows how peers can dedicate part of their network resources to form a dedicated core network. For example, A may expose some network elements to the other peers, which can be used by B or D to interconnect, either to A, or between each other through the core network of A. Also, C and D may decide to put some network resources in a pool, forming another, joint, core network. Typically, a core network formed by multiple peers is exposed as one single core network by a broker, which then delegates incoming requests to the individual administrators of the peers.

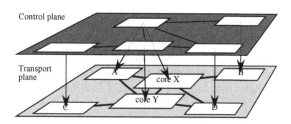

**Fig. 4.** Example of the distributed control model

## 4  Model Usage

In Table 2, we give a list of viable mappings between the current interconnection points to the models described, based on our observation of current exchanges.

**Table 2.** Applicable models for each type of interconnection point

|  | Internet Exchange | Mobile Exchange | Optical Exchange | Point of Presence |
|---|---|---|---|---|
| Autonomous control model | ✓ | ✓ |  | ✓ |
| Federated control model | ✓ | ✓ | ✓ | ✓ |
| Distributed control model |  |  | ✓ |  |

Stateless Internet and mobile exchanges use the autonomous control model, since no request needs to be sent to the core network administrator to exchange data between peers. If the Internet or mobile exchange is stateful, it can be either of these two models.

A POP typically uses the autonomous control model, because the configuration is mostly static and peers have no direct control over the inner working of the facility. However, if peers of a POP can decide on the policy, the federated control model is used.

If optical exchanges offer multiple services, standardized service discovery and service invocation are required. Both the federated and distributed control models offer this feature in a scalable way using pluggable services (a service oriented architecture). The distributed control model is more complex than the other models, and thus harder to deploy, because there is no longer a single entity that acts as a broker broker.

## 5  Future Trends

Large data transport on long distances is most efficient over the lowest possible layers, and peers and their users demand more flexibility to set up circuits with known quality of service (QoS) between domains. Interconnection points down in the protocol stack can offer this flexibility.

Technologies change over time, just as the requests from the users. We have reasons to believe that the current optical (transport) exchanges and Internet exchanges converge into optical exchanges that support all the required services. First there is a tendency for current optical exchanges to provide network services, and a future service might be multiparty peering like in a LAN-based Internet exchange. Secondly, Internet exchanges tend to offer more services which are now regarded as optical exchange functions, like private circuits between two peers[7]. Third, there is a tendency to build Internet exchanges and optical

---

[7] For example, the Amsterdam Internet Exchange AMS-IX already provides private interconnects and closed user groups.[16]

exchanges at the same locations[8], which indicates a possible economic advantage of combining exchanges on the same physical location.

Open control is a mind shift compared to most current exchanges. With closed control, peers sometimes have the ability to change the state of one or more network elements in a core network, but their requests are evaluated against the policy set by the exchange. With open control on the other hand, the peers decide on the policy and the exchange enforces it for them. Even if peers are in control, they do not experience it that way unless their requests are promptly answered by an automated ensemble. Thus, automation of exchanges is a necessity for this paradigm change to happen.

We also recognize a trend to let end users control the network resources as they want. For example UCLP supported by CANARIE is a control mechanism driven by users. Whether the exposition of network elements and network services will continue is yet unclear. If low layer network connections are exposed to users, authorization becomes more important to prevent abuse. Monitoring is important for peers and end-users to check if and where failures occur. This is part of our future research direction.

# 6   Conclusion

Formerly, discussions about optical or lambda exchanges have been hampered by a lack of common terminology. In this paper we identified ambiguous terms, in particular on "open exchanges", and presented a consistent terminology, based on experiences in the GLIF community. We introduced multiple models for exchanges that we offer to use as reference points to the community. We did show that the terminology can be used to classify the existing exchanges according to the models that we introduced. While we are confident that the models are workable, we hope they are found as fruitful to others as they are to use in discussions on the difference between Internet exchanges and optical exchanges.

# Acknowledgment

Part of this research is done under the GigaPort Next Generation project led by the Dutch National Research Network (SURFnet), and the Interactive Collaborative Information Systems (ICIS) project. Both projects are supported by the Dutch Ministry of Economic Affairs, grant numbers BSIK03020 and BSIK03024.

The authors wish to thank John Vollbrecht from Internet2, Henk Steenman and Job Witteman of the AMS-IX, and members of the GLIF community for their discussions and proof-reading.

---

[8] For example, Chicago, New York and Amsterdam.

# References

1. Global Lambda Integrated Facility http://www.glif.is/
2. Terminology discussion in the GLIF community (September 2005) http://www.glif.is/list-archives/tech/msg00019.html
3. Dijkstr, F., de Laat, C.T.A.M.: Optical Exchanges, GRIDNETS conference proc. (October 2004)
4. Dijkstra, F., et al.: extended version of A Terminology for Control Models at Optical Exchanges http://www.science.uva.nl/~fdijkstr/
5. Considerations for a telecommunications management network, ITU recommendation M.3013 (February 2000)
6. The terms economic ownership and legal ownership are common economic terms. E.g. Harrison, A., in Definition of economic assets (January 2006) http://unstats.un.org/UNSD/nationalaccount/AEG/papers/m4EconAssets.pdf
7. Ong, L.Y.,(eds.), et al.: Intra-Carrier E-NNI Signaling Specification, OIF specification OIF-E-NNI-Sig-01.0 (February 2004)
8. Takeda, T., et al.: Framework and Requirements for Layer 1 Virtual Private Networks, draft-ietf-l1vpn-framework, Work in Progress (January 2007)
9. Berger, L., et al.: Generalized Multi-Protocol Label Switching (GMPLS) Signaling Functional Description, RFC 3471 (January 2003)
10. Chinoy, B., Salo, T.: Internet Exchanges: Policy-Driven Evolution, Harvard Workshop On Co-Ordination Of The Internet, J.F. Kennedy School Of Government(September 1996)
11. Huston, G.: Interconnection, Peering, and Settlements. In: Proc. of Inet'99 (June 1999)
12. Norton, W.: Internet Service Providers and Peering. In: Proc. of NANOG 19 (May 2001)
13. Blyth, K.J., Cook, A.R.J.: Designing a GPRS roaming exchange service, Second International Conference on 3G Mobile Communications Technologies (March 2001)
14. Tomic, S., Jukan, A.: GMPLS-Based Exchange Points: Architecture and Functionalilty Chapter 8. In: Emerging Optical Network Technologies Architectures, Protocols and Performance, October 2004, Springer, Berlin Heidelberg (2004) ISBN 0-387-22582-X
15. Qiao, C., Yoo, M.: Optical Burst Switching (OBS) – A New Paradigm for an Optical Internet. J. of High-Speed networks, pp. 69–84 (1999)
16. Amsterdam Internet Exchange, Services provided by the AMS-IX http://www.ams-ix.net/services/

# Self-forming Network Management Topologies in the Madeira Management System

Liam Fallon[1], Daryl Parker[1], Martin Zach[2], Markus Leitner[2], and Sandra Collins[1]

[1] Ericsson Ireland Research, Ireland
{liam.fallon,sandra.collins,daryl.parker}@ericsson.com
[2] Siemens AG, Austria
{martin.zach,markus.leitner}@siemens.com

**Abstract.** This paper describes a novel approach to network management topologies where multiple customized topologies are self-configured, self-optimized, and maintained automatically by the underlying network of elements. An implementation of these self-forming management topologies as developed in the Celtic European research project Madeira is described. The self-forming topologies use peer-to-peer communication facilities provided by the Madeira platform running on each network element and give a view of the complete network topology, with customization optimised for individual management functionality. Finally, experiences in utilising these topologies are described, highlighting the benefits of this novel approach.

**Keywords:** network management topology, self-formation, self-configuration.

## 1 Introduction

Most network management systems (NMS) in service today use layered management topologies that are a variant of the model proposed in the ITU standards [1] [2] originating from the late 80's. The network management topology in this model is a representation of the interconnectivity between the network elements (NEs) and the management systems, and can be characterized as centralized and hierarchical. This hierarchy introduces different levels of abstraction – from element management of individual NEs up to business management at the top of the Telecommunication Management Network (TMN) pyramid [1].

Management functions in each element manager read data from NEs connected to them to build internal logical topology mappings. Likewise, management functions in each network manager read data from element managers connected to them to build a logical topology mapping. Thus management information flow in both directions – up and down this static hierarchy – is cascaded, with information mapping performed at each layer. One consequence is, from a functional point of view, the five FCAPS disciplines remain rather separated. Interactions between these disciplines typically happen at higher management layers, or even through a human operator.

There are a number of drawbacks to this approach. There is a single network management topology in the network, it is static in nature: it is a representation of the

A.K. Bandara and M. Burgess (Eds.): AIMS 2007, LNCS 4543, pp. 61–72, 2007.

connectivity of the management system for the network. This topology is not necessarily optimal for every management function. It becomes very difficult to build advanced management functions that work across managers; as each manager is only aware of its local topological information and that of its subordinate NEs. As a consequence, this architecture inhibits managers at the same level from sharing topological information. This is a critical issue for multi-vendor, multi-technology management systems. Compounding the problem is the scale, transience, and diversity of elements in evolving networks. The task of keeping topology mappings consistent in dynamic networks is increasingly difficult; with more development effort required to keep track of what is managed rather than being focused on improving the management of the services the network provides.

Motivated by these issues we present a novel implementation of self-configuring, self-optimizing management topologies, based on a peer-to-peer (P2P) approach to network management, developed and implemented in the CELTIC research project Madeira [3]. The remainder of this paper is structured as follows: chapter 2 briefly summarizes related work; chapter 3 presents an overview of the self-organizing cluster topology mechanisms of the Madeira solution while chapter 4 provides details of the implementation. Chapter 5 describes our experiences of using such topologies in a test network and simulation environment. Chapter 6 concludes the paper and outlines future work.

## 2  Related Work

Networks which are predominantly static in nature are inherently straightforward to manage using existing TMN principles. In contrast, the networks we address in this paper have highly dynamic topologies. The target network we selected as our test-bed for the Celtic project Madeira is a large-scale wireless Ad-hoc network.

A centralised approach typically results in a high message overhead introducing a large waste of bandwidth; a critical resource in wireless environments. There are two potential approaches available to a central manager; polling or asynchronous notifications. Either approach has been seen to be inefficient, particularly for polling [4]; both approaches result in the central manager being a single point of failure, and bottleneck in the network. Therefore, this approach is not considered appropriate for large-scale wireless environments.

There exists however a number of management architectures currently used for Ad Hoc networks, based on a combination of both distributed and hierarchical approaches. The most notable of these systems can be found in [4], [5] and [6]. These proposals are largely based on specific clustering techniques: [4], [7] and [8] respectively. The superpeer management service described in [9] uses proximity based message broadcasting and NE capabilities to find and elect superpeers, building a single level topology that is optimized for latency. A taxonomy of various distributed management paradigms has been compiled in [10]. With respect to their taxonomy, our Madeira approach might be classified as following the strongly distributed hierarchical paradigm, with the additional advantage of using a completely dynamic hierarchy. The use of a dynamic hierarchy allows the Madeira system to adapt to network failures and state changes, that [11] argues is essential to effective management of future large scale dynamic networks which must exhibit adaptive, decentralized control behaviours.

# 3 Madeira Management Topologies in Overlay Networks

An overlay network [12][13] is a logical network built on top of another network, with overlay nodes connected by virtual or logical links, each corresponding to a path, perhaps through many physical links, in the underlying network. The Madeira platform [3] is based upon the concept of Adaptive Management Components (AMCs); containers on NEs that run management software entities. AMCs provide services to those entities so that they can manage the NEs on which they are running and communicate with entities running on other NEs. This distributed management system has many advantages including low bandwidth usage, low message consumption, and scalability for large, dynamic networks.

It is evident however, that such an approach conflicts with some assumptions from a classical NMS approach. Traditional architectures assume a network with a relatively static hierarchical topological structure, in which:

- Aggregation and delegation occurs only as data moves up and down the hierarchy.
- Connections in the management hierarchy are controlled; adding and removing entities to a management structure is assumed to be a static task.
- The absence of a management entity is usually assumed to be an error.

In contrast, in the Madeira management overlay, element management and parts of network management run on NEs in the network itself in a flat peer-to-peer manner. Information is exchanged on east-west interfaces, allowing the distributed management system to understand its local environment and carry out environment-specific management tasks autonomically. Furthermore NEs can appear and disappear in normal operation, behaviour that conventional network management systems do not expect and has difficulty managing. The Madeira platform accommodates such behaviour through the use of management clusters which self-organise into a logical hierarchical structure, which can interact with management systems built using traditional management approaches. In this way the Madeira platform provides the base for building distributed and cooperative network management applications. The remainder of this chapter gives an overview of the functional aspects of the Madeira management clusters, with implementation details covered in chapter 4.

## 3.1 Topologies of Clusters and Cluster Heads

Management clusters are distributed structures that are formed in an ad-hoc manner by a set of co-operating NEs for the purpose of managing some network feature or function. Fig. 1 shows a network with its NEs formed into management clusters for two hypothetical management functions X and Y. These management clusters self-organize into a cluster hierarchy made up of cluster members and cluster heads. Each cluster hierarchy constitutes a topology and many such cluster topologies may coexist, customised for one or more management functions.

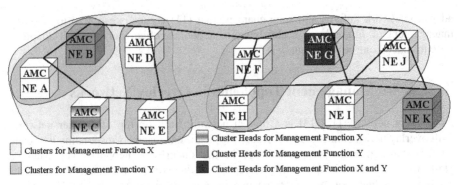

**Fig. 1.** Management Clusters for Management Functions X and Y

The cluster head (or super peer) is the NE within a cluster that is elected to coordinate and publish the topology of that cluster. A cluster head may also aggregate and correlate data for a cluster or act as a mediation point. The cluster topology of a management function is tuned for that particular management function. A topology used by a fault management application is optimized for root cause detection of common faults on low level cluster heads, thus reducing the resources needed in higher level cluster heads. Cluster heads that correlate alarms are chosen because they have high processing power and reasonable memory availability.

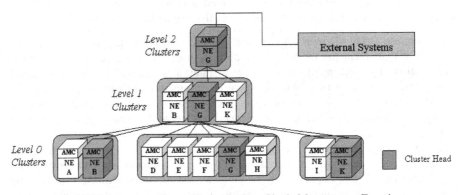

**Fig. 2.** Management Cluster Hierarchy for a Single Management Function

Fig. 2 shows an example of a cluster hierarchy for a single management function. An NE in a level n cluster is the cluster head from a level n-1 cluster. NEs in a level n cluster elect a cluster head which represents the level n cluster in the level n+1 cluster. The hierarchy is self-configuring and re-forms dynamically and seamlessly whenever NEs are added, moved, or removed. New clusters may appear, merge, split, or disappear within a topology. Promotion and demotion of cluster heads may occur. New levels may appear or levels may disappear in the hierarchy of a topology. The topology on a single NE, a sub-tree of a topology or an entire topology can also be manually reset by a network operator or an external system if required.

The mechanisms for the formation of clusters, election of cluster heads, and supervising the levels in a hierarchy are controlled via parameters[1]. A topology may re-form if any of the parameters that influence it are changed during network operation, causing the structure to self-optimize based on the prevailing network conditions. Parameters can be altered dynamically by direct operator intervention, automatically using policies [14], or as a result of changes in the network state.

Users of a topology such as an external system may register for topological events. Notification subscriptions may vary in scope from, an entire topology, a sub-tree of a topology, or a single NE. Examples of predefined events include:

- a NE being added to or removed from a cluster
- a NE is promoted to or demoted from being a cluster head
- a NE is promoted to or demoted from being the top NE in a topology

A management function may issue events specific to its function; for example a FM application may report correlated faults as events.

# 4   An Algorithm for Self-forming Topologies

In this chapter, we introduce the main components and use case interactions in the Madeira implementation of self-forming topologies.

## 4.1   Topology Entities

The building block for all topologies is a Topology Entity (TE). A TE runs in the AMC of each NE for every topology that the NE is a part of. The TE is responsible for building and maintaining a local view of its topology for the NE on which it runs. The TEs for a particular topology communicate and co-operate to build and maintain the entire topology for the network as shown in Fig. 3.

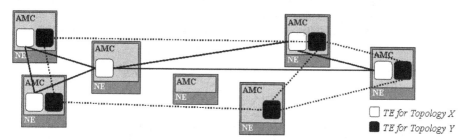

**Fig. 3.** Topology Entities for Two Management Functions Running in AMCs

All TE software components are identical. A full topology is an aggregation of all local topology information for the TEs in that topology. A key characteristic to note is

---

[1] Parameters might include type, technology, NE resource or service capabilities, NE and neighbour location, availability, accessibility, cost of use, topology structure and NE membership in other topologies.

that when a topology is fully formed, it exists logically as a hierarchical layered structure, even though it is instantiated in a flat management overlay. A TE manages the structure of a topology for its local NE, keeping track of relevant data for the NE itself and the logical connections the NE has with TEs in other NEs.

If a TE appears at a certain level in a topology, it must also appear at every level below that level. A TE has either the role of cluster head or member at a particular level. A TE must be a cluster member at the highest level that it exists at in the hierarchy and a cluster head at every other level. A TE records its role at each level in a table. If a TE has a cluster member role at a level, the TE records the address of its cluster head and a flag indicating if that TE is the top cluster head. If a TE is a cluster head at a level, it records the addresses of each of the cluster members. Fig. 4 shows the structure of the TE tables for the topology shown in Fig. 2.

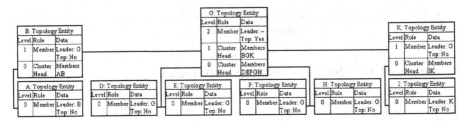

**Fig. 4.** Topology Entity Tables for a Topology

## 4.2  Role Controllers

TEs communicate with each other to build and maintain topology structures, using role controllers to keep track of the topology at each level. Therefore, a TE has a Head Role Controllers (HRC) for each level at which it is a cluster head and a single Member Role Controller (MRC) for its highest topology level. The HRCs and MRCs at a particular level in the topology co-operate with each other to maintain clusters and handle the topology at that level for the entire topology or for sub-trees of the topology. Fig. 5 shows the HRC and MRC co-operation for the topology of Fig. 2.

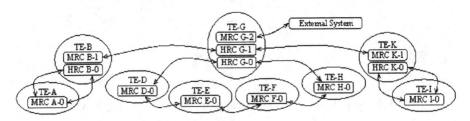

**Fig. 5.** HRCs and MRCs Co-Operating at Topology Levels

## 4.3  Cluster Formation

In the following sections we present the TE lifecycle and describe various interactions for building, maintaining, and using network management cluster topologies.

**Initial Start of TE.** When a TE starts, it initializes its topology data table and inserts a table entry at level 0 indicating that the TE is a member of a topology at that level and has no cluster head. It starts a MRC at level 0.

**MRC Start and Restart.** When the MRC starts at a given level, it realises that it is a member of a cluster with no cluster head. If the MRC had assumed it was the cluster head at the top of a topology and had set the "top" flag, that flag is cleared. The MRC issues a not top of topology event to any external entities that have subscribed for that event. This sequence is shown in Fig 6 a).

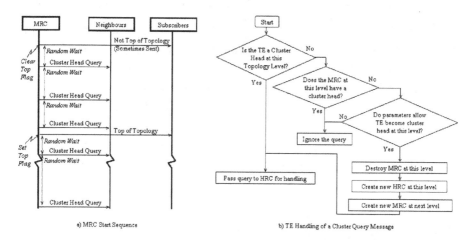

a) MRC Start Sequence            b) TE Handling of a Cluster Query Message

**Fig. 6.** Starting MRCs and Cluster Head Election

The MRC waits for a parameterized random time period and sends a multicast or broadcast cluster head query with its address and the topology level to a parameterized set of neighbours. By default the query is sent to all neighbours 1 hop away for MRCs at level 0, two hops away for MRCs at level 1 and so on. While the MRC receives no reply, it periodically re-sends the cluster head query. If no neighbours running a HRC or MRC for the topology and level in question exist, then the MRC will receive no reply. If a HRC receives a cluster head query and decides not to admit the MRC in question into its cluster, the HRC will not reply to the MRC. If after a parameterized number of resends no reply is received, the MRC assumes it is a cluster member at the top of a topology, sets the "top" flag for that level, and issues a top of topology event to its subscribers.

**Cluster Head Promotion.** Fig. 6 b) shows how a TE handles a cluster head query. If it is already a cluster head at a level, it passes the message to the HRC at that level. If it is a cluster member at that level and has a cluster head, it drops the message, allowing the TE with the HRC for its cluster to handle the message.

If the TE is a cluster member but not a cluster head at that level, then there are two cluster members at the same level with no cluster head. The TE checks its topology

68    L. Fallon et al.

parameters and, if the check permits, promotes itself to cluster head. It does this by destroying the MRC at that topology level, starting a HRC at that topology level, and starting a MRC for the next topology level. The cluster head query is passed to the HRC for handling.

When the HRC starts, it initializes a list to hold the addresses of its cluster members. Initially, this list includes just the address of the TE itself. It issues a cluster head promoted event to its subscribers.

**Cluster Member Addition.** Fig. 7 a) shows the message sequence used to add members to a cluster. A cluster head query may be handled by any HRC that is running or is started at the topology level specified in the query. If after checking its parameters the HRC decides to admit the new member, it reserves a place for the member and replies with a cluster head query reply. On receipt of the reply, the MRC checks its parameters to see if it is still allowed to become a member of the cluster of that HRC and if yes, sends a member confirmation message to the HRC. A MRC may receive more than one reply to a cluster head query. It always responds to and joins the cluster of the first HRC that replies and is acceptable, ignoring all other replies. The cluster member supervision on those HRCs removes the MRC reservation after a certain timeout has expired.

When the HRC receives a cluster member confirmation, it confirms the MRC as a member of its cluster and issues a cluster member added event to its subscribers. If the MRC had previously assumed it was at top of the topology it clears its top of topology flag and issues a not top of topology event to its subscribers.

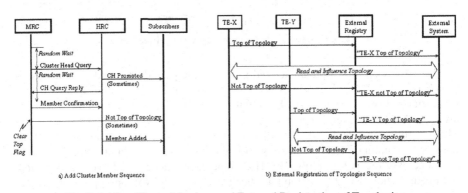

Fig. 7. Adding Cluster Members and External Registration of Topologies

**Cluster Member and Cluster Head Supervision.** Once the cluster head and cluster member relationships have been established a supervision process is initiated to monitor these relationships. A cluster head periodically polls its members to ensure that they still exist. When a MRC is polled, its HRC expects a reply to its poll within a certain time. If the MRC does not reply within the time period, the HRC removes the MRC from its cluster. Once a cluster head has completed its member scan, if the HRC itself is the only member of the cluster, the TE demotes the HRC to a MRC.

Similarly the MRC expects to be polled by its cluster head periodically; if it is not polled by its cluster head for a set time period, the MRC assumes its cluster head has disappeared, and the MRC restarts itself.

**Cluster Head and Cluster Member Orderly Removal and Shutdown.** If a cluster member shuts down or restarts, its MRC sends a leave cluster message to its HRC if it has a cluster head. If the MRC had assumed it was the cluster member at the top of a topology and had set the "top" flag, that flag is cleared and MRC issues a not top of topology event to its subscribers. If the MRC is not polled for a set time period, or it gets an error when communicating with its cluster head, it assumes its cluster head has disappeared. In all these cases, the MRC restarts itself.

If a HRC cannot communicate with a MRC; when a HRC to MRC poll fails; or when a HRC itself is shut down, the HRC removes the MRC from its member list and issues a cluster member removed event to its subscribers. Similarly when a cluster head is shut down or restarted, it sends a cluster head shutdown message to all its cluster members and issues a cluster head demoted event to its subscribers.

**Registration of Topologies and Communication with External Systems.** When a cluster head realises that it is the top cluster head in a topology, it registers itself using a Top of Topology Event with an external registry such as a UDDI repository as being the entity that is publishing information externally for its topological hierarchy. An external system can subscribe to registry get the address of the top TE and can then open a direct communication session with that TE as shown on Fig. 7 b).

External systems may be informed that an address they are using is no longer valid, if the registry receives the top and not top events, ensuring connectivity to external systems even in case of unplanned outages of the top level TE.

# 5   Using Self-forming Topologies in Management Applications

In order to validate our approach, we have built two distributed management applications using self forming topologies; an inventory retrieval application and a fault management application [15]. The validity of these applications for management of a real network has been shown on our test network, and we are currently performing a scalability analysis in a large-scale simulated environment.

## 5.1  Madeira Test Network

Our test network consists of 12 identical NEs[2] wirelessly connected using OLSR [13]. The topmost cluster head (CH) runs Apache Tomcat [16]; applications use it and Apache Pubscribe [17] to publish their interfaces. A test OSS on a PC external to the network communicates with the topmost cluster head using web services. In our tests we did not observe a significant performance difference in the algorithm for various network configurations for the NEs.

The parameters used to determine the topology are set statically or using policies[3] as detailed on the table below:

---

[2]  HP tc4200, 1.73GHz CPU, 512MB RAM, 802.11 B/G interface., and Ubuntu Linux OS.
[3]  Policies are implemented as in the FM application [14].

**Table 1.** Parameter Values used to Determine the Topology in the Madeira Test Network

| Parameter | Value | Explanation |
|---|---|---|
| MaxClusterSize | 3 | Maximum NEs per cluster |
| SecsHoldReservation | 5 | Time before CH cancels member reservation |
| SecsBetweenMemberPolls | 25 | CH polling interval for member polls |
| SecsWaitMemberReply | 5 | Time CH waits for a reply to a member poll |
| SecsMinChSearchDelay | 5 | Minimum time a member waits before CH search |
| SecsRangeChSearchDelay | 10 | Window after minimum wait before CH search starts |
| SecsWaitChPoll | 45 | Member wait interval before assuming CH lost |
| MemberQueriesBeforeTop | 3 | CH queries before member becomes top |

The structure of the topology built by the algorithm is largely influenced by the start-up sequence of the NEs. When all the NEs are switched on simultaneously[4], it is difficult to predict where the NEs will appear in the resultant cluster topology. If however the NEs are started in sequence, the behaviour of the algorithm generally exhibits the following pattern. The first NE started becomes a level 0 cluster member, while the second NE becomes a level 0 cluster head and a level 1 cluster member. As more NEs are switched on, they become level 0 cluster members until the maximum number of NEs allowed in the cluster is reached. The next NE to be switched on becomes a level 0 cluster member in a new cluster, and the following NE becomes a level 0 cluster head for the new cluster, and generally becomes the level 1 cluster head. The algorithm continues in this way to build up the entire topology.

The time for topology formation to reach stability is highly dependant on the timeout values, see Table 1. Shutting down or restarting a cluster head causes part of the topology to be reformed, often resulting in a new cluster head being elected. When the algorithm has completed topology formation, the topmost NE starts Apache Tomcat and registers its address with the external UDDI repository. From this point on, the test OSS can use the inventory and fault management applications.

The inventory application publishes inventory information for all NEs by delegating queries from the topmost cluster head down through the topology, so that each subservient cluster head builds and aggregates the topology for its own cluster.

Our fault management application [15] demonstrated that the distributed approach exhibits a number of benefits, including scalability and robustness, inherent consistency between CM and FM related information, and the fact that simple alarm correlation rules are sufficient even for complex network scenarios. Apart from functional tests - the FM application worked well for faults like NE and communication link outages - we have performed extensive performance tests, with alarm rates of up to 10 per second processed by cluster members and cluster heads.

## 5.2 Madeira Simulation

A simulation environment is being used to assess the scalability of the Madeira management approach in general and self-forming topologies in particular. The preliminary results for a typical NE shown on Fig. 8 demonstrate the scalability of the Madeira management approach. Simulations of up to 100 NEs are tested, and show

---

[4] A rather unrealistic scenario in a real network.

that the approach is scalable; NE CPU and memory usage stabilise after an initial increase, and the bandwidth usage by a NE is relatively low and constant for the entire simulation. Results for CPU and memory usage for cluster heads and the cumulative bandwidth use of the algorithm for all NEs in the network will be published when the simulation work concludes.

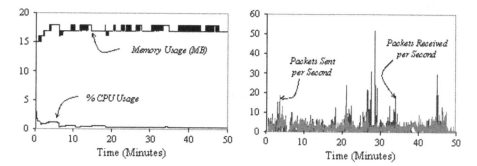

**Fig. 8.** Preliminary Results from Simulation Runs

## 6   Conclusions and Outlook

In this paper, we have described the Madeira implementation of self-forming network management topologies. We have shown how logical, self-configuring, self-optimising, dynamic topologies can be deployed. Management systems no longer have to synchronise or manually configure topologies, and can delegate configuration and optimisation of topologies to NEs, while controlling their formation using parameters and policies. Management systems can monitor changes in topologies by registering for events rather than having to read and map changes themselves.

The use of management function-specific topologies means that topologies can be customised for particular management functions and can be self-optimised at run time to cater for changing conditions in the network, facilitating flexibility in the operator's management portfolio. Another advantage is that any NE can address other NEs in its topology cluster and so is aware if its environment, facilitating distributed autonomic management at local level. A cluster head can co-ordinate the management of that cluster, correlating data and acting as a mediation point, hence minimising delay, message overhead, and bandwidth consumption. This means that management applications can be built and run in a much more distributed manner than in a traditional management approach, facilitating autonomic management and reducing operator expenditure.   In some cases, vendor-specific element and network management can be replaced by external systems that connect directly to distributed management functionality integrated on NEs.

We have also described the test scenarios carried out on the Madeira test-bed which demonstrate the validity of this distributed self-forming topology approach, in particular for two implemented applications; namely inventory and fault management.

The Madeira project is carrying out further research in the application of self-forming management topologies for distributed network management, and the scalability of the clustering approach is being evaluated using network simulators. Preliminary results show that the approach is scalable; the CPU and memory usage level out after an initial increase, and the bandwidth usage is relatively low and constant for the entire simulation.

# References

1. ITU-T Recommendation M.3000, Overview of TMN Recommendations, ITU, Geneva, Switzerland (2000)
2. ITU-T Recommendation M.3010, Principles for a Telecommunications Management Network, ITU, Geneva, Switzerland (2000)
3. Arozarena, P., Frints, M., Fallon, L., Zach, M., Serrat, J., Nielsen, J., Fahy, C., Gorgalas, N.: Madeira: A peer-to-peer approach to network management. Wireless World Research Forum 16, Shanghai, China (2006)
4. Chen, W., Jain, N., Singh, S.: ANMP: Ad Hoc network management protocol. IEEE Journal on selected areas in communications, vol. 17(8) (1999)
5. Shen, C-C., Srisathapornphat, C., Jaikaeo, C.: An Adaptive Management Architecture for Ad Hoc Networks. IEEE Communications Magazine, pp. 108–115 (February 2003)
6. Sivavakeesar, S., Pavlou, G., Bohoris, C., Liotta, A.: Effective Management Through Prediction-based Clustering for Next Generation Ad Hoc Networks. In: Proc. of ICC 2004. France (June 2004)
7. Jaikaeo, C., Shen, C.-C.: Adaptive Backbone-Based Multicast for Ad Hoc Networks. In: Proc. of ICC 2002, New York, USA (April 2002)
8. Sivavakeesar, S., Pavlou, G., Liotta, A.: Stable Clustering Through Mobility Prediction for Large-Scale Multihop Intelligent Ad Hoc Networks. In: Proc. of WCNC 2004. Atlanta, USA (March 2004)
9. Jesi, G.P., Montresor, A., Babaoglu, O.: Proximity-Aware Superpeer Overlay Topologies, In: Proc. of Selfman 2006, Dublin, Ireland (June 2006)
10. Martin-Flatin, J., Znaty, S., Hubaux, J.: A Survey of Distributed Enterprise Network and Systems Management Paradigms. Journal of Networks and Systems Management 7(1), 9–26 (1999)
11. Adam, C., Lim, K.S., Stadler, R.: Decentralizing Network Management, KTH Technical Report (December 2005)
12. Andersen, D., Balakrishnan, H., Kaashoek, M., Morris, R.: The Case for Resilient Overlay Networks. Proc. HotOS VIII, Schloss Elmau, Germany (May 2001)
13. RFC3626 - Optimized Link State Routing Protocol, (OLSR) (October 2003)
14. Marin, R., Vivero, J., Nguyen, H., Serrat, J., Leitner, P., Zach, M., Fahy, C.: A Distributed Policy Based Solution in a Fault Management Scenario, Proc. of GLOBECOM 2006, San Francisco, USA (November 2006)
15. Leitner, M., Leitner, P., Zach, M., Collins, S., Fahy, C.: Fault Management based on peer-to-peer paradigms. In: Proc. of IM, to appear (2007)
16. The Apache Tomcat Servlet Engine http://tomcat.apache.org
17. The Apache Pubscribe Web Services Notification (WSN) Implementation http://ws.apache.org/pubscribe

# Activity-Based Scheduling of IT Changes

David Trastour[1], Maher Rahmouni[1], and Claudio Bartolini[2]

[1] HP Labs Bristol, UK
[2] HP Labs Palo Alto, USA
{david.trastour,maher.rahmouni,claudio.bartolini}@hp.com

**Abstract.** Change management is a disciplined process for introducing required changes onto the IT environment, with the underlying objective of minimizing disruptions to the business services as a result of performing IT changes. Currently, one of the most pressing problems in change management is the scheduling and planning of changes. Building on an earlier mathematical formulation of the change scheduling problem, in this paper we take the formulation of the problem one step further by breaking down the changes into the activities that compose them. We illustrate the theoretical viability of the approach, discuss the limit of its applicability to real life scenarios, describe heuristic techniques that promise to bridge the scalability gap and provide experimental validation for them.

## 1 Introduction

As defined in the IT infrastructure library (ITIL, [1]), *change management* is a disciplined process for introducing required changes onto the IT environment. A good and effective change management process must minimize disruptions to the business services as a result of performing IT changes.

The main driver for IT organisations to adopt ITIL is the need to improve service quality [2]. Change management has a direct impact on service quality as it tries to understand and reduce risks. This makes change management a major ITIL process, often implemented early on when adopting ITIL, alongside incident management and configuration management.

Our research agenda in change management is driven by the results of a survey with IT change managers and practitioners in 2006 [3]. The survey highlighted that currently, the top three problems in change management are: 1) scheduling and planning of changes, 2) handling high number of urgent changes, and 3) dealing with ill-definition of request for changes. To respond to these challenges, we have projects underway on assessment of risk in change management, on assisted design of changes and on business-driven scheduling of changes. In this work, we formalize the change scheduling as an optimization problem and we develop methods to solve it to optimality. We build on our previous work by extending our conceptual model for change scheduling and breaking down the changes into the activities that compose them. As an example, we reuse the calculation of business impact defined in [5] and use it as the objective function of the optimization problem.

A.K. Bandara and M. Burgess (Eds.): AIMS 2007, LNCS 4543, pp. 73–84, 2007.

The problem with scheduling changes is that IT practitioners have little visibility into business risk and impact of changes onto customers. In order to make as much information as possible transparently available to all the stakeholders, ITIL recommends the creation of a change advisory board (CAB). The typical CAB is made up of decision-makers from IT operations, application teams, and business units—usually dozens of people—who meet weekly to review change requests, evaluate risks, identify impacts, accept or reject changes, and prioritize and schedule the ones they approve. However, CAB meetings are usually long and tedious and consume a great amount of time that could be made available to deal with change building, testing and deployment, with consequent benefit for the IT organization's efficiency. The problem is further complicated by the ever increasing number of changes and the constantly growing complexity of IT infrastructure. It is not uncommon for CABs to receive several hundreds of changes per week (such volume of change has been observed in HP outsourcing customers).

Besides the negative impact on efficiency imposed by CAB meetings, various other factors impact the effectiveness of the change management process, the effect of which could be mitigated by careful scheduling:

- because of the complexity of infrastructures and the number of possible stakeholders, CABs can't accurately identify "change collisions" that occur when two simultaneous changes impact the same resource or application;
- it is difficult to understand cross-organization schedules since large organizations have multiple CABs with no coordination between them.

In this paper, we discuss how our approach to activity-based scheduling of IT changes allows us to tackle these problems. The remainder of this paper is structured as follows. In section 2 we introduce concepts and design relevant data structures that are the bases for the formalization of the activity-based change scheduling problem (presented in section 3). In section 4 we provide experimental validation of the approach. We discuss related work in section 5 and draw our conclusions in section 6.

## 2 Related Work

Our work belongs to the research domain in IT service management, and in particular of business-driven IT management (BDIM). For a comprehensive review of business-IT management, see [9]. The research in Business-driven IT management covers automation and decision support for IT management processes, driven by the objectives of the business.

The novelty of the work presented here, (as well as for [5] that preceded it), is that our approach targets the dimensions of *people* and *processes* in IT management rather than the *technology* dimension of it as the most notable early efforts in business-driven IT management do, in particular the ones that were applied to (see [9,10,11,12,13,18] for service level management, [12,14,15] for capacity management, and [19] for security management on the service delivery side of ITIL [1]).

More relevant to our line of research are BDIM works that touch on IT support processes, such as incident management, problem management, change management itself and configuration management. The management by business objectives (MBO) methodology that we described in [16] - and that we applied there to incident management – is also the driver for this work. However, the focus of this paper is on the solution of the scheduling problem itself, whereas in our previous paper we did lead to the formulation of (mixed integer programming) incident prioritization problem, but we touched on it just as an example of putting the MBO methodology to work. Besides, the scheduling problem considered here reaches a far deeper level of complexity than the incident prioritization problem.

Coming to change management, Keller's CHAMPS [17] (CHAnge Management with Planning and Scheduling) is the seminal work. At a first level of analysis, the formulation of the scheduling problem that we present here can look very similar to the scheduling optimization problem that CHAMPS solves. While this provide mutual validation of both approaches, it has to be noted that CHAMPS addresses the automation aspects of the change management process and deals in particular with software deployment, whereas in this work we look at scheduling as a decision problem, offering support for negotiation of the forward schedule of change in CAB (change advisory board) meetings. In particular, CHAMPS assigns activities to servers, whereas in our formulation activities are assigned to technicians and affect configuration items. Another significant difference in the two approaches is that this work takes into account the IT service model: hardware components, applications and services and their dependencies. This allows us to model and avoid conflicts between changes.

With respect to our previous work, in [4] we introduced a mathematical formulation of the business impact of performing IT changes. In [5], we presented a conceptual model of change scheduling and evaluated the business impact of a change schedule. While the algorithm presented in [5] was only dealing with assigning changes to change windows, here we take the scheduling problem to the next level of detail, by actually scheduling down to the level of the single change activities composing the change, and producing detailed schedules for maintenance windows. [5] also concentrated on providing a plausible business-oriented utility function to maximize, whereas here we are here agnostic as far as the objective function is concerned.

Finally, scheduling is a field which has received a lot of attention. A great variety of scheduling problems [20] have been studied and many solution methods have been used. Staff scheduling problems in particular have been well studied [Ernst]. Our problem can be seen as a generation of a generalized resource constraint scheduling problem [21]. Our problem has the additional difficulty that one need to avoid conflicting change activities on IT components.

## 3   Change Scheduling

As seen in the introduction, CAB members need to have up-to-date change information to be able to make good decisions. Such information includes the detailed designs of changes, the topology of the underlying IT infrastructure and services, the calendars of change implementers. We now briefly recall the sections of the conceptual model presented in [5] that are relevant to our more detailed problem description. We extend the model to include the notion of change activities. We then move on to presenting the mathematical formalization of the activity-based scheduling problem.

We first need a model of the IT services that are under change control. ITIL calls configuration item any component of the IT infrastructure (hardware or software) that is required to deliver a service. The configuration management database (CMDB) holds the collection of configuration items, along with their dependencies. We model the CMDB as a directed graph where the nodes are configuration items and where edges represent direct dependencies between configuration items. Such dependencies can be containment dependencies (i.e. a web server instance runs a given server) or logical dependencies (i.e. a J2EE application depends on a database server).

A *request for change (RFC)* represents a formal proposal for a change to be made. The RFC contains a high-level textual description of the change. It also specifies an implementation deadline, by which the change must be implemented. Penalties may apply if not.

During the planning phase of the change management process, the high-level description of the change contained in the RFC is refined into a concrete *implementation plan*. The implementation plan describes the collection of *activities* and *resources* (people, technology, processes) that are required to implement the change. The plan also specifies dependency constraints between activities. As commonly done in project management [6], the dependency constraints are expressed in the form of a lag time and a dependency type, *finish-before-start, start-before-finish, finish-before-finish* or *start-before-start* constraints.

A change activity represents an elementary action that must be performed in order to complete a step of the change implementation. An activity has an associated expected duration and requires a set of implementation resources. As seen previously, it might also depend on other activities. Finally, a change activity may affect one or more configuration items.

An implementation resource is any technical resource that is required to perform a change activity, such as a change implementer or a software agent. Our model attaches an hourly cost to each implementation resource.

Finally, change windows are pre-agreed periods of time during which maintenance can be performed for an IT service. Such windows are usually found in service level agreements (SLA) or operating level agreements (OLA).

With this conceptual model in mind, we can define the activity-based scheduling problem. Our solution to the problem consists of two phases. In the first phase, changes are assigned to pre-defined change windows. This is modeled in figure 1 with the *change window assignment* association. In the second phase, activities are assigned to implementation resources within each change windows, and this results in an *assignments* being created.

If we look at the activity-based scheduling problem as an optimization problem, several objective functions can be considered: minimizing the total cost of implementing changes, maximizing the number of changes to implement or minimizing the downtime of certain applications. We thoroughly discussed alternative objective functions definition in [5]

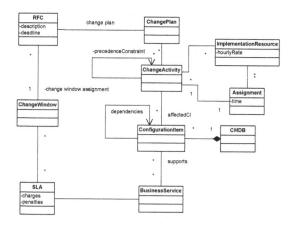

**Fig. 1.** Change scheduling conceptual model

and will not go into nearly as much detail in this paper. However, the objective function does play a role in the mathematical formulation of the problem, and we will cover it from this point of view in the following section

## 4  Mathematical Formulation of the Activity-Based Change Scheduling Problem

Let $C = \{c_i : 1 \leq i \leq N\}$ be the set of changes that have been designed, built and tested and are ready to be scheduled. Each change $c_i$ is composed of a set of activities $A_i = \{a_{i,j} : 1 \leq j \leq |A_i|\}$, where each activity $a_{i,j}$ has an estimated duration $\delta_{i,j}$.

The scheduling of changes is done over a given time horizon. Let $W$ be the number of predefined change windows $w : 1 \leq w \leq W$ that are pre-allocated within this time horizon. We refer to time within each change window through the index $t : 0 \leq t < \Delta_w$.

Let $\{r_k : 1 \leq k \leq R\}$ be the set of implementation resources that are necessary to implement changes. Let $\kappa_{k,w,t}$ be the capacity of resource $r_k$ at time $t$ in window $w$. This capacity allows us to model both the availability of a resource (when $\kappa_{k,w,t} = 0$ the resource is unavailable) and the degree of parallelism of a given resource (a resource can perform up to $\kappa_{k,w,t}$ activities in parallel). Let $\rho_{i,j}$ be the set of resources that are necessary to implement activity $a_{i,j}$.

To represent conflicts between changes, we also need a model of the service hierarchy and of the configuration items that are being changed. Let $\{i_l : 1 \leq l \leq I\}$ be the set of configuration items. Let $\tilde{A}_l$ be the set of activities that directly impact configuration item $i_l$. Let $D_l$ be the set of configuration items that depend on $i_l$ (i.e. the transitive closure of its direct dependants).

Possible solutions to the scheduling problem are characterized by the binary variables $u_{i,w}$ and $x_{i,j,k,w,t}$. The variables have the following meaning: $u_{i,w}$ is equal to 1 if change $c_i$ is scheduled in change window $w$, and is equal to 0 otherwise. $x_{i,j,k,w,t}$ is equal to 1 if the implementation of activity $a_{i,j}$ by the resource $r_k$ **starts** in change window $w$ at time $t$ and is equal to 0 otherwise. Finally the variables $l_{l,w,t}$ will be used to represent resource locking in order to avoid conflict; more specifically $l_{l,w,t}$ is equal to 1 when the configuration item $i_l$ is locked by a change activity at time $t$ in change window $w$.

We now model the constraints of the problem. When omitted, the ranges for each index are as follows: $i:1\leq i\leq N$, $j:1\leq j\leq |A_i|$, $k:1\leq k\leq R$, $w:1\leq w\leq W$, $t:0\leq i<\Delta_w$, and $l:1\leq i\leq I$.

$$\sum_{l=1}^{W} u_{i,k} \leq 1 \quad \forall i \tag{1}$$

$$\sum_{j=1}^{|A_i|}\sum_{k=1}^{R}\sum_{t=1}^{T_w-1} x_{i,j,k,w,t} = u_{i,k}\cdot\sum_{j=1}^{|A_i|}|\rho_{i,j}| \quad \forall i, \forall w \tag{2}$$

$$x_{i,j,k,w,t} = 0 \quad \begin{cases} \forall i,\forall j,\forall k,\forall w \\ \forall t:\Delta_w - \delta_{i,j} + 1\leq t<\Delta_w \end{cases} \tag{3}$$

Equation (1) ensures that each change is executed at most once. In equation (2) we make sure that if a change is scheduled to be executed in a change window, then all the activities that it comprises of are implemented within that change window. This also ensures that a change cannot span several change windows, which is undesirable as this situation would leave the infrastructure in an unknown state and would likely result in service unavailability.

Equation (3) ensures that any activity that is started in a change window is completed within the bounds of the change window.

$$\sum_{t=0}^{T_w-1} x_{i,j,k,w,t} = u_{i,w} \quad \begin{cases} \forall i,\forall j,\forall w \\ \forall k:k\in \rho_{i,j} \end{cases} \tag{4}$$

$$x_{i,j,k,w,t} = 0 \quad \begin{cases} \forall i,\forall j,\forall w,\forall t \\ \forall k:k\notin \rho_{i,j} \end{cases} \tag{5}$$

Equations (4) and (5) guarantee that the appropriate resources are used in the implementation of each activity. In particular, (4) states that if the change is scheduled for a given window, then sometime during that window all the necessary resources are scheduled to start working on it. Conversely, (5) prevents this from happening if the for the resources that are not required.

As far as capacity constraints are concerned, their expression in terms of the $u_{i,w}$ and $x_{i,j,k,w,t}$ variables does not come naturally. However, we observe that they can naturally be expressed via a binary variable signaling when an activity is being executed (recall that $x_{i,j,k,w,t}$ only specifies when the activity starts). To this end, we introduce the auxiliary variable $z_{i,j,k,w,t}$, whose value is 1 at all time during activity execution and 0 otherwise. $z_{i,j,k,w,t}$ is in turn best calculated through the introduction of two more auxiliary variables: $s_{i,j,k,w,t}$, that is indefinitely equal to 1 after the activity started and 0 otherwise; and $f_{i,j,k,w,t}$, that is indefinitely equal to 1 after the activity finished and 0 otherwise.

$$s_{i,j,k,w,t} = \sum_{\tau=0}^{t} x_{i,j,k,w,\tau} \quad \forall i, \forall j, \forall k, \forall w, \forall t \tag{6}$$

$$f_{i,j,k,w,t} = \sum_{\tau=0}^{t-\delta_{i,j}} x_{i,j,k,w,\tau} \quad \forall i, \forall j, \forall k, \forall w, \forall t \tag{7}$$

$$z_{i,j,k,w,t} = s_{i,j,k,w,t} - f_{i,j,k,w,t} \quad \forall i, \forall j, \forall k, \forall w, \forall t \tag{8}$$

The interpretation of these auxiliary variables is best understood graphically, as shown in the table below.

**Table 1.** Illustration of problem variables for an activity of duration 5

| $t$ | 0 | 1 | 2 | 3 | 4 | 5 | 6 | 7 | 8 | 9 | 10 |
|---|---|---|---|---|---|---|---|---|---|---|---|
| $x_{i,j,k,w,t}$ | 0 | 0 | 0 | 1 | 0 | 0 | 0 | 0 | 0 | 0 | 0 |
| $s_{i,j,k,w,t}$ | 0 | 0 | 0 | 1 | 1 | 1 | 1 | 1 | 1 | 1 | 1 |
| $f_{i,j,k,w,t}$ | 0 | 0 | 0 | 0 | 0 | 0 | 0 | 0 | 1 | 1 | 1 |
| $z_{i,j,k,w,t}$ | 0 | 0 | 0 | 1 | 1 | 1 | 1 | 1 | 0 | 0 | 0 |

Capacity constraints can now be quite naturally expressed:

$$\sum_{i=1}^{N} \sum_{j=1}^{|A_i|} z_{i,j,k,w,t} \leq \kappa_{k,w,t} \quad \forall k, \forall w, \forall t \tag{9}$$

The auxiliary variable f and s come very useful also when specifying precedence constraints between change activities. For example, we can naturally express a *finish-before-start* precedence constraint between two activities $a_{i,j_1}$ and $a_{i,j_2}$ with equation (10). $\lambda_{i,j_1,j_2}$ represent an additional *lag* that can be modeled if needed.

$$\sum_{w=1}^{W}\sum_{t=0}^{T_w-1} f_{i,j_1,k,w,t} - s_{i,j_2,k,w,t} \leq \lambda_{i,j_1,j_2} \quad \forall k, \forall w, \forall t \tag{10}$$

*Start-before-finish, start-before-start* and *finish-before-finish* constraints are expressed through similar linear compositions of $s_{i,j,k,w,t}$ and $f_{i,j,k,w,t}$.

The following constraints deal with the possibility of conflicting change activities on the infrastructure.

$$\sum_{a_{i,j}\in \bar{A}_l} \frac{1}{|\rho_{i,j}|} \cdot \sum_{k=1}^{R} z_{i,j,k,w,t} = l_{l,w,t} \quad \forall l, \forall w, \forall t \tag{11}$$

$$l_{l,w,t} \leq l_{l',w,t} \quad \forall l,l': l' \in D_l, \forall w, \forall t \tag{12}$$

Equation (11) ensures that the lock $l_{l,w,t}$ is set and that, among the activities that have an effect on the configuration item $i_l$, only one activity is active at a time (possibly using several resources $\rho_{i,j}$). Equation (12) states that all dependent configuration items $D_l$ are affected when the configuration item $i_l$ is being worked on.

Other additional constraints can be imposed to make the model work in a practical setting. For example, one could require to have a minimum number of changes scheduled (i.e. 90% of changes must be scheduled). Or change managers and supervisors may want to restrict some changes to take place within certain given change windows, or to restrict the permissible schedules of some activities in other ways. The expression of these additional constraints lends itself quite usefully to the case in which only a marginal re-scheduling is necessary due to the incumbency of some changes. In this case, the user may want to prevent re-scheduling of changes whose implementation date is approaching. All these constraints can be naturally expressed through linear combinations of the $u_{i,w}$ and $x_{i,j,k,w,t}$.

In order for the problem formulation to be complete, we now express its *objective function*. Depending on the requirements of the change managers and supervisors, different instances of objective function could be used. As an example, when we minimize the total cost of implementing changes, including the estimated business impact [4], the objective function becomes:

$$\text{minimize} \sum_{w=1}^{W}\sum_{i=1}^{N} \phi_{i,w}.u_{i,w} \tag{13}$$

This completes the theoretical development of the activity-based change scheduling problem. In the next section we will discuss experimental validation of the method described here.

## 5  Experimental Validation

We have implemented the mathematical programming formulation presented in this paper using CPLEX [7]. Due to the complexity of the problem definition, it turns out that in the worst case scenario our formulation does not scale up to a number of changes in the order of the hundreds. This formulation has however been a valuable instrument to better understand user requirements, as it allowed us to quickly capture and test additional user constraints, and to compare alternative objective functions such as the minimization of the makespan or of the number of conflicts.

For practical applications of the algorithm, we therefore need to develop heuristic solutions, while we will still use the complete formulation to validate the accuracy of the heuristics for low-dimension cases. We therefore developed a priority-based list scheduler [8] where the business impact plays the role of the priority function.

To compare the performance of the two implementations and to gauge the quality of the solutions produced by the priority-based list scheduler, we have developed a random generator of changes and resources. The generator takes as input: the number of change requests submitted per day, the average number of activities per change, the number of managed services, the number of configuration items and the number of available implementers. The changes and resources generator produces the following:

* service model along with the dependencies between configuration items;
* service level agreement penalties;
* for each change, its type (emergency, routine and normal) and its implementation deadline. For example, the deadline of an emergency change is set to 2 to 4 days from its submission date on average;
* for each change, its reference random plan, modeled as a dependency graph between activities;
* for each activity, its duration, its required locks on configuration item and its required resources.

We have run series of experiments comparing both implementations with different loads of changes and resources. We have fixed the number of services to 20, the number of configuration items to 100, the average number of activities per change to 5 and we varied the number of changes and the number of resources as shown in Table 2.

**Table 2.** Experiments with varying load

|  | Activities per Change | Changes | CIs | Services | Resources |
|---|---|---|---|---|---|
| Example 1 | 5 | 30 | 100 | 20 | 5 |
| Example 2 | 5 | 90 | 100 | 20 | 10 |
| Example 3 | 5 | 300 | 100 | 20 | 38 |
| Example 4 | 5 | 600 | 100 | 20 | 70 |

The results of our experiments are shown in Table 3. Both algorithms were run on an HP Workstation XW8200 with a 3.2 GHz Xeon processor and 2GB RAM. For each implementation, Table 3 shows the processing time needed to schedule the examples defined in Table 2 as well as the estimated overall business impact. The business impact of assigning a change to a change window is calculated by summing up the following three components:

1. Cost of implementing the change: each resource has an hourly rate
2. Potential revenue loss: estimated loss in revenue due to the degradation of services impacted by the change.
3. Penalties incurred from the violation of service level agreements including penalties for missing deadlines.

**Table 3.** Comparison between PLS and CPLEX implementations

|  | Priority list scheduler | | CPLEX scheduler | |
|---|---|---|---|---|
|  | Processing Time | Overall Impact | Processing Time | Overall Impact |
| Example 1 | 0.5 sec | $24 K | 40 sec | $18K |
| Example 2 | 8 sec | $155K | 4 hours | $70K |
| Example 3 | 97 sec | $376K | ** | ** |
| Example 4 | 531 sec | $948K | ** | ** |

For low-dimension examples (less than a hundred changes), the CPLEX scheduler produces the optimal solution within an acceptable time. As the number of changes gets bigger, the processing time grows exponentially, making it impossible to apply it to real IT environments (thousands of changes per month). In examples 3 and 4, the scheduler ran over 12 hours without producing a result while the list scheduler took less than 10 minutes.

Through analyzing the results produced by both implementations for small examples, there are some improvements that could be made to the list scheduler for producing better results. One improvement is to try to fit more changes into each change window by scheduling activities with smaller *mobility* (distance between its earliest possible assignment and its latest possible assignment) first, while giving priority to the highest impacted changes. Another improvement would be to sort the changes not according to their impact over one change window but over two or more change windows. As an example, let's take two changes c1 and c2 and two change windows cw1 and cw2 and let's assume that the impact of assigning:

- c1 to cw1 is $10K
- c1 to cw2 is $15K
- c2 to cw1 is $8K
- c2 to cw2 is $24K

If we assign c1 to cw1 and c2 and cw2, the overall impact is $34K, but if we assign c2 to cw1 and c1 to cw2, the overall impact is $23K.

# 6  Conclusions

Building on an earlier mathematical formulation of the change scheduling problem, in this paper we presented a methodology and a tool which pushes the formalization of the problem to the next level of detail, by breaking down the changes into the activities that compose them. We illustrated the theoretical viability of the approach, discuss the limit of its applicability to real life scenarios, describe heuristic techniques that promise to bridge the scalability gap and provide experimental validation for them.

In conducting our experiments and showing the prototype to domain experts, it emerged that end users would found it difficult to deal with schedules that are automatically generated. The tool we have produced assumes that the knowledge regarding change activities is complete and accurate. This is not necessarily the case in a production environment and may lead to problematic schedules. Rather than having a fully automated procedure, domain experts expressed the need to incrementally schedule sets of changes and to preserve pre-existing assignments as much as possible. They also recommended that all constraints should not be treated with the same importance and that some constraints should be relaxed based on preferences and user feedback. Our immediate next steps are to address these issues.

Further along our research path we plan to take into account the fact that changes may fail during the course of their implementation, thereby possibly invalidating current schedules. We will do so by accommodating for back-out change plans in our schedule. The challenge ahead of us is that to indiscriminately account for each and every change failure in our models will most likely be overkill. Techniques assessing the likelihood of a change to fail given past history and present conditions look like a promising avenue to assess risk of failure and only scheduling for possible back-out if the change has a non-negligible likelihood of failing.

# References

1. IT Infrastructure Library, ITIL Service Delivery and ITIL Service Support, Office of Government Commerce, UK (2003)
2. ITIL Change Management Maturity Benchmark Study, White Paper, Evergreen, http://www.evergreensys.com/whitepapers_tools/whitepapers/cmsurveyresults.pdf.
3. The Bottom Line Project. IT Change Management Challenges – Results of 2006 Web Survey, Technical Report DSC005-06, Computing Systems Department, Federal University of Campina Grande, Brazil (2006)
4. Sauvé, J., Rebouças, R., Moura, A., Bartolini, C., Boulmakoul, A., Trastour, D.: Business-driven support for change management: planning and scheduling of changes. In: State, R., van der Meer, S., O'Sullivan, D., Pfeifer, T. (eds.) DSOM 2006. LNCS, vol. 4269, pp. 23–25. Springer, Heidelberg (2006)
5. Rebouças, R., Sauvé, J., Moura, A., Bartolini, C., Boulmakoul, A., Trastour, D.: A decision support tool to optimize scheduling of IT changes. In: Proc. 10th IFIP/IEEE Symposium on Integrated Management (IM2007), Munich (May 2007)
6. Elmaghraby, E., Kamburowski, J.: The Analysis of Activity Networks under Generalized Precedence Relations (GPRs). Salah Management Science 38(9), 1245–1263 (1992)
7. ILOG Inc, ILOG CPLEX 10.1 user's manual and reference manual

8.  Coffman, G.: Computer and Job-shop Scheduling Theory.Wiley and Sons Inc.(February 1976)
9.  Sauvé, J.P., Moura, J.A.B., Sampaio, M.C., Jornada, J., Radziuk, E.: An Introductory Overview and Survey of Business–Driven IT Management. In: Proceedings of the 1st IEEE/IFIP International Workshop On Business-Driven IT Management (BDIM06), pp. 1–10
10. Liu, Z., Squillante, M.S., Wolf, J.L.: On maximizing service-level agreement profits. In: Proceedings of the ACM Conference on Electronic Commerce (2001)
11. Buco, M.J. et al.: Managing eBusiness on Demand SLA Contracts in Business Terms Using the Cross-SLA Execution Manager SAM, International Symposium on Autonomous Decentralized Systems (April 2002)
12. Sauvé, J., Marques, F., Moura, A., Sampaio, M., Jornada, J., Radziuk, E.: SLA Design from a Business Perspective. In: Schönwälder, J., Serrat, J. (eds.) DSOM 2005. LNCS, vol. 3775, Springer, Heidelberg (2005)
13. Aib, I., Sallé, M., Bartolini, C., Boulmakoul, A.: A Business Driven Management Framework for Utility Computing Environments, HP Labs Bristol Tech. Report 2004-171
14. Aiber, S., Gilat, D., Landau, A., Razinkov, N., Sela, A., Wasserkrug, S.: Autonomic Self–Optimization According to Business Objectives. In: Proceedings of the International Conference on Autonomic Computing (2004)
15. Menascé, D., Almeida, V.A.F., Fonseca, R., Mendes, M.A.: Business-Oriented Resource Management Policies for e-Commerce Servers, Performance Evaluation 42, Elsevier Science, 2000, pp. 223–239. Elsevier, North-Holland, Amsterdam (2000)
16. Bartolini, C., Sallé, M., Trastour, D.: IT Service Management driven by Business Objectives – An Application to Incident Management. In: Proc. IEEE/IFIP Network Operations and Management Symposium (NOMS 2006) (April 2006)
17. Keller, A., Hellerstein, J., Wolf, J.L., Wu, K., Krishnan, V.: The CHAMPS System: Change Management with Planning and Scheduling. In: Proceedings of the IEEE/IFIP Network Operations and Management Symposium (NOMS 2004), April 2004, IEEE Press, New York (2004)
18. Bartolini, C., Sallé, M.: Business Driven Prioritization of Service Incidents. In: Sahai, A., Wu, F. (eds.) DSOM 2004. LNCS, vol. 3278, Springer, Heidelberg (2004)
19. Wei, H., Frinke, D., Carter, O., et al.: Cost–Benefit Analysis for Network Intrusion Detection Systems, In: Proceedings of the 28th Annual Computer Security Conference (October 2001)
20. Pinedo, M.: Scheduling: Theory, Algorithms, and Systems. Prentice Hall
21. Demeulemeester, E.L., Herroelen, W.S: A Branch-And-Bound Procedure for the Generalized Resource-Constrained Project Scheduling Problem. Operations Research 45(2), 201–212 (1997)

# Estimating Reliability of Conditional Promises

Alva L. Couch, Hengky Susanto, and Marc Chiarini

Tufts University, Medford, Massachusetts, USA
alva.couch@cs.tufts.edu, hsusan0a@cs.tufts.edu, mchiar01@cs.tufts.edu

**Abstract.** Using conditional promises, the reliability of promises can be measured without reference to the reliability of the issuing agent, by defining notions of when conditions operate and when promises are expected to be fulfilled. This inspires an analytical method that attributes promise failures to incomplete knowledge rather than agent unreliability. This analysis allows agents to choose between conditional offers of service based upon statistical measures of the completeness of stated conditions.

## 1 Introduction

Conditional promises were introduced in [1] to describe situations in which one agent promises to serve another agent whenever its own requirements are met. However, there has been little discussion of how an agent might interpret such conditional promises, or the limits of conditioning as a mechanism. In this paper, we explore how agents can interpret conditional promises and make decisions based upon statistical measures.

The most important claim in the following treatment is that *the reliability of a conditional promise is a more appropriate basis for trust than the reliability of an agent*. Previous work on promises measures "agent reliability" as a statistical function[2,3,4]. We contend that this is not realistic, because the reliability of promises varies with the kind of promise.

For example, the authors are not reliable concert violinists, and a promise to personally perform a violin concerto is not credible when made by any one of us. However, the authors are reasonably adept at managing systems, so that a promise to manage systems has more credibility. Statistical measures of agent reliability might prohibit us from managing systems, just because we suffer from the delusion that we are also adequate concert violinists!

Our second claim is that *reliability of a specific conditional promise is a measure of completeness of its conditions as a model of its requirements*. This Bayesian world-view is partly inspired by the thinking of E. T. Jaynes[5], and is actually a form of "maximum entropy assumption." Even when probabilistic analysis indicates that a promise is *an unreliable hypothesis*, this is not sufficient evidence that its *source* is unreliable; the promise may be unreliable for external reasons having nothing to do with the originating agent. In Jaynes' methodology, it is an analytical error to use promise reliability as a measure of reliability of the issuing agent without compelling evidence that the agent has complete responsibility for and control over that behavior.

A.K. Bandara and M. Burgess (Eds.): AIMS 2007, LNCS 4543, pp. 85–96, 2007.

For example, even if we are superb concert violinists, if we do not manage to play the violin concerto we promised to play, this is not incontrovertible evidence of our reliability or lack of reliability as violinists; there may be some other factor (e.g., entropy) contributing to our lack of performance. It could be, e.g., that we have no reliable access to a violin at the time we are expected to play, or even that we have the flu and cannot play because we are ill. It could even be that someone smashed our only violin just before the concert. Thus our promise should not be "I will play a violin concerto", but rather something like "I will play a violin concerto, given that I can obtain a violin, am not ill, it is functional, and I have practiced enough.". The unconditional promise "I will play a violin concerto" is not convincing evidence that the agent is "dishonest" or "unreliable"; it is simply "incomplete"[1].

## 2    Background

The background and notation for this paper have been developed in [6] (to appear in the same publication and conference) and are briefly summarized here before turning to new material.

A *promise*[1,4,7,8] is a commitment from one sender to one recipient involving one information packet called a "promise body". We can think of each promise as a triple $\langle s, r, b \rangle$ where $s$ is a sender, $r$ is a recipient, and $b$ is a "promise body" describing some commitment of $s$ to $r$.[2]

A *conditional promise* is a construction in which one sender promises a particular promise body conditionally, based upon the existence of other commitments [6,4]. In general, we write $(p|q_1, \ldots, q_k)$ for a conditional promise, where $p$ and $q_1, \ldots, q_k$ are "primitive" promises of the form $\langle s, r, b \rangle$.

A particular promise is called *operative* in the context of a particular agent if it is known to be valid in that context, and *inoperative* otherwise. There are two ways to become valid/operative: through being explicitly promised to the agent, or through being a conditional result of other promises becoming operative. All unconditional promises are always operative. The conditional promise $(p|q_1, \ldots, q_k)$ means that $p$ is operative whenever all of $q_1, \ldots, q_k$ are operative.

The typing system for promise bodies $b$ has been studied in [8]. In this paper, we are actually describing part of a theory of types; it would be just as valid to write $(\langle s, r, b \rangle | p)$ as $(\langle s, r, (b|p) \rangle)$; one can (and probably should) characterize the conditions as being part of the body rather than being separate entities.

---

[1] In our specific case, the promise should be more of the form, "We will play you a violin concerto when pigs fly." There is strong experimental evidence that this is a highly reliable promise, and this does not preclude making some conditional promise later (after one of us has actually learned to play the violin) that has a weaker set of conditions. By issuing promises with inherently false conditions, we might be able to achieve fairly high reliability ratings as agents, but those ratings would be meaningless.

[2] We depart from the pictorial notation used in other papers and utilize traditional graph notation in order to more easily specify derived graphs.

Our notation, however, allows us to think of promises as independent from the body of a promise, which helps us notate complex relationships clearly without defining the type of $b$.

Each agent's view of the world can be partly represented as a set of conditional and unconditional promises $C$ received by and issued by the agent. One way to think of $C$ is to consider it as a *set of hypotheses* that can be true or false in specific instances.

**Definition 1.** *For a set of (conditional and unconditional) promises $C$, we notate the operative promises that result from that set as $\rho(C)$.*

These are the union of the primitive promises in $C$, together with the consequents $p$ of conditional promises $(p|q_1, \ldots, q_k) \in C$ where all $q_i$ are operative in $C$. It is also important for us to understand when two representations $C$ and $D$ of promises represent the same situation:

**Definition 2.** *Two sets of promises $C$ and $D$ are equivalent iff $\rho(C) = \rho(D)$, i.e., they represent the same sets of operative promises.*

## 3    Observability

In the unconditional model of promises, there is no need to consider whether an agent can determine if a promise is operative; all promises are primitive and thus operative when received. In the conditional model, it becomes important to distinguish between what each agent "knows" about the promises that it sends or receives, because conditions that cannot be observed cannot possibly be verified. This work is based upon the concept of observability as first described in [9].

**Definition 3.** *In the context of an agent $X$, a promise $p$ is observable if $X$ can determine with certainty when $p$ is operative, and unobservable otherwise.*

This is a different kind of observability than observing whether a promise is *reliable*; in this case, it is the operative nature only that is observed.

Many promises that can occur as conditions are not guaranteed to be observable. The promise $\langle s_1, r_1, b_1 \rangle | \langle s_2, r_2, b_2 \rangle$ contains a condition $\langle s_2, r_2, b_2 \rangle$ that is not guaranteed to be observable by $r_1$ unless $s_2$ or $r_2$ is equal to $r_1$. It is not guaranteed to be observable by $s_1$ unless $s_2$ or $r_2$ is equal to $s_1$. It is not guaranteed to be *mutually observable* by $s_1$ and $r_1$ unless either $s_2 = s_1$ and $r_2 = r_1$, or $s_2 = r_1$ and $r_2 = s_1$. Observability of a promise is of little value unless both sender and receiver of each promise can observe equally.

In practice, third-party constructions are common, e.g., "I will give you DNS if I get file service from a third party." In a third-party condition, there is no commitment on the part of the *receiver* to track (or even to have the ability to track) whether the antecedent promises are operative. Consequently, the sender has no knowledge of the receiver's abilities. Thus any promise involving a third-party commitment requires more machinery in order to become operative.

In our previous paper[6], for a primitive promise $p$, the promise $\langle s, r, \kappa(p) \rangle$ means that $s$ agrees to inform $r$ as to whether $p$ is operative. The promise

$\langle r, s, U(\kappa(p)) \rangle$ is a promise by $r$ to use the information about $p$ provided by $s$. One way to resolve the observability quandary is for each agent to send a $U(\kappa(p))$ promise to each agent that is a potential issuer of a currently unobservable promise $p$. This is a request for knowledge of whether $p$ has been issued. If each potential issuer responds with a $\kappa(p)$ promise, then observability is assured.

## 4  Assumptions

In this paper, we assume that:

1. Agents are connected by reliable network connections and all promises are reliably delivered from sender to receiver.
2. All promises in agent conditions are observable (by means of $\kappa$ or some other abstraction).
3. All operative promises for an agent may be tested via repeated, discrete trials that indicate success or failure.
4. Conditional probabilities of promise success during these trials are stationary (i.e., the probability of success for a particular conditional promise does not vary in time).

These assumptions simplify the following discussion, but leave many issues to be addressed in future work.

## 5  Reliability

Observability simply means that we can determine whether a commitment is present; whether the commitment is honored is a separate thing.

**Definition 4.** *From the point of view of an agent $X$, a promise $\langle s, r, b \rangle$ is re-liable if whenever it is operative, it is also functional according to some test of behavior (that corresponds to the contents of the promise body $b$).*

Practical promises cannot ever be entirely reliable, and an agent cannot predict and/or condition its promises against all possible forms of future failure. Many failure modes are not easily detectable themselves, even from the point of view of the promiser.

  For example, it is of little value for an agent to try to report that its outgoing communication channels are overloaded, because a message that might *notify* an agent that the problem exists would have to contend with the *cause* of the problem. It is equally amusing to consider how an agent would inform another that an entity *between* them is interfering with or even spoofing their attempts at communication. But in practical terms, "interference" can take much more subtle forms, including presence of unknown bugs in software, latent conditions in configuration exposed by client-server interactions, etc.

  Computing the experimental reliability of an unconditional promise is straightforward.

**Definition 5.** *The reliability of an unconditional promise is the probability that a trial of the promise commitment will succeed.*

If reliability is stationary (i.e., the probability is not time-varying), one estimate of reliability is the ratio of "number of successes" to the "number of trials". This becomes an estimate of "average reliability" rather than "reliability" whenever reliability varies with time.

To compute the reliability of a conditional promise, one must account for whether conditions are operative:

**Definition 6.** *The* reliability *of a conditional promise is the probability that its commitment will be delivered when it is operative in the context of the observing agent.*

The experimental reliability of a conditional promises is thus the ratio of "number of successes while conditions are operative" to "number of trials while conditions are operative".

It is important to distinguish between a "failed promise" whose trials indicate failure rather than success, and a "broken promise" that is contradicted by some newer promise. Whether a promise succeeds or fails contributes to its reliability, but if it is explicitly broken, no more measurement of its success is meaningful because the commitment it represents is no longer present. Reliability measurements must account for changes in which promises are operative due to broken promises and other forces, such as time-varying promise scoping[6].

In other work, the reliability of a promise is combined with that of other promises to obtain a concept of agent reliability. While this is a sound idea when considering security of a system, it does not represent the case where an agent simply does not know enough to appropriately condition a promise. It is safe to assume that an agent *cannot* know the complete conditions under which a promise will be fulfilled, so that the failure to fulfill a promise is a *failure of agent knowledge* rather than *failure of an agent*.

One can embody this assumption by thinking of a failed promise $p$ as having some invisible condition, call it $\varepsilon(p)$, that causes the failure by its absence. If $S$ is a set of conditions that we think should be operative before $p$ is operative, we can think of the "realistic" promise $p|S$ as having imperfect reliability, while the "ideal" promise $p|S \cup \{\varepsilon(p)\}$ exhibits perfect reliability[3]. To understand how unreliable a specific promise can be, we can quantify the probability that $S$ is operative while $\varepsilon$ is not. A failure of $p$ with $S$ operative means that $\varepsilon(p)$ is *not* operative for some undisclosed reason[4]. It is also possible that $\varepsilon(p)$ represents time-varying or unobservable conditions.

This world-view has a profound effect upon how we analyze sets of conditional promises. As a human example, when we promise to pay our tax bills, we do not mention the idea that we might not have enough money at some point in the future. This "sin of omission" might be considered the true source of unreliability, *not the agent*. This omission is part of the content of $\varepsilon$.

---

[3] The resemblance between $\varepsilon(p)$ and system entropy is purely intentional!

[4] It is perhaps useful to consider $\varepsilon(p)$ as the "set of latent preconditions of $p$"[10].

Another example is that of a web server $W$ that promises service to client $M$ with the constraint of "delivery $< 100$ms" and the condition "fileserver $F$ delivery $< 25$ms". If $F$'s promise is inoperative (and observable by $W$), then so is that of $W$, and $M$ is aware that it has no guarantee. However, it may be the case that $W$ constrains itself to less than 50 simultaneous client requests at any one time *without* telling $M$. This is essentially a promise to itself. Suppose that $M$ obtains the promise of service from $W$ and attempts to use that promise as the 51st client. Service will be denied and the promise will fail, because the *hidden* $\varepsilon$ condition "number of concurrent requests $< 50$" is inoperative.

# 6   Condition Graphs

To compute sample probabilities of conditional promise reliability, one can use condition graphs. A condition graph is a representation of the dependencies between promises held or promised by a specific agent.

**Definition 7.** *The "condition graph" $G = \langle P, Q \rangle$ corresponding to a set of conditional promises $C$ is formed as follows. The nodes of the condition graph are subsets of primitive promises; $P$ is a subset of the powerset of all primitive promises contained in $C$ as unconditional promises or primitive elements of conditionals. For each conditional promise $p|S$ in the graph, where $S$ is a set of promises that must become operative before $p$ is operative, construct a directed edge in $G$ from $S$ to $\{p\}$ (the singleton set containing $p$).*

In other words, there is an edge in $G$ for each *way* in which a promise $p$ can become operative. If a node $p$ in $G$ has two incoming edges, this represents two ways in which the node can become operative, e.g., $p|q$ and $p|r$. The edge $(\{q, r\}, \{p\})$, by contrast, indicates that both $q$ and $r$ must be operative before $p$ is operative under that rule. All arrows are sufficient but not necessary, and $p$ can become operative by other means, including simply being promised unconditionally in $C$. Figure 1 shows a simple condition graph. We indicate unconditional promises via boldface circles around symbols.

Condition graphs allow one to calculate dependencies between promises.

**Definition 8.** *In a condition graph $G$, a subset of promises $S_1$ controls a subset of promises $S_2$ if whenever every promise in $S_1$ is operative, every promise in $S_2$ is also operative.*

As an example, consider the graph for $\{(p|q, r), (q), (r|s)\}$. In this graph, $\{s\}$ controls $\{p\}$, because if $s$ is operative, $r$ is operative, and $q$ is always operative, so $p$ is operative. But we could also say that $\{s\}$ controls $\{p, q, r\}$. The notion of control is that of a guarantee; if $s$ is operative, what other promises are guaranteed to be operative as well?

One construction will greatly reduce the complexity of calculating conditional relationships.

**Definition 9.** *Two condition graphs $G$ and $H$ are equivalent iff they express the same control relationships.*

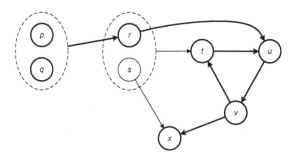

**Fig. 1.** A simple condition graph comprising the set of promises $\{(r|p, q), (t|r, s), (t|v),$ $(u|t), (u|r), (v|u), (x|v), (x|s)\}$. $p$ and $q$ are unconditional promises and are thus operative. Following the operative edges, we see that every promise except $s$ is made operative. $s$ is inoperative because it is not promised unconditionally.

**Lemma 1.** *Any condition graph $G$ with a strongly connected component $V$ of primitive promises is equivalent with a graph $G'$ in which $V$ is represented as a single node (set) $v$.*

*Proof.* Recall that a strongly-connected component of $G$ has the property that there is a path from any node to any other. In a condition graph, these paths represent control relationships. Thus if any one of these nodes becomes operative, all others are operative as well. We construct $G'$ from $G$ as follows:

1. Add a new node $v$ to the graph, representing the set of nodes in the strongly-connected component.
2. Change all edges pointing to nodes in $V$ (including those within the component) to point to $v$.
3. Remove $V$.

Claim: this new graph embodies the same control relationships. To see this, consider what happens when any one node $n \in V$ becomes operative. In $G$, this makes the component operative. In $G'$, this has the same effect, in the sense that the set representing the component becomes operative, because of the arrow from $n$ to $v$. Any other arrow into a member of $V$ in $G$ has the same effect when pointed at $v$ in $G'$. □

It is sometimes useful to connect the graph with more edges than the explicit promises allow. The most important implicit relationship is that of subsets.

**Definition 10.** *The completion $\omega(G)$ of the condition graph $G$ includes the edges in the condition graph, as well as edges from set $S_1$ to set $S_2$ whenever $S_1 \supset S_2$.*

It should be obvious that this does not change inferences of what is operative: $\rho(\omega(G)) = \rho(G)$.

Completions also make it easy to describe how to compute control dependencies:

**Theorem 1.** *In a condition graph* $G$, *the maximal set of nodes controlled by a subset* $S$ *is the union of every subset* $S'$ *reachable from* $S$ *in the completion* $\omega(G \cup \{S\})$.

*Proof.* The point of the completion is to take every subset relationship into account. We can demonstrate this by induction on the size of the control subset $S$. If $|S| = 1$, the lemma is trivially true, because all promises that $S$ controls are directly connected by paths of singletons (recalling that all edges in the completion lead to smaller subsets and singletons). If the lemma is true for $|S| \leq k$, then for $|S| = k + 1$, we can compute the sets of controlled promises by looking at the edges exiting $S$ and from all subsets of $S$ that appear within the completion. Since these edges always connect to sets of size less than $S$ (by construction) the inductive hypothesis applies to these sets, and the union of all operative nodes found by following the paths from each of these sets is maximal.
□

The point of this lemma is to give an easy way to compute the effect of making a set of nodes operative. To compute the effects, one utilizes breadth-first search of the completion graph, progressing along all paths starting at the set and stopping when cycles are detected.

## 7   Computing Reliability

In simplifying the calculation of reliability, we are aided by condition graphs. The edges in the graph are control relationships, so each edge can be labeled with a tally of successes and failures, as well as a binary flag denoting whether the source of the edge is operative. Each time a promise is tested for success or failure, we increment the tallies on all *incoming* edges that are operative. This is a quick operation once the condition graph is built, even if promises become inoperative over time, as described in [6].

Observations made by one agent are less useful than observations made over a population of agents. For promise sets consisting of only primitive promises, it is valuable to average the accuracies for promises $\langle s, r, b \rangle$ as measured by each recipient $r$, as a measure of the reliability of agent $s$ [2]. For conditional promises, we must consider instead how one would cluster tuples of the form $\langle s, r, b \rangle | S$. One way to cluster these is to hold $s$, $b$, and $S$ constant and tally over all $r$, as a measure of the reliability of promises of the kind $\langle s, *, b \rangle | S$.

In clustering statistics for several agents, it helps to have a notion of condition graph that spans agents.

**Definition 11.** *Two promises* $p$ *and* $q$ *held by different agents are comparable if one can transform* $p$ *into* $q$ *by replacing each reference to the recipient of* $p$ *with a reference to the recipient of* $q$.

For example, $p = \langle s, r, b \rangle | \langle r, s, c \rangle$ and $q = \langle s, t, b \rangle | \langle t, s, c \rangle$ are comparable, because one can transform $p$ into $q$ by replacing $r$ with $t$.

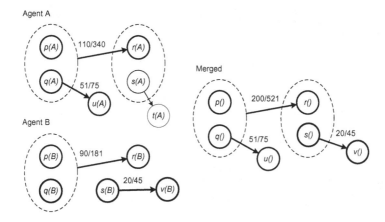

**Fig. 2.** Clustering statistics from multiple agents requires adding tallies for edges representing comparable promises

Each set of comparable promises forms a *promise pattern* originating from a specific sender and containing a free variable for the recipient. In the case above, if the free variable is $X$, the pattern is $\langle s, X, b \rangle | \langle X, s, c \rangle$.

**Definition 12.** *Given a set of condition graphs from multiple agents, the* merged condition graph *is formed as follows (Figure 2):*

1. *Merge comparable nodes into single nodes.*
2. *In each case where all nodes in a set are comparable between two or more agents, merge comparable sets.*
3. *Replace edge label statistics (successes/total trials) exiting merged nodes or sets with sums of statistics (over both numerator and denominator) for the merged nodes or sets.*

This accomplishes the same calculation that we described before: the graph represents statistics for particular $\langle s, *, b | S \rangle$ patterns.

In the merged condition graph, the sample probability labeling each edge is a measure of the reliability of a promise pattern originating from a particular server. This can be used to globally compare reliability of the same service from different servers, or to test hypotheses about causes of unreliability.

## 8    Reasoning About Reliability

Agents can utilize annotated condition graphs to reason about whether promises are appropriately conditioned or not. When the set of promises $C$ contains two different conditional promises with the same consequent $p$, it is possible to compute which set of conditions is more reliable in assuring $p$ over time.

Figure 3 depicts an example of this calculation. In (a), an agent has observed the success of condition sets $\{s, t, u\}$ and $\{s, t, u, d\}$ over ten trials, where $d$

becomes operative and inoperative during the trials due to broken and resent promises or time-varying constructions[6]. Promise $f$ is not considered, as it remains inoperative throughout all trials. After 1000 trials (b), the success rate indicates that when $d$ is operative, the promise tends to fail *more* often. Since the set of promises $\{s, t, u\}$ is sufficient to make $p$ operative, the agent may wish to negotiate that future offers of $p$ not be conditioned upon $d$, so that $d$ can remain inoperative.

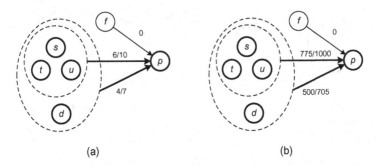

(a)                                            (b)

**Fig. 3.** Reliability estimates for conditional promise $p$ after (a) 10 trials and (b) 1000 trials

More generally, the question arises as to whether any agent contains conditions that could make a promise more reliable or unreliable than those stated by its sending agent. It is possible for agents to calculate reliability measures of *hypothetical* conditional relationships other than those asserted by the sending agent, and to experimentally determine the "best set of conditions" for assuring a behavior.

Suppose, for example, that we suspect that a particular promise $p$ is a hidden prerequisite for promise $q|S$, even though it does not appear in $S$ as a prerequisite. We construct a promise pattern for the promise $q|S$ and locate all agents holding comparable promise. For each comparable promise $q'|S'$, we instruct the agent to form an extra edge representing the *hypothetical* promise $q'|S' \cup \{p\}$. This hypothetical promise is constructed so that instances on every agent are comparable, so statistics can be gathered and combined to form a global estimate of its reliability.

## 9   Conclusions

We have presented a new method for analyzing the reliability of promises issued by an agent, to replace methods for analyzing agent reliability as a whole. Reliability is analyzed relative to how an agent *scopes* and *qualifies* its offers for service, which gives agents the opportunity and motivation to learn how to qualify their behaviors more accurately. If agents are responsible only for their actions, then we can distinguish between "good" and "bad" agents, but if they are instead responsible for their knowledge, they can grow in knowledge over time, and make more intelligent promises as a result.

In this paper we have assumed that there is perfect observability of promises by each agent, reliable communications between all agents, and that arbitrary promises can be observed and tested. Without these assumptions, one cannot always easily combine reliability results from different agents. For example, suppose we have two agents $X$ and $Y$ holding promises $p|S$ and $p|S'$, respectively. The reliability of $p|S$ and $p|S'$ are likely to differ for unequal $S$ and $S'$. But even if $X$ and $Y$ hold the same promise $p|S$, it is possible that their abilities to observe $S$ differ for some reason external to the promise $p|S$. E.g., one agent might not hold the necessary "knowledge"$(\kappa)$ promises, or unreliable network communications might make $\kappa$ commitments impossible to honor, leading to non-comparable measures of reliability. In order for us to cluster and combine statistics collected by multiple agents, the promise, the observability of its conditions, and the ability to observe failures must be the same for both agents. This is a matter for future study.

As well, real systems do not obey stationary probability distributions and exhibit entropic behavior as a result of causes other than holding or not holding promises. The "entropy condition" $\varepsilon(p)$ to which we have neatly attributed all failures of conditional promises does not consist solely of promise conditions, and we cannot eliminate that condition through promises alone. It is not yet clear how to determine whether our model of promise-based conditions is as complete as possible or not.

What is the limit of this technique? Perfect reliability is impossible, and near-perfect reliability may well require a large number of conditions. But agents can do what humans do already: promise based upon conditions that seem to be most important. Principal axis analysis could easily identify these conditions.

By considering the reliability of promises, rather than reliability of the agent, we allow agent knowledge to evolve over time, and allow future networks to accept value wherever it evolves.

# References

1. Burgess, M.: An approach to understanding policy based on autonomy and voluntary cooperation. In: Schönwälder, J., Serrat, J. (eds.) DSOM 2005. LNCS, vol. 3775, pp. 97–108. Springer, Heidelberg (2005)
2. Bergstra, J., Burgess, M.: Local and global trust based on the concept of promises. Technical Report PRG0606, University of Amsterdam (September 2006)
3. Burgess, M., Fagernes, S.: Pervasive computer management: A smart mall scenario using promise theory. In: Proceedings of First IEEE International Workshop on Modelling Autonomic Communication Environments (MACE2006), p. 133 (2006)
4. Burgess, M., Fagernes, S.: Pervasive computer management: A model of network policy with local autonomy. IEEE Transactions on Networking (submitted) (2006)
5. Jaynes, E.T.: Probability Theory: the Logic of Science. Cambridge University Press, Cambridge (2003)
6. Couch, A., Susanto, H., Chiarini, M.: Modeling change without breaking promises. In: Proceedings of AIMS-2007 To appear (preprint) (February 2007)

7. Burgess, M., Begnum, K.: Voluntary cooperation in pervasive computing services. In: LISA, USENIX, pp. 143–154 (2005)
8. Burgess, M., Fagernes, S.: Promise theory - a model of autonomous objects for pervasive computing and swarms. In: ICNS, p. 118. IEEE Computer Society, Los Alamitos (2006)
9. Couch, A., Sun, Y.: On observed reproducibility in network configuration management. Science of Computer Programming 53, 215–253 (2004)
10. Kanies, L.: Isconf: Theory, practice, and beyond. In: Proceedings of the Seventeenth Systems Administration Conference (LISA XVII) (USENIX Association: Berkeley, CA), p. 115 (2003)

# Modeling Change Without Breaking Promises

Alva L. Couch, Hengky Susanto, and Marc Chiarini

Tufts University, Medford, Massachusetts, USA
alva.couch@cs.tufts.edu, hsusan0a@cs.tufts.edu, mchiar01@cs.tufts.edu

**Abstract.** Promise theory defines a method by which static service bindings are made in a network, but little work has been done on handling the dynamic case in which bindings must change over time due to both contingencies and changes in policy. We define two new kinds of promises that provide temporal scope for a conditional promise. We show that simple temporally-scoped promises can describe common network behaviors such as leasing and failover, and allow an agent to completely control the sequence of sets of promises to which it commits with another agent, over time. This allows agents to adapt to changing conditions by making short-term bilateral agreements rather than the long-term unilateral agreements provided by previous promise constructions.

## 1  Introduction

*Promise theory*[1,2,3,4] provides a mechanism by which one can model intelligent autonomous service binding between clients and services. A *promise* has three parts:

1. A *sender s* that is committing to a particular behavior.
2. A *receiver r* that is receiving that commitment.
3. A *body b* of information describing the commitment.

We can describe the promise between nodes $s$ and $r$ as a labeled edge $\langle s, r, b \rangle$ and the sum total of all promises among a set of nodes as a *promise graph* $G = \langle V, E \rangle$, where $V$ represents all nodes (agents), and each edge $e \in E$ is a labeled directed edge of the form $e = \langle s, r, b \rangle$, with source $s$, destination $r$, and label $b$.[1]

Promise theory allows one to easily characterize the function of network services in terms of promises between entities. For example, we can describe DNS, file service, and web service in terms of kinds of promises[5]. For ease of notation, we utilize wildcards to denote promises to everyone: $\langle s, *, b \rangle$ means "$s$ promises $b$ to every node", while $\langle *, r, b \rangle$ means that "$r$ is promised $b$ by every node."

Prior work on promise theory identified three kinds of promises: "regular", "use", and "coordination". A *regular promise* is a commitment to provide some service (e.g. $b$), while a *use promise* is a commitment to use some service

---

[1] We find it instructive to utilize the notation of traditional graph theory, instead of the labeled arrow notation introduced by Burgess et al. This notation allows us to construct derived graphs with a simple notation.

A.K. Bandara and M. Burgess (Eds.): AIMS 2007, LNCS 4543, pp. 97–108, 2007.
© Springer-Verlag Berlin Heidelberg 2007

(e.g., $U(b)$). A "coordination promise" obligates one agent to follow the "instructions" given by another agent (e.g., $C(b)$). In addition, a "commitment promise"[2] is a special kind of promise body $b$ representing the commitment of a *non-returnable investment*. In this paper, we do not consider commitment promises, and use the term "commitment" to refer more generically to any promise made.

Recently, *conditional promises* were introduced in order to encode simple interactions between promises[3,6,7,8]. A conditional promise is a promise that is contingent upon the validity of other specified promises.

**Definition 1.** *A promise is* primitive *if it consists of a single promise body, transmitted from a single originator to a single recipient, with no conditions stated.*

A conditional promise is a promise that is held by an agent, but whose validity is contingent upon the validity of other stated promises[1]:

**Definition 2.** *A conditional promise has the form* $(p|q_1, q_2, \ldots, q_k)$ *where* $p$ *is a* consequent *primitive promise and* $q_1, q_2, \ldots, q_k$ *are antecedent primitive promises.*

A primitive promise $p$ can be thought of as a conditional promise $(p|)$ with an empty set of antecedents. In the above definition, each of $p$ and $q_1, \ldots, q_k$ are promises with sender, receiver, and body, e.g., $q_i = \langle s_{qi}, r_{qi}, b_{qi} \rangle$. At this point, the values of $s_{qi}$, $r_{qi}$, and $b_{qi}$ are unconstrained, though we will discuss later what it means for such a promise to be meaningful in the context of a particular agent.

The purpose of a conditional promise $(p|q_1, \ldots, q_k)$ is to state conditions under which a consequent promise $p$ is considered to be valid. To make discussion easier, we will refer to a promise that is valid in a particular context as *operative* in that context, and a promise that is not valid as *inoperative*. A promise that is not valid but could potentially become valid in the future is *latent*.

**Axiom 1.** *All primitive promises in a set* $C$ *are operative with respect to* $C$.

**Axiom 2.** *A conditional promise* $c = (p|q_1, \ldots, q_k)$ *is operative with respect to a set of conditional promises* $C$ *precisely when each of* $q_1, \ldots, q_k$ *is operative with respect to* $C$.

**Definition 3.** *For a conditional promise* $c = (p|q_1, \ldots, q_k)$, *we say* $p$ *is operative (with respect to* $C$) *whenever* $c$ *is operative (with respect to* $C$).

A conditional promise describes *one way* that a primitive promise can become operative. It can also become operative, e.g., by being promised explicitly and unconditionally, or by being a consequent of some other conditional promise whose antecedents are operative. Thus the conditional construction is *sufficient but not necessary*; it is quite possible that the consequent of a conditional becomes operative by means other than that particular conditional.

One simple extension of basic conditional promises allows conditional promises to express arbitrary zeroth-order logical statements inside conditions as *sets* of simple conditional promises.

**Definition 4.** *If p is a promise, then the promise ¬p is the assertion that p is not operative, which is operative exactly when p is not operative.*

**Theorem 1.** *A conditional promise involving any of the logical operators → (implication), ↔ (equivalence), ∧ (conjunction), ∨ (disjunction) or ⊕ (exclusive-or) in the condition can be represented as a set of conditional promises of the above form.*

*Proof.* Note first that conditional promises are conjunctions: $(p|q_1, \ldots, q_k)$ means $(p|q_1 \wedge \cdots \wedge q_k)$. Disjunctions are represented by sets of promises: The single conditional $(p|q_1 \vee q_k)$ is equivalent to the set of conditionals $\{(p|q_1), \ldots, (p|q_k)\}$. Exclusive-or is represented as a set of alternatives: $(p|q \oplus r)$ means $\{(p|q \wedge \neg r), (p|\neg q \wedge r)\}$. Implication $(p|q \rightarrow r)$ means $p|\neg q \vee r$, which expands to $\{(p|\neg q), (p|r)\}$. Equivalence is similar. □

In this paper, we intentionally avoid first-order logical constructions such as quantifiers and variables. One reason for this is that we seek to extend the capabilities of the configuration management tool CFEngine[9,10,11,12,13], which contains only the ability to interpret zeroth-order logical expressions[14]. Another reason for excluding quantifiers is that a condition that uses quantification over a finite, known set is logically equivalent to a set of zeroth-order conditionals: if $S = \{s_1, \ldots, s_n\}$, then the set $\{(p|\forall(x \in S)x)\}$ is equivalent to the set $\{(p|s_1, \ldots, s_n)\}$ (which we can notate as $(p|S)$ without ambiguity), while the set $\{p|\exists(x \in S)x\}$ is equivalent to the set $\{(p|s_1), (p|s_2), \ldots, (p|s_n)\}$. Thus, we can express a first-order condition involving quantification over finite sets of promises as a *finite set of conditional promises* in our notation.

## 2   Related Work

Burgess et al. continue to refine promise theory and its domains of applicability. The basic framework above was described in [1], including conditional promises. We differ from this view in one important respect: Burgess suggests that temporal logic cannot be used due to lack of knowledge of prerequisites. We show in this paper that a simple concept of sequencing, based upon mutual observability, is sufficient to allow simple kinds of temporal constructions.

[2] explores the use of voluntarily collaborating agents to perform system administration tasks in an uncertain environment with minimal trust. We agree with these conclusions, but also believe that more trust is possible with the addition of new kinds of promises, described here.

[4] contrasts promise theory with traditional control theory and introduces the notion of promise *reliability* (probability that a promise will be kept) to reduce promise graphs and enable spectral analysis of relationships. This is one approach to understanding evolution of services; our model is complementary to this and involves hard bindings that change over time.

In [7], Bergstra and Burgess apply promise theory to modeling trust relationships, reputation, and expectation. Their discussion of how bundled promises (made in parallel) should affect trust includes an XOR scenario in which mutually exclusive conditional promises act like a switch. This inspires our temporal operators, which are used in a similar manner.

In [3], Burgess and Fagernes introduce the Common Currency Equivalent Graph and extract eigenvectors from its matrix representation to determine the sustainability of network policy. The paper remarks on chains of conditional promises requiring an external mediating component to act as a broker. This informs our own ideas regarding knowledge binding.

Note that while we add operators that allow a new kind of dynamic scoping, at any particular time, our promise network is reducible to one in which the scoping operators do not appear. Thus all prior results apply, except that the "hard bindings" in our networks can change over time.

There has also been much work on how promises can be reasoned about within an agent. This requires a policy that is (regardless of representation) equivalent to a set of first-order rules[15]. While this is an important topic, we avoid specifically describing policies here, and concentrate instead on what a particular set of promises means, and how that meaning can evolve over time, regardless of "why" specific promises were made or what policies caused them to be promised.

## 3   Temporal Scoping

One limit of prior promise theory is that although one can prove that a set of promises creates a functional network, there is no mechanism by which promises can change over time except by "breaking promises". A "broken promise" occurs when an agent promises something contradictory to a prior promise. The receiving agent may consider this as evidence of untrustability in its trust model[7]. Thus promise-based networks evolve toward a state of stability that is immutable unless agents break their promises.

Then how do promise networks react to changes in policy and needs? At present, the only way an agent can be ready for change (without explicitly breaking promises) is to fail to commit to a particular course of action. For example, if an agent $X$ is offered the same service from servers $A$, $B$, and $C$, and $X$ commits to use one exclusively, then it is implicitly promising – forever – not to use the others, until it breaks that promise. Thus the agent must maintain relatively weak bindings with others in order to remain ready to change bindings without breaking promises. This means, in turn, that the potential servers $A, B, C$ can never know client $X$'s full intent; even if $X$ intends to use $A$ exclusively, it cannot make that intent clear unless it also – in the future – potentially issues a contradictory promise. Agents unable to promise to use services represent points of instability in a network, rather than points of stability. A new notion is needed, that allows an agent to be predictable (and commit to a particular course of action) *for some period of time* and then make choices about future action.

## 3.1   $\alpha$ and $\tau$

In this paper, we suggest two mechanisms for "scoping" promises in time by means of two new promise bodies. The promise body $\tau(t)$ is operative from the time that it is received to the time $t$ time units in the future. The promise body $\alpha(p)$ is operative from the time it is received to the time that primitive promise $p$ becomes operative (Figure 1). If $p$ is already operative then $\alpha(p)$ never becomes operative.

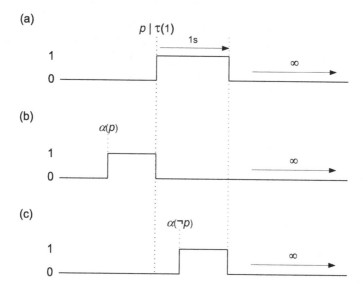

**Fig. 1.** Temporal scoping. (a) The $\tau$ promise is given such that $p$ is operative for one second. (b) The $\alpha$ promise is operative until $p$ becomes operative. (c) The $\alpha$ of a negated promise $p$ is operative until $p$ becomes non-operative.

To simplify notation, we often omit details that can be inferred from context. Since $\alpha$ and $\tau$ only make sense in conditional promises, it is implicit that their initiator is the sender in the consequent and that their receiver is the receiver in the consequent. Thus we will write $(\langle s, r, b \rangle | \alpha(p))$ to mean $(\langle s, r, b \rangle | \langle s, r, \alpha(p) \rangle)$ and $(\langle s, r, b \rangle | \tau(t))$ instead of $(\langle s, r, b \rangle | \langle s, r, \tau(t) \rangle)$. Thus we will refer to the *promises* $\alpha(p)$ and $\tau(t)$ without confusion.

$\tau$ and $\alpha$ allow one to make conditional promises whose consequents are operative for a limited time. The promise $(p | \tau(t))$ means that $p$ is operative for time $t$, and then inoperative thereafter. Likewise, the promise $(p | \alpha(q))$ means that $p$ is operative until replaced by a "presumably better" promise $q$.

This means, in particular, that any promise containing an (unnegated) $\alpha$ or $\tau$ condition may be *permanently deleted* from an agent's knowledge base after the state transition from operative to inoperative has been accomplished. In other words, $(p | \alpha(q))$ and $(t | \tau(t))$ (and any conditional promises containing them) have a *limited lifetime* that is the temporal scope implied by their conditionals. Once $\alpha$ and $\tau$ become inoperative, they never become operative again, and any promise they condition can be forgotten forever.

Conversely, any promise containing the *negation* of an $\alpha$ or $\tau$ construction cannot become operative *until* the clause is fulfilled. $(p|\neg\alpha(q))$ means that $p$ becomes operative only when $q$ has become operative. Likewise, $(p|\neg\tau(t))$ means that $p$ becomes operative after time $t$. This means that after any negation of $\alpha$ or $\tau$ becomes operative, it can be *omitted from the conditional expression that contains it* from then on.

Combining negative and positive temporal operators allows one to specify any scope whatever in time. For example, $(p|\neg\tau(t_1), \tau(t_2))$ means that $p$ becomes operative from the time $t_1$ units in the future, until the time $t_2$ units in the future. Likewise, $(p|\neg\alpha(q), \alpha(r))$ says that $p$ becomes operative from when $q$ becomes operative, to when $r$ becomes operative.

### 3.2   Leasing

Several simple examples can illustrate the utility of $\alpha$ and $\tau$ in modeling common service binding behaviors. A lease is a time-limited promise. The use of a lease is – in turn – similarly limited in time. Let us model a typical DHCP lease in promise theory:

1. The client requests a lease. Requests are not promises.
2. $\langle s, c, b\rangle|\tau(t), \langle c, s, U(b)\rangle$: each server responds with a time-limited offer.
3. $\langle c, s, U(b)|\tau(t)\rangle$: the client responds to one server with an acceptance.

(See Figure 2a).

### 3.3   Gating

Another common situation is that a client wants to commit to a service until it decides to do otherwise. We can accomplish this via an "abstract" promise. An abstract promise has a body that has no behavioral effect nor any effect upon commitment except to gate a condition. Let us rewrite the leasing example to be gated instead:

1. The client requests a lease.
2. $\langle s, c, b\rangle|\langle c, s, U(b)\rangle$: each server responds with a conditional offer.
3. $\langle c, s, U(b)\rangle|\alpha(\langle c, s, \text{not}\rangle)$: the client responds with a gated acceptance, where the abstract body "not" represents the promise that ends the commitment.
4. $\langle c, s, \text{not}\rangle|\tau(0)$: the client, when it wishes to disconnect, issues a "gate promise".

The last is a promise that becomes operative and non-operative at a single time, thus nullifying $\alpha$ in the previous promise (and, in doing so, nullifying the entire promise) but becoming inoperative itself immediately after (Figure 2b). Note that gating can be coded in either direction. One could, e.g., allow the server to renege instead of the client, via:

$$\langle c, s, U(b)\rangle | \alpha(\langle s, c, \text{not}\rangle)$$

or even allow either to unilaterally back out of the agreement, via:

$$\langle c, s, U(b)\rangle | \alpha(\langle c, s, \text{not}\rangle), \alpha(\langle s, c, \text{not}\rangle)$$

A gated promise avoids "breaking promises" by declaring in advance which promises *will* become inoperative, and the events that will make them inoperative.

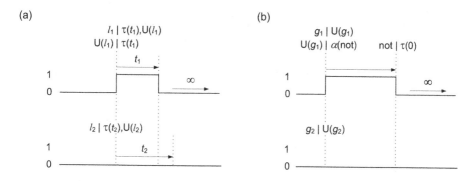

(a)

$l_1 | \tau(t_1), U(l_1)$
$U(l_1) | \tau(t_1)$
$t_1$

1

0

$\infty$

$l_2 | \tau(t_2), U(l_2)$

$t_2$

1

0

(b)

$g_1 | U(g_1)$
$U(g_1) | \alpha(\text{not})$     not $| \tau(0)$

1

0

$\infty$

$g_2 | U(g_2)$

1

0

**Fig. 2.** (a) Lease (promise) $l_1$ is operative, conditioned on a use promise and the time being less than the current time plus $t_1$. Lease $l_2$ never becomes operative. (b) Gating. Promise $g_1$ is operative until such time as its recipient decides otherwise. $g_2$ never becomes operative.

## 4   Observability and Knowledge

Before we can utilize timing and gating in more complex situations, we need to grapple with exactly when $\alpha$ and $\tau$ conditions make sense. A key element of promise theory is that an agent only has access to the promises that it makes and receives. In the above examples, it is clear what $\alpha$ and $\tau$ mean, because they involve only two servers with some concept of shared knowledge, but in more complex constructions, one must be careful not to write conditional expressions with no reasonable meaning. The constructions that are meaningful are those in which the agents involved in a promise transaction *can mutually observe the outcome* of the transaction. This is an extension of the principles of observability discussed in [16].

Consider, first, the case of one agent $X$ making a promise conditioned by $\tau(t)$ to another agent $Y$. The outcome of this promise is trivially mutually observable, because both agents can start a clock and make the promise inoperative after time $t$. No further communication is necessary in order to observe the effect.

In this paper, we assume that there is "reliable communication" between agents. Thus, if an agent sends a promise to another, that promise is guaranteed to be received. We are aware that this assumption is *not* made in most of current promise theory. But it is a valid assumption in many of the networks that promise theory attempts to model.

### 4.1 Observing $\alpha$

Now consider the more complex case of $\alpha(p)$. This promise is not mutually observable unless it is made between a sender and receiver that match those in $p = \langle s, r, b \rangle$. $(\langle s, r, b_2 \rangle | \alpha(\langle s, r, b_1 \rangle))$ and $(\langle r, s, b_2 \rangle | \alpha(\langle r, s, b_1 \rangle))$ make sense, but mentioning promises in $\alpha$ involving any external agent not equal to $s$ or $r$ does not make sense.

In general, it makes little sense for an agent to promise something conditionally unless it already holds a guarantee sufficient for it to believe that it can observe the conditions itself and thus know whether the promise is binding or not. Likewise, it makes little sense for the receiving agent to agree to react to a change in state unless it can observe the change whenever it occurs.

**Definition 5.** *A promise $\langle s, r, b \rangle$ is observable by an external agent $x$ not equal to $r$ or $s$ if $x$ holds sufficient promises to be able to determine with certainty whether $\langle s, r, b \rangle$ is operative in $r$ (and $s$).*

Obviously, $\alpha(p)$ is observable exactly when $p$ is mutually observable between sender and receiver.

### 4.2 Knowledge and $\kappa$

But how can an agent $x$ learn of a promise between two other agents $s$ and $r$? By definition, this is a communication between $s$ and $r$ with no intermediary. There is no standard mechanism other than to embed the promise in a body of another promise between some agent and $x$.

**Definition 6.** *Given a promise $p = \langle s, r, b \rangle$, the promise body $\kappa(p)$ means that "I will provide knowledge of whether the promise $p$ is operative."*

It is reasonable for either $s$ or $r$ to communicate this information to a third party $x$; e.g., the promises $\langle s, x, \kappa(\langle s, r, b \rangle) \rangle$ and $\langle r, x, \kappa(\langle s, r, b \rangle) \rangle$ are both reasonable[2]. $\kappa$ represents an *offer* to communicate this information, while $U(\kappa(\langle s, r, b \rangle))$ represents a commitment to *interpret* this information. Further, once promises $\kappa(p)$ and $U(\kappa(p))$ have been exchanged by a server agent $x$ and a client agent $y$, it makes sense for conditional expressions sent from $x$ to $y$ to contain $\alpha(p)$, even though $p$ may not involve $x$ and $y$.

The addition of $\kappa$ makes it possible to scope promises based upon knowledge of those made between other agents, in particular, $\alpha(p)$ makes sense as a condition

---

[2] Note that this information is similar to a "reification" in a resource description framework, and is of the form "$s$ claims that $\langle s, r, b \rangle$ holds."

even if $p$ is not a promise to the recipient. It is important to remember, however, that without a commitment to report ongoing state of an agent $s$ to an agent $x$, $x$ cannot be sure that it is completely aware of the relevant state of $s$. Likewise, an agent $x$ receiving such information, unless it agrees to *use* it, cannot be expected to react to it.

Note that unlike $\alpha(p)$, which is abstract, $\kappa(p)$ and $U(\kappa(p))$ are promises that make sense as consequents, and do not concern the state of $p$, but rather an intent to *communicate* that state from sender to receiver. It thus makes sense to consider "foreign" conditions (that do not share sender and receiver with the consequent promise) to be inoperative unless a $\kappa$-binding is in effect.

These new promise bodies – together with conditional promises – give us a variety of ways to express complex temporal relationships and state changes.

### 4.3   Failover

Normally, in a non-failover situation, we have a situation of offer and use promises: $\langle s, c, b \rangle$ and $\langle c, s, U(b) \rangle$. The server agent promises until its death, and the client agent promises until its death, respectively.

Failover is represented as a conditional promise network in which the failure of one service triggers a response from another server. We need several components to make this work.

1. $\langle s_1, *, b \rangle$: The original server $s_1$ promises to provide the service to everyone.
2. $\langle s_2, *, b \rangle$: the backup server $s_2$ promises to provide the service to everyone.
3. $\langle c, s_1, U(b) \rangle$: the client promises to use the original server until it or the client fails.
4. $\langle c, s_2, U(b) \rangle | \alpha(\langle s_1, c, b \rangle)$: in a failover situation, the client promises to use the failover server if the original server fails, until the original server comes alive again.

When the first server fails, the client is *not* breaking its promise to use the failed server; *but it must receive a new promise from the original server in order to continue*. Note that the backup server is only utilized until the client receives a valid promise from the original server.

But the above picture is not complete, because the last promise above *cannot be directly observed*. Without further information, that promise is nonsense. One way to fix this is to create a knowledge binding from server $s_1$ to server $s_2$: $\langle s_1, s_2, \kappa(\langle s_1, c, b \rangle) \rangle$, as well as a usage-of-knowledge binding in return: $\langle s_2, s_1, U(\kappa(\langle s_1, c, b \rangle)) \rangle$.

### 4.4   Complex Time-Varying Behavior

Suppose we wish to utilize the temporal calculus to describe a state machine for the state of a particular agent, where states will change over time due to external events or timeouts. The temporal operators are powerful enough to describe any such state machine:

**Theorem 2.** *Suppose agent A wishes to program a time progression on agent B in which promises $p_1, p_2, \ldots, p_k$ become exclusively operative in sequence. This can be accomplished with conditional promises, $\alpha$, and negation.*

*Proof.* Let $\{p_i\}$ be a set of promises to transition between, and let $\{s_i \mid i = 1, \ldots, k+1\}$ be a set of "abstract" promises whose assertion by any means "gates" the promises $\{p_i\}$ by accomplishing state changes. Let the promise set $C$ contain:

$$p_1 \mid \neg\alpha(s_1), \alpha(s_2)$$
$$p_2 \mid \neg\alpha(s_2), \alpha(s_3)$$
$$p_3 \mid \neg\alpha(s_3), \alpha(s_4)$$
$$\cdots$$
$$p_i \mid \neg\alpha(s_i), \alpha(s_{i+1})$$
$$\cdots$$
$$p_k \mid \neg\alpha(s_k), \alpha(s_{k+1})$$

Now we can accomplish state changes via the gate promises $s_i|\tau(0)$. If these are asserted in order, then promise $s_i|\tau(0)$ makes promise $p_i$ operative and promise $p_{i-1}$ non-operative. In this way, the target agent transitions in sequence between states $p_1$ to $p_k$.  □

The same construction can be utilized to cycle through any number of sets of promises, over time or in reaction to events.

Note that these transitions can only happen *once* because of the self-canceling behavior of $\alpha$. Once $\alpha$ has done its work, it becomes permanently inoperative and its rule effectively disappears. Thus:

**Corollary 1.** *An agent can achieve a cyclic behavior in a set of promises sent to another agent only by re-promising clauses that have become permanently non-operative.*

Note that any such control structure, once promised, can be eradicated as well:

**Corollary 2.** *The state machine in the previous proof can be erased from the target Y by the agent X, as needed.*

*Proof.* The state machine consists of one-time transitions based upon asserting certain events. When these transitions are used, they become permanently inoperative. To erase the state machine, one must take it through its transitions, after which each one becomes inoperative.

This is complicated unless one remembers that one can assert *any* state for a short time, or even for no time at all. To erase a rule, one makes its un-negated antecedents operative for a short time, then makes them inoperative again.  □

Thus conditional promises provide a way both to accomplish state changes and to erase the mechanism that enables them, as needed.

## 4.5   Calculating Operative Promises

Temporal promises add no major complexity to the calculation of which promises are operative or not.

**Theorem 3.** *At a particular time t, on a particular agent X, the calculation of whether a particular promise is operative can be done in two phases: first eliminating scoping rules, then interpreting pure conditionals.*

*Proof.* First suppose there is an abstract promise called "true" that is operative at all times. Create a pure conditional network $C'$ from the temporo-conditional network $C$ as follows:

1. Remove the whole promise for any $\tau$ or $\alpha$ conditions that have expired. $\tau$ expires when its time is up, while $\alpha$ expires when the event for which it is watching has been observed.
2. Replace all operative $\tau$ and $\alpha$ with "true".

Claim: the operative promises in the resulting network are equivalent with the operative promises in the original network. First, by definition of conditional promises and the temporal operators, all temporal operators expire at the end of their events. This means we can safely discard them, as they cannot become operative *again*. Second, when a condition is true in a conditional, the operative effect is that it is simply operative, and does not depend upon its temporal qualities. If for example we have $p|q_1, q_2, \ldots, q_k$, and we know $q_i$ is operative, then $p|q_1, \ldots, q_{i-1}, \text{true}, q_{i+1}, \ldots, q_k$ has the same effect as the previous one on $p$. The negation of "true", if it appears, behaves properly and one can delete the conditional promise containing it from the set of promises to be considered.   □

As a corollary, any promise whose temporal conditions aren't operative can be discarded as obsolete. This helps us "tidy up" promise space.

# 5   Conclusions

We have demonstrated that extending conditional promises with temporal promises $\alpha$ and $\tau$ (as well as negation) allows one to synthesize common network behaviors such as leasing and event-driven reaction. This mechanism allows an agent to almost completely control other agents' views of its commitments, over time. At any particular time, however, the commitments binding upon agents are analyzable via normal promise theory. Since temporally scoped promises become permanently inoperative after their conditions become inoperative, the promises an agent holds can be "tidied" by removing permanently inoperative conditionals.

Many questions remain to be answered. What is the most efficient way to compute the operative promises? Are there operators more efficient than the proposed operators? What depictions of conditional and temporal state are useful? There are more questions than answers.

One thing is certain, however: the ability for two agents to agree to forget a promise after a specific time is both useful and necessary in modeling contemporary networks.

# References

1. Burgess, M.: An approach to understanding policy based on autonomy and voluntary cooperation. In: Schönwälder, J., Serrat, J. (eds.) DSOM 2005. LNCS, vol. 3775, pp. 97–108. Springer, Heidelberg (2005)
2. Burgess, M., Begnum, K.: Voluntary cooperation in pervasive computing services. In: LISA, USENIX, pp. 143–154 ( 2005)
3. Burgess, M., Fagernes, S.: Pervasive computer management: A model of network policy with local autonomy. IEEE Transactions on Networking (submitted) ( 2006)
4. Burgess, M., Fagernes, S.: Promise theory - a model of autonomous objects for pervasive computing and swarms. In: ICNS, p. 118. IEEE Computer Society, Los Alamitos (2006)
5. Burgess, M., Couch, A.: Modeling next generation configuration management tools. In: LISA, USENIX, pp. 131–147 ( 2006)
6. Aredo, D., Burgess, M., Hagen, S.: A promise theory view on the policies of object orientation and the service oriented architecture (preprint) (submitted) (November 2006)
7. Bergstra, J., Burgess, M.: Local and global trust based on the concept of promises. Technical Report PRG0606, University of Amsterdam (2006)
8. Burgess, M., Couch, A.: Autonomic computing approximated by fixed-point promises. In: Proceedings of First IEEE International Workshop on Modeling Autonomic Communication Environments (MACE), pp. 197–222 ( 2006)
9. Burgess, M.: A site configuration engine. In: Computing systems, vol. 8, p. 309. MIT Press, Cambridge MA (1995)
10. Burgess, M., Ralston, R.: Distributed resource administration using cfengine. Softw. Pract. Exper. 27(9), 1083–1101 (1997)
11. Burgess, M.: Automated system administration with feedback regulation. Software practice and experience 28, 1519 (1998)
12. Burgess, M.: Cfengine as a component of computer immune-systems. Proceedings of the Norwegian conference on Informatics (1998)
13. Burgess, M.: Configurable immunity for evolving human-computer systems. Science of Computer Programming 51, 197 (2004)
14. Alva, L., Couch, D., Gilfix, M.: It's elementary, dear watson: Applying logic programming to convergent system management processes. In: LISA '99: Proceedings of the 13th USENIX conference on System administration, Berkeley, CA, USA, USENIX Association, pp. 123–138 ( 1999)
15. Bergstra, J., Bethke, I., Burgess, M.: A process algebra based framework for promise theory. Technical Report PRG0701, University of Amsterdam (2007)
16. Couch, A., Sun, Y.: On observed reproducibility in network configuration management. Science of Computer Programming 53, 215–253 (2004)

# Norms and Swarms

Mark Burgess and Siri Fagernes

Oslo University College
`mark.burgess@iu.hio.no`
`siri.fagernes@iu.hio.no`

**Abstract.** This paper describes a position for work in progress. We offer a definition of a "swarm" using the management concepts of promises and information rather than the programmed rules commonly used to mimick swarm behaviour. We look for a general and underlying meaning to swarms as a form of organization. Noting that swarms lead to an autonomous reduction of total information of the ensemble of agents, we propose that our definition of swarming suggests criteria for achieving fully decentralized, ad hoc network management without dedicated specialist controllers.

## 1  Introduction

The concept of a swarm has captured the imagination of many authors, both for engineering solutions, technologies and algorithms within distributed systems[1]. The apparent success of 'natural' swarms in accomplishing complex tasks, with each entity in the swarm performing rather simple actions, is compelling and mimics existing distributed algorithms for routing etc[2]. Swarm-inspired methods are often associated with multi-agent systems[3], and ant-inspired routing algorithms are perhaps the best known example of computing mechanisms that claim such inspiration[4]. In the natural sciences authors have also considered mathematical models that mimic swarming behaviour[5] in order to predict and compare clouds to observed swarms.

The concept of swarming has remained somewhat unclear however (dare we call it a "buzz word"?). We question the usefulness of the the way in which many authors model swarms, as if they were constellations held together by unknown forces. As an abstract concept one can do better than simply mimicking nature. What is it that actually constitutes as a swarm then? Answers bring forth many ideas in both physical science and computing, but it seems clear that the phenomenon of swarming has something to do with *collective organization*, and that it is a social phenomenon which brings individual parts into an effective whole, without a concerted controller. It is therefore natural to suppose that system management would also have something to learn from swarms, especially for ad hoc collaborations.

A second concept of interest in social networks is that of a *norm*. A norm is considered to be a aspirational goal for a population. We can think of it as a kind of *goal policy*, in the jargon of management. Unlike a swarm, which is

A.K. Bandara and M. Burgess (Eds.): AIMS 2007, LNCS 4543, pp. 109–120, 2007.

centred around what is actually representative for a population of self-controlled entities, a norm is like a flame we would like our swarm to fly towards. The concept of a norm, or policy goal is a desirable management paradigm for external control. The distinction between these swarms and norms is of basic interest to management.

In this paper we shall not be interested in algorithms that claim to draw inspiration from swarming, nor in reproducing the measurable physical signatures of swarming, rather we are interested in extracting the central principles of the phenomenon itself, from a behavioural viewpoint. We want to identify what it is that makes swarms a successful behavioural strategy. We shall use promise theory[6,7,8] for this, as it is a natural way to model the behaviour of autonomous parts within a collective.

Our motivation is to see if we can identify a swarm concept in network management, whose principles teach us something about successful management strategy. Thus, we begin by asking:

- Why do swarms emerge? (Agent behaviour)
- How do swarms emerge? (Initial conditions, minimum conditions, etc)
- How can swarm modelling enlighten problems in management of systems?

We consider first some remarks from the literature for later comparison. Next we define some metric criteria for swarms. Finally we propose a high level understanding of swarms in terms of *promises*.

## 2    Swarm Fundamentals

The traditional approach in *swarm engineering* (or swarm intelligence) is to design and create a 'population' of agents or robots that are all configured with a specific *goal*. We find this to be misleading as it explicitly precludes emergent phenomena. Our own notion of swarms is closer to the pervasive computing scenario, where a large number of autonomous entities move around and interact, both with each other and the environment, without any pre-designed behaviour. They have certain similarities, experience both potential risks and benefits in their interactions, and potentially profit from active participation in collaborative behaviour. We propose that a swarm model could apply to this scenario.

Swarm models aim to understand the behaviour of populations of 'agents', inspired for instance by ants building nests or collecting food, flocks of birds flying in certain formations etc. In a swarm, each individual 'agent' makes decisions about its own behaviour without a 'global' programme or overview. For instance, a bird makes a decision on how to fly in a flock based on observations of its neighbours, not on the overall movement of the flock.

There is a presumed advantage to having individual parts (computing devices or humans) forming cooperative structures instead of performing alone. The same idea is often assumed to be desirable in network management, without necessarily being understood from a model. We could view this from two angles:

1. *Local perspective:* An individual in a swarm might achieve more as a part of a 'team' than on its own.
2. *Global perspective:* If we are managing an entire ensemble of agents, a swarm might solve the management problem with fewer resources.

So how do we identify and nurture characteristics that lead to beneficial collective behaviour?

When imagining a swarm, many of us will naturally think of a spatial cluster of parts, moving together somehow. Although reasonable, this cannot be a sufficient condition for a swarm, as there are many reasons why agents might be localized, e.g. a pile of leaves blown by a gust of wind, or a number of cars forced to follow the only road available could satisfy this condition, but no one would claim that these examples exhibited self-determined, collective behaviour. Kazadi[9] defines a swarm as follows:

> *A set of two or more independent agents all acting in a common environment, in a coherent fashion, generating an emergent behaviour.*

This suggests that some self-determined behaviour must emerge from an ensemble of agents (without being obviously designed into the ensemble). What is unclear in this definition is what is meant by "independent". Many authors also use the term *autonomous agent* (with a variety of meanings)[3]. In most cases the definition of independent or autonomous involves some "cheating" – i.e. although each agent works alone, there is a centrally defined program that coordinates their behaviours. Kazadi characterizes *emergent behaviour* as follows:

> *the behaviour of the swarm is a result of the interactions of the swarm with its environment or members, but not a result of direct design. Emergent behaviour requires inter-agent communication, which need not be direct.*

This quotation raises many questions, but highlights the need for some interaction between the parts of a swarm. Let us consider the issues in turn.

**Ensemble Localization.** We remarked above that one of the features commonly associated with swarms is that of localization around some centre. Natural swarms are spatial clusters, but we could imagine clustering also in any measurable parameter belonging to an abstract metric space that characterizes agents, e.g. device configuration parameters or policy parameters.

Let us consider such a metric space with generalized coordinate $x$, measured relative to an arbitrary origin. A distribution of distances $|x|$ from the origin, denoted by $p(|x|)$ is a normalized probability density function for agents within the space (see fig 1). We define localization to mean a peak in the probability distribution. If we use the normalized Shannon entropy (or information[10]) as a scalar measure of the distribution

$$S = \frac{-\int dx\, p(x) \log p(x)}{S_{\max}} \quad \in [0,1].$$

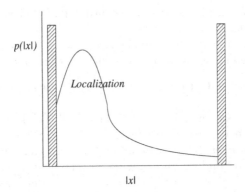

**Fig. 1.** Localization in a spatial distribution, with boundary conditions

then localization means that $S < S_{\max}$, i.e. there is some tendency to favour a particular location within the space. Localization is a *statistical observable*. It could be barely visible in a highly delocalized ensemble, or sharply focused when agents are touching. The Shannon entropy $S$ of an ensemble is therefore a characteristic parameter which measures the extent of its localization. We propose that it makes no sense to specify an arbitrary threshold on this localization, rather we should label swarms with a localization parameter. This is often governed by limitations of communication, and it is the attraction that derives from the communcation that answers the question of *how* swarm behaviour is favoured.

Note that the space in the figure has boundary conditions, denoted by the hatched bars, that prevent agents from existing outside the bounded region. Confinement by boundary is not swarm behaviour, it is an environmental constraint. We now define a norm as a pre-specified localization:

**Definition 1 (Norm).** *A norm is an externally specified distribution $p(|x|)$ within a given metric parameter space.*

**Communication and coordination.** A basis for agent interaction that could lead to localization is inter-agent *communication*, which is categorized as either *direct* or *stigmergic*. Direct (active) communication is a signal sent from one agent to another. A stigmergic communcation implies that an intermediary was involved, such as posting a sign or leaving a trail to follow. Cars following a road do not communicate stigmergically via the existence of the road, they simply have no alternative but to follow it; but cars in a traffic jam, which try to follow other cars they see to be moving on successful routes, are communicating by visual signals. Observation is thus a form of communication (we call it passive communication).

**Persistent emergent behaviour.** The final characteristic of a swarm is that it must exhibit some resultant behaviour collectively that is not evident in the behaviours of the individual agents. For instance, flocks of birds form co-moving formations, ants form food distribution networks and build nests. The emergent behaviour must persist over time, as the distributions of agents evolve; i.e. as agents change their parameters or positions in the relevant configuration space, the average properties of the swarm must persist. Thus we propose:

**Definition 2 (Swarm).** *A swarm is an ensemble of agents that uses communication to reduce its total information with respect to any abstract measuring classification, and which exhibits emergent behaviour.*

## 3   Behaviour and Promises

Promise theory is a high level description of constrained behaviour in which ensembles of agents document the behaviours they promise to exhibit. Agents in promise theory are truly autonomous, i.e. they decide their own behaviour, cannot be forced into behaviour externally but can voluntarily cooperate with one another[6].

Promises made by agents fall into two basic categories, promises to provide something or offer a behaviour $b$ (written $a_1 \xrightarrow{+b} a_2$), and promises to accept something or make use of another's promise of behaviour $b$ (written $a_2 \xrightarrow{-b} a_1$). A successful transfer of the promised exchange involves both of these promises, as an agent can freely decline to be informed of the other's behaviour or receive the service.

Promises can be made about any subject that relates to the behaviour of the promising agent, but agents cannot make promises about each others' behaviours. The subject of a promise is represented by the promise body $b$, which consist of two essential parts: a promise *type* ($\tau$) and a *constraint* ($\chi$) which indicates what subset of behaviours are promised from within the domain of all behaviours of that type. Finally, the *value* of a promise to any agent is a numerical function of the constraint e.g. $v_{a_1}(a_1 \xrightarrow{+b} a_2)$, and is determined and measured in a currency that is private to that agent. Any agent can form a valuation of any promise that is knows about. One would like to know: what promises are necessary and sufficient for the formation of swarms and norms? We shall make some proposals here, without proof.

## 4   Inter-agent Distance and Norms in Promise Space

Norms are not promises: they are aspirations or potential promises that someone would like to see under idealized conditions. In practice, perhaps only a fraction of a population will choose to promise behaviour that lies within a norm. Nevertheless, we can describe norms in terms of the promises we would like agents to make. Promises are an ideal language for parameterizing norms.

We postulate here for simplicity a hypothetical external observer who can measure all of the agents on a common scale relative to a fixed origin (like Maxwell's daemon). This is important, as autonomous agents can each judge the world according to a different standard. A norm is then often a specific value of a constraint. $\chi = \chi_{norm}$, or a focused distribution in general. A trend is an empirical localization with an ensemble average $\langle \chi \rangle = E(\chi) \equiv \int d\chi \, p(\chi)\chi / \int d\chi$. If the trend is not equal to the norm, then we can say that there is a deviation from the norm.

The similarity of two distributions is measured by their mutual information $I(p; q)$[10]. If the mutual information is zero, then they are only coincidentally similar. A norm is normally a desire to achieve a low informational entropy clustering of the agents about a normative configuration.

In management terms we understand that a localization or normalization is a strategy for reducing the amount of information needed to manage a group of agents by making them as similar as possible (the "keep it simple" rule). The introduction of a low entropy "attractor" norm is one approach to this, but only if the agents will naturally adopt it. We must therefore understand the reasons why autonomous agents would comply or succeed in reaching goals.

## 5   Swarms of Promises

Basic requirements for coordinated behaviour are i) Communication: agents must be able to identify one another and promise behaviours or reject others' promises. For a cluster we need ii) Localization: promises to minimize the total information. A swarm requires in addition iii) Emergence: a common emergent behavioural promise to a hypothetical observer, and finally iv) Persistence: the emergent behaviour and localization must persist or change only slowly compared to the reliabilities of the individual agents.

### 5.1   Inter-agent Communication

The basis of any swarm is a sufficient communication between the elementary parts. This interaction is what actually 'binds' the agents together. In a promise theory representation, communication is not represented in detail (there are no events, no explicit time), there is only implied by promises to send or to receive. Kazadi defines communication as

> any action of one agent which influences the subsequent behaviour of one or more other agents in the system, directly or indirectly.

Promise theory does not normally discuss actions. The question thus becomes what promises should be made to ensure the necessary interactions. The guarantee of influence from one agent to another requires a promise to send and a promise to receive, regardless of whether the signal is active (message), passive (observation), direct (transmission) or stigmergic (through a relay).

| Signal/promise types | +promise | -promise |
|---|---|---|
| Direct | be detectable to neighbours | observe neighbours |
| Stigmergic | leave message | read message |

In graph terms we propose that a necessary condition for a swarm is thus that the graph of neighbour interactions must be strongly connected in the promise types contributing to emergent promises.

## 5.2   Emergent Behaviour

Emergent behaviour is thus posited as a criterion for an ensemble of agents to qualify as a swarm. To model this, we first require emergent behaviour to be measured by the same standard as planned behaviour. Even though emergent behaviour is, by definition, not promised explicitly by any agent, we imagine it represented as a promise to a hypothetical external observer or arbitrator of swarm behaviour (like Maxwell's daemon). The observer must be external in general to be able to observe the swarm, as individuals cannot necessarily observe (communicate with) all other agents in the ensemble.

**Proposition 1 (Common behaviour to a hypothetical observer).** *A necessary condition for a swarm is that every agent promises some common behaviour to a hypothetical external observer or* arbitrator *concerning its emergent behaviour.*

In ref. [7] we have demonstrated how a set of promises between specific agents acts as a label that identifies a group. Similar ideas fit well with principles of social organization that have been applied to P2P networks[11].

A second property of emergent behaviour is that is not explicitly planned by the agents themselves. It emerges from the binding promises, combined with the random changes that input information from the environment in which agents move or change their configurations. We therefore define emergent behaviour as follows:

**Definition 3 (Emergent behaviour).** *A promise-role is an emergent behaviour if the entire ensemble of agents' promises induces a new set of promises, by virtue of cooperation, from each agent in the ensemble to any arbitrating agent, hypothetical or real.*

We can use the proposed theory of measurement from ref. [7] to explain this (fig. 2). On the left of the figure we see the constellations of promises observed. On the right, a reinterpretation of the relevant promises that are cooperative, implying the existence of a (possibly unreliable) promise to an external third party.

If all agents had a deterministic ability to observe or communicate with one another one would have rigid formations rather than swarms. The swarm property derives from the unreliability of the promises made to all agents in the swarm, from the inevitable interactions with the environment. In computer engineering terms, we can think of the (un)reliability of promises being kept as the existence of an *ad hoc* overlay network between agents that is used to implement the promises. Effectively, agents in a swarm fall in and out of the swarm depending on their ability to keep their promises of visibility and mutual observation.

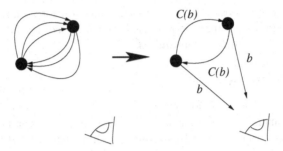

**Fig. 2.** Emergent behaviour – a hypothetical promise to combine the individual promises between agents, promised to an external observer or arbitrator

For example, flocking birds promise each other to stay close together, follow magnetic lines and avoid turbulence and collisions. The emergent result of this is that they promise to collaborate to reduce their surface area against attack, navigate as a group and adjust their formations aerodynamically and minimize their information. All birds in the flock make the same effective set of promises which can be understood by an external observer as emergent goals. These are precisely the promise roles.

We propose a stability requirement for the preservation of the low entropy structure:

**Proposition 2 (Persistent behaviour).** *A necessary condition for a swarm is that the ensemble's localization changes only adiabatically i.e. $\frac{1}{S}\frac{dS}{dt} \ll 1$ and the width $\frac{1}{\sigma}\frac{d\sigma}{dt} \ll 1$, where $S$ is the entropy of the ensemble promises and $\sigma$ is the standard deviation of the ensemble promises.*

**Typed Swarms.** As promise theory is based on types, swarms also have types. An agent can therefore belong to more than one swarm. Could this lead to a conflict of interest for an agent? This depends on the ontological classification of promise types. If swarms occur in entirely disconnected spaces, there will be no conflict. A "design strategy" for avoiding management conflicts is to clearly separate promise types into mutually exclusive categories.

## 6   To Swarm or Not to Swarm: A Dilemma?

Why might agents choose to enter a swarm? Let us sketch a possible answer. This question can be restated as follows: what benefit do autonomous devices get from coordinating their behaviour? This is a question that calls forth many prejudices about management.

As swarms consist of purely autonomous individuals, no outside forces or agents can *a priori* cause an agent to change its behaviour. To predict whether a swarm will emerge from a group of selfish-minded individuals, we must study the potential economic benefit of promises. The real challenge here is to identify the relevant *currencies* that motivate the agents.

Traditionally, game theoretical models use the well-known *Prisoner's Dilemma* model and its tit-for-tat strategy for inducing cooperative behaviour. The threat for retaliation for non-cooperative is crucial to the economic incentive. In a swarm, the picture is quite different. The basic choice of an agent is to either join a group, or act on its own. Joining the group typically implies certain emergent (rather than direct) benefits. Another difference from the 'Prisoner's Dilemma'-scenario, is that the risk of 'free-riders' is effectively reduced due to the coarse graining of payment[1] that can occur when there is a one-time payment for a service quota (as in a fixed-price contract). The economics of swarms is the key to understanding their longevity and stability. Space limitations prevent us from discussing this further here[13].

# 7    Applications to Ad Hoc Network Management

The emergent properties of swarms arise from the interplay between inter-agent promises. These make agents reduce their differences and increase the reliability of the (ad hoc) "overlay" network that enables communicative cooperation. All management in unreliable systems can be viewed as ad hoc network management[14]. In [15,16,17] the authors highlight some of the ideas we touch upon here in describing the management of ad hoc networks.

An example of how swarms emerge to provide coordinated behaviour in response to the economics of the environment was presented in ref. [18], which involved a so-called *smart shopping mall*, or shopping mall with the additional feature of wireless networks, enabling the mall to provide enhanced services to its customers. Each of the customers, in addition to the shops, mall management and ISP providing the infrastructure, were thought of as an autonomous agent in this scenario. The autonomous nature of the interaction between the agents implies potential risks for the agents, in addition to a range of benefits, all dependent on the overall agent behaviour.

Depending on the dynamics, interaction patterns and individual choices made by each of the customers, shops and other 'actors' in this scenario, certain promise-role structures emerged. The promise-role of a specific agent was determined by the *types* of both given and received promises by that agent, in addition to *which* agents it would form a relationship with through promises. These structures could aid us in monitoring such communities, simplifying the process of predicting several aspects of environments of autonomous entities, for

---

[1] In ref. [12] this phenomenon is illustrated by comparing swarm behaviour to the sharing of *open source* software on the Internet. The author argues how the majority of the consumers of such information never contribute themselves, but that this does not harm the community of contributors. Even if the number of contributors is low compared to the overall size of the 'population', there are enough contributors to provide a valuable information to the entire community. The fact that a non-contributor is taking advantage of a piece of information, does not induce any additional cost to the providers as long as the cost model is sufficiently coarse grained, and might actually help the survival of the contributors.

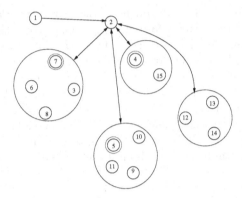

**Fig. 3.** In ref. [18] we show how promise-roles emerge as a result of the economically supported promises of boundedly rational agents

instance the risk of unwanted selfish behaviour. Related to the emerged roles of the individual agents, several *groups* of agents evolved.

We propose the emergence of promise-roles and groups in this promise community as an example of emergent behaviour in a swarm of autonomous agents. The emergent behaviour is both economic and associative.

## 8   Conclusions

We have used the distinct ideas of norms (social ideals) and swarms (emergent behavioural condensates) to discuss the management of heterogeneous and volatile populations of agents. Our description uses only two ideas: promises (behavioural constraints) and configuration probabilities (information). Promises give us a way of defining emergent behaviour formally, without losing a grasp of the high level issues. Our work differs from other swarming work in that we suggest properties for swarm behaviour; we do not program agents to behave "like a swarm".

We propose that communication allows agents to make similar choices (in some physical or abstract space). This has the effect of reducing the total information in the system (as with graph reducibility). With less information, the cost of management is reduced, since "management" implies that one invests work to track and change system information. A *norm* is the aspiration to make all agents alike, leading to maximal reduction of information but not necessarily through inter-agent communication. Simply making all agents the same does not reduce the cost of management if the same total amount of information has to be tracked on each agent.

A swarming agent must balance the cost of non-cooperation against the value it places on individual autonomy. This is a calculation that involves relating multiple currencies: currencies of survival, security, effort and perhaps even money. The economics of this scenario have not been studied in detail, and we aim to do so in future work. Each agent makes its judgement based on private information available only to it.

We aimed to explain the distinction between system behaviours that were self-determined, those that are engineered by global policy, and those that are simply random chance. Now we see that norms are engineered, as in centralized policy management. This is expensive to enforce and inflexible, since no agent can outsource any part of the enforcement. Swarms are relatively cheap and adaptable, but less predictable. Both norms and swarms are subject to the same unreliabilities. Cheaper yet is when agents are forced into similarity by the boundary conditions of the environment itself. In such a situation, the freedom of a swarm approach can quickly adapt, but trying to impose a norm that was different from the environmental attractor would seem expensive and foolish, yet that is often what management systems advocate.

Does our story about swarming autonomous agents have anying to do with ordinary management systems? Autonomy plus promises gives us the entire spectrum of architectural management paradigms. If agents promise to follow instructions from a common source they mimic centralized management. What the swarm phenomenon shows us is that centralized management is not a prerequisite for stable and efficient behaviour and it suggests us an economic explanation for why.

We have sketched what we consider to be a thought-provoking model for classifying and measuring the cost of management strategies for pervasive and ad hoc networks. Work is needed to explore the details and implications of the model. We shall return to the many outstanding issues in future work.

This work is supported by the EC IST-EMANICS Network of Excellence (#26854)

# References

1. Bonabeau, E., Dorigo, M., Theraulaz, G.: Swarm Intelligence: From Natural to Artificial Systems. Oxford University Press, Oxford (1999)
2. Huitema, C.: Routing in the Internet, 2nd edn. Prentice-Hall, Englewood Cliffs (2000)
3. Wooldridge, M.: An Introduction to MultiAgent Systems. Wiley, Chichester (2002)
4. Di Caro, G., Dorigo, M.: Antnet: Distributed stigmergetic control for communications networks. Journal of Artificial Intelligence Research 9, 317–365 (1998)
5. Arlotti, L., Deutsch, A., Lachowicz, M.: On a discrete boltzmann type model of swarming. Math. Comp. Model 41, 1193–1201 (2005)
6. Burgess, M.: An approach to understanding policy based on autonomy and voluntary cooperation. In: Schönwälder, J., Serrat, J. (eds.) DSOM 2005. LNCS, vol. 3775, pp. 97–108. Springer, Heidelberg (2005)
7. Burgess, M., Fagernes, S.: Pervasive computing management: A model of network policy with local autonomy. IEEE Transactions on Software Engineering, page (submitted)
8. Burgess, M., Fagernes, S.: Voluntary economic cooperation in policy based management. IEEE Transactions on Network and Service Management, page (submitted)

9. Kazadi, S.: Swarm Engineering. PhD thesis, California Institute of Technology (2000)
10. Cover, T.M., Thomas, J.A.: Elements of Information Theory. J.Wiley & Sons, New York (1991)
11. Hales, D., Edmonds, B.: Applying a socially inspired technique (tags) to improve cooperation in p2p networks. IEEE Transactions on Systems, Man and Cybernetics vol. 35, pp. 385–395
12. Heylighen, F.: Open Source Jahrbuch, chapter Why is Open Access Development so Successful? Stigmergic organization and the economics of information
13. Burgess, M., Fagernes, S.: On the economics of swarms (In preparation) (2007)
14. Burgess, M., Canright, G.: Scaling behaviour of peer configuration in logically ad hoc networks. IEEE eTransactions on Network and Service Management 1, 1 (2004)
15. Festor, O., Badonnel, R., State, R.: Management of mobile ad-hoc networks: Information model and probe-based architecture. Journal of Network Management 15, 335–347 (2005)
16. Festor, O., Badonnel, R., State, R.: Fault montoring in ad-hoc networks based on information theory. Networking, pp. 427–438 (2006)
17. Badonnel, R., State, R., Festor, O.: Probabilistic management of ad-hoc networks. In: Proceedings of 10th IFIP/IEEE Network Operations and Management Symposium NOMS (2006)
18. Burgess, M., Fagernes, S.: Autonomic pervasive computing: A smart mall scenario using promise theory. In: Proceedings of the 1st IEEE International Workshop on Modelling Autonomic Communications Environments (MACE); Multicon verlag 2006, pp. 133–160 (2006) ISBN 3-930736-05-5

# Providing Seamless Mobility in Wireless Networks Using Autonomic Mechanisms

John Strassner, Barry Menich, and Walter Johnson

Motorola Labs, 1301 East Algonquin Road, Mail Stop IL02-2240
Schaumburg, IL 60196 USA
{john.strassner,barry.menich,walter.johnson}@motorola.com

**Abstract.** Existing wireless networks have little in common, as they are designed around vendor-specific devices that use specific radio access technologies to provide particular functionality. Next generation networks seek to integrate wide-area and local-area wireless systems in order to provide seamless services to the end user. This would provide freedom of movement between indoor/outdoor and metropolitan/enterprise coverage while maintaining continuity of applications experience. Seamless Mobility is an experiential architecture, predicated on providing mechanisms that enable a user to accomplish his or her tasks without regard to technology. This paper examines how autonomic mechanisms can satisfy some of the challenges in realizing seamless mobility solutions.

**Keywords:** autonomic computing, causal determinacy, data model, information model, key quality indicator, key performance indicator, seamless mobility.

## 1 Introduction

Historically, management of wireless operations in wide-area mobile networks was vested in the OMC-R (Operations and Maintenance Center – Radio) network element [1][2] and attendant management software. Performance management statistics, alarms, and call logs are obtained, calculated and analyzed, enabling computation of key performance and quality indicators (KPIs and KQIs) to determine the quality of the system and its components. This provides a machine-interpretable view of system quality as perceived by the end user.

The individual management and optimization of any one type of wireless system is very challenging, and up to now, has given rise to mechanisms that are specific to a particular type of radio access technology (RAT). This presents a daunting set of challenges for current RATs, due to their non-compatible standards and vendor-specific differences in implemented functionality, as well as for future multi access mode devices [3] and cognitive networks [4]. However, the vision of Seamless Mobility [5] is even more ambitious. Seamless Mobility is the natural progression of enhanced mobility enabled by cellular and wireless technologies. For example, the cell phone is used not only to stay in touch, but to snap photos, share videos, play music, send text messages and more.

A.K. Bandara and M. Burgess (Eds.): AIMS 2007, LNCS 4543, pp. 121–132, 2007.

## 2  The Vision of Seamless Mobility

Businesses are gaining competitive advantage through innovative applications that empower their increasingly mobile employees and customers, and end-users are now starting to expect a world of easy, uninterrupted access to information, entertainment, and communication across diverse environments, devices and networks. Businesses want anywhere, anytime communications to provide enhanced productivity to their workforce. Consumers are equally eager for personalized services that make it easy to access and share digital content when, where and how they want it. Network operators seeking an edge in a changing marketplace are exploring new approaches to delivering this content in a timely and cost-effective manner.

Seamless Mobility, and its vision of seamless service delivery, requires significant changes to existing wired and wireless network management systems. For example, when handover from one wireless system to another wired or wireless system is performed, a "seam", or discontinuity, is created that interrupts the continuity of application experience. In this paper, we will describe two types of changes – more automation of tasks previously done manually, and embedding intelligence in devices as well as networks and systems that enables the OMC-R to reason (from evidence) about what is causing service disruptions and, in the cases where a fix is not known, deduce how to fix the problem(s).

Motorola's vision of Seamless Mobility is to provide simple, uninterrupted access to any type of information desired at any time, independent of place, network and device. Seamless Mobility is an experiential architecture that captures the current context of what the user is doing, so that services that the user desires can be optimized. In earlier work, we have developed a novel context model that provides a first step in solving this difficult problem that is part of our FOCALE [6] architecture; this will be explained in more detail in Section 5.

## 3  Wireless Networking Management Fundamentals

Quality problems in existing wireless systems are difficult to determine. Network engineers must piece together different statistics, logs, and other data to *infer* problems and their causes. If data collected at the OMC-R is not sufficient to determine the cause of failures, "drive testing" (a process in which a person walks or drives around the wireless system coverage area to verify performance levels) is used. However, this approach ignores other aspects (e.g., equipment availability or poor quality) that could be potential causes, as well as calls failing for multiple reasons.

### 3.1  The Nature and Use of Call Detail Logs

Clearly, the costs associated with drive-testing of systems scales with the size of the system; the costs associated with human-in-the-loop analysis of call logs and ensemble statistics is equally intolerable. The preferred solution is automating the collection and analysis of key data leading to causal determination.

The Call Detail Log (CDL) is the primary source of information regarding call behavior in a CDMA system. Each log entry is a collection of attributes captured for a call and stored upon call termination. Broadly speaking, typical attributes collected in a CDL relate to pieces of infrastructure equipment used during the life of the call, radio frequency (RF) measurements made at certain times, a record of call behavior (handoffs, packets transmitted, etc.) and an indication of how the system classified the call (coarse classification) upon call termination [2]. This final, coarse classification is used in establishing the statistical performance of the system (success rate, dropped call rate, access failure rate, etc.) that is eventually incorporated into key performance information and reported to operations personnel.

The CDL contains attributes that are observational in nature, causal in nature, and some attributes that are both. CDL data can be augmented by using the SU as a means to collect either per-call or continuous measurement information. An example of an SU instrumented with specialty software for collecting RF measurements and air interface messaging using the OMA-DM standard [7] is [8].

Combining CDL data with SU data can help evaluate and diagnose wireless system performance issues, especially if the data relating to the same call from the CDL and the subscriber unit can be correlated. This information can be used to identify many issues such as coverage problems, interference, suboptimal neighbor list construction, and uplink/downlink imbalances, among others. Correlation is hard due to the natural temporal separation created through the collection process.

## 3.2 Key Performance and Quality Indicators

Performance of cellular systems includes the monitoring of terrestrial networking data as well as RF data. Simple Network Management Protocol (SNMP) data forms part of the Internet protocol suite used by network management systems. SNMP data can be used to form Key Performance Indicators (KPIs) and Key Quality Indicators (KQIs) [10]. KPIs and KQIs are monitored to track the performance and/or reliability of the system against a specific Service Level Agreement (SLA) [10]. KPIs are quantifiable measurements that reflect the critical successful or unsuccessful factors of a wireless system. KQIs provide an indicator for a specific performance aspect of the product or product components (e.g., service or service elements) and draw their data from a number of sources including KPIs. SLAs are formal negotiated agreements or contracts (or part of one) between two parties which are designed to create a common understanding about the services, priorities, and responsibilities that a wireless system provider guarantees to their customers.

Several KPIs can be formed using data from the CDMA system's CDL records and SUs. We defined the following KPIs: Dropped Call Rate, Setup Failure Rate, Bad Quality Rate, Call Blocking Rate, Call Setup Blocking Rate, and Call Handoff Blocking Rate (examples for UMTS are given in [11]). In general, the KPI rates were generated by calculating a rate based on forming a ratio of negative examples as compared to the total number of examples over a particular window length. The KQIs defined for our project were Voice Service Quality and Network Service Availability, both of which were formed using the above KPIs. The system level KQIs and KPIs both use a windowing function for the purpose of smoothing or otherwise shaping the resulting CDL rates to avoid short term temporal or spatial anomalies that could result in violating an SLA when unwarranted. Our project adopted simple SLAs that were based on violating a KQI threshold that was defined by a novel policy language.

### 3.3 Causal Analysis

Once an SLA agreement is violated, the cause for why the violation occurred must be determined and corrective action taken. In our system, an SLA violation maps to a KQI violation that determines the equipment(s) needing further inspection. This is accomplished by rank ordering the equipment KPIs and KQIs across all system elements and choosing the piece (or pieces) of equipment with the worst performing indicators. Once the identity of the equipment requiring further inspection is determined, a casual analysis is carried out.

KQI violations are analyzed using a supervised rule-based expert system classifier that operates on negative call examples (i.e., calls that failed in some manner), where the classification rules have been derived via domain expert guidance and individually proven in empirical trials. However, we made two important changes to normal classification operations. The first is that a negative call example can be assigned to more than one class, since calls may fail for multiple reasons. The second is that we don't use an explicit classification rule to represent implied causal precedence, due to the characteristics of CDMA, (e.g., equipment failures would cause coverage problems). Thus, equipment failures and coverage failures are treated as mutually exclusive failure causes during the classification process.

At the end of the classification process, the counters (corresponding to the class assignments) are tallied and the results rank-ordered in the form of a Pareto [12]. Based on the distribution of results, a cause and a remediation for the distribution are specified to the operations personnel. The operations personnel then have the option to take direct action on this information or perform further analysis in order to determine how to improve the overall wireless network health and operation. The Pareto information is stored along with wireless network performance after the corrective action has taken place and used as input to learning algorithms to better predict the corrective action or actions that should be taken in a given situation.

## 4   Salient Features of Autonomic Networking

This section will first define autonomic computing, and then discuss the difference between it and autonomic networking.

### 4.1 Autonomic Computing

The purpose of autonomic computing is to manage complexity. The name was chosen to reflect the function of the autonomic nervous system in the human body. By transferring more manual functions to involuntary control, additional resources (human and otherwise) are made available to manage higher-level processes.

The fundamental management element of an autonomic computing architecture is a control loop, as defined in [13][14][15]. This control loop starts with gathering sensor information, which is then analyzed to determine if any correction to the managed resource(s) being monitored is needed (e.g., to correct "non-optimal", "failed" or "error" states). If so, then those corrections are planned, and appropriate actions are executed using effectors that translate commands back to a form that the managed resource(s) can understand. This usually results in the reconfiguration of that managed resource, though it can cause the reconfiguration of other managed resources that are affecting the state of the managed resource that is being monitored.

The Autonomic Element is a building block, in which the autonomic manager communicates with other types of autonomic and non-autonomic managers using the sensors and effectors of the autonomic manager. IBM's version is shown in Figure 1.

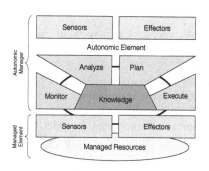

**Fig. 1.** IBM's Control Loop

The autonomic manager provides the overall guidance for the autonomic element in collecting, analyzing, and acting on data collected from the managed resource via its sensors. It consists of four parts that govern the functionality of the control loop. The monitor portion gathers data, filters and collates it if required, and then presents it to the analysis portion. The analysis portion seeks to understand the data, and to determine if the managed resource is acting as desired. The planning part takes the conclusions of the analysis part and determines if action should be taken to reconfigure any managed resources, using predefined policies that establish the goals and objectives that the autonomic manager enforces. The execute portion translates the plan into a set of commands that direct any reconfiguration required.

## 4.2  Autonomic Networking

The motivation behind autonomic networking is to identify those functions that can be done without human intervention to reduce the dependence on skilled resources for managing devices, networks, and networked applications. If the autonomic network can perform manual, time-consuming tasks (such as configuration management) on behalf of the network administrator, then that will free the system and the administrator to work *together* to perform higher-level cognitive functions, such as planning and optimization of the network.

Motorola has defined a new management approach that is equally appropriate for legacy devices and applications as well as for next generation and cognitive networks. One difference between autonomic computing and autonomic networking is that the latter must cope with and coordinate *multiple* control mechanisms (used by different networks), which the former usually doesn't consider. Our FOCALE architecture was designed to support this need as follows. Multiple networks and network technologies require multiple control planes that can use completely different mechanisms; this makes managing an end-to-end service difficult since different management mechanisms must be coordinated. FOCALE addresses this through model-based translation (see section 5.3). Second, in current environments, user needs and environmental conditions can change without warning. Therefore, the system, its environment, and the needs of its users must be continually analyzed with respect to business objectives. FOCALE uses inferencing to instruct the management plane to *coordinate the (re)configuration of its control loops* in order to protect the current business objectives. This is unique to autonomic networking.

# 5  Applying FOCALE to Wireless Network Management

This section describes the adaptation of our FOCALE architecture to meet the needs of wireless networks.

## 5.1  Introduction

FOCALE was built to apply autonomic principles to network management. As such, it is different than common autonomic architectures, which are applied to non-networking components of IT systems.

FOCALE stands for **Foundation – Observation – Comparison – Action – Learn – rEason**, which are the six key principles required to support autonomic networking. These principles are used to manage complexity while enabling the system to adjust to the changing demands of its users and environmental conditions. In order for the network to dynamically adjust the services and resources that it provides, its components must first be appropriately (re)configured as needed. Assume that behavior can be defined using a set of state machines, and that the configuration of each device is determined from this information. FOCALE is a closed loop system, in which the current state of the managed element is calculated and compared to the desired state (defined in the state machines). Any variance from the desired state is analyzed to ensure that business goals and objectives are still being met. If they are, the system will keep monitoring state (though it may need to change what is being monitored); if they aren't, then the system executes a set of configuration changes to fix the problem(s). Equally important, the results of these changes are observed to ensure that the system reacted as expected.

However, since networks are complex, highly interconnected systems, the above approach is modified in several important ways. First, FOCALE uses multiple control loops, as will be explained below. Second, FOCALE uses a combination of information models, data models, and ontologies for three things: (1) to develop its state machines, (2) to determine the actual state of the managed element, and (3) to understand the *meaning* of sensor data so that the correct set of actions can be taken. Third, FOCALE provides the ability to change the functions of the control loop based on context, policy, and the semantics of the data as well as the current management operations being processed. Fourth, FOCALE uses reasoning mechanisms to generate hypotheses as to why the actual state of the managed element is not equal to its desired state, and develops theories about the system. Finally, FOCALE uses learning mechanisms to update its knowledge base.

## 5.2  The Control Loops of FOCALE

Figure 2 shows that in reality, there are two different types of control loops in FOCALE (as opposed to one, which is pictured in most other autonomic systems). The desired state of the managed resource is pre-defined in the appropriate state machine(s), and is based on business goals [16] [17] [18]. In our case, we use KPIs and KQIs of SLAs to define these business goals. The top control loop (maintenance) is used when no anomalies are found (i.e., when either the current state is equal to the actual state, or when the state of the managed element is moving towards its intended goal).

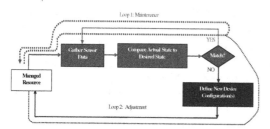

**Fig. 2.** The Two FOCALE Control Loops

The bottom (adjustment) control loop is used when one or more reconfiguration actions must be performed.

FOCALE uses multiple control loops (Figure 2 shows two for simplicity) to provide better, more flexible management. In network management, correcting a problem may involve more actions affecting more entities than the original managed entity in which the problem was noticed. Put another way, why should a control loop designed for monitoring be useful for performing a completely different action?

The use of two different control loops, one for maintenance operations and one for reconfiguration operations, is fundamental to overcoming the limitations of using a single static control loop having fixed functionality. Since FOCALE is designed to *adapt* its functionality as a function of *context*, the control loop controlling the reconfiguration process must be able to have its functionality adapted to suit the vendor-specific needs of the different devices being adapted.

Another important reason to use multiple control loops is to protect the set of business goals and objectives of the users as well as the network operators. The implementation of these objectives is different and sometimes in conflict – having a single control loop to protect these objectives is simply not feasible.

The reconfiguration process uses dynamic code generation based on models and ontologies [16] [17] [18] [19]. The models are used to populate the state machines that in turn specify the operation of each entity that the autonomic system is governing. The management information that the autonomic system is monitoring signals any context changes, which in turn adjusts the set of policies that are being used to govern the system, which in turn supplies new information to the state machines. The goal of the reconfiguration process is specified by the state machines, which defines the (re)configuration commands required.

### 5.3 Model-Based Translation

Existing RF networks have little in common from a management perspective, as they are designed around vendor-specific devices that use specific radio access technologies to provide particular functionality. This is why management standards such as SNMP are in and of themselves not enough to describe management data.

FOCALE associates one or more ontologies with its DEN-ng based [21] data and information models. This enables ontologies to represent relationships and semantics that cannot be represented using UML. For example, even the latest version of UML doesn't have the ability to represent the relationship "is similar to" because it doesn't define logic mechanisms to enable this comparison. Note that this relationship is critical for heterogeneous end-to-end management, since different devices have different languages, programming models, and side effects [17].

The autonomic manager uses the ontologies to analyze sensed data to determine the current state of the managed entities being monitored. Often, this task requires inferring knowledge from incomplete facts. For example, consider the receipt of an SNMP alarm. This is a potentially important fact, especially if the severity of the alarm is assigned as "major" or "critical". However, the alarm in and of itself doesn't provide the business information that the system needs. Which customers are affected by the alarm? Which Service Level Agreements (SLAs) of which customers are effected? These and other questions are critical in enabling OSSs and BSSs to decide which problems should be worked on, and in what order.

Given the above example, FOCALE tries to determine automatically (i.e., without human intervention) which SLAs of which customer are impacted. Once an SLA is identified, it can be linked to business information, which in turn can assign the priority of solving this problem. FOCALE uses a process known as semantic similarity matching [20] to establish additional semantic relationships between sensed data and known facts. This is required because, in this example, an SLA is not directly related in the model to an SNMP alarm. Inferencing is used to establish semantic relationships between the fact that an SNMP alarm was received and other facts that can be used to determine which SLAs and which customers could be affected by that SNMP alarm.

### 5.4 Context-Driven Policy Management

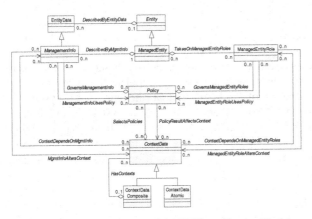

**Fig. 3.** Simplified Form of the DEN-ng Context Model

A simplified form of the DEN-ng context model is shown in Figure 3. This context model is unique, in that it relates Context to Management Information to Policy [21]. At a high level, this model works as follows: Context is used to determine the working set of Policies that can be invoked at any given time; this working set defines the set of Profiles and Roles that can be assigned, which in turn governs functionality that can be invoked or provided. Significantly, this model also defines the set of management information that is used to determine how the Managed Element is operating. Note that this *proactive definition* of *how* to determine whether a component or function is operating correctly is very important to the central concept of governance.

The SelectsPolicies aggregation defines a given set of Policies that should be loaded based on the current Context. The association PolicyResultAffectsContext enables Policy results to influence Context. For example, if the execution of a Policy succeeds, then the current Context doesn't change; alternatively, if the execution of the Policy fails, then the Context changes. Managed Entity Roles are used to describe the state of the Managed Entity, and are then linked to both Policy and Context by the four aggregations shown. Specifically, Policy is used to define which management information will be collected and examined; this management information in turn affects policy. Context defines the management info to monitor, and the values of these management data affect context, respectively.

## 5.5  A New Type of Autonomic Manager

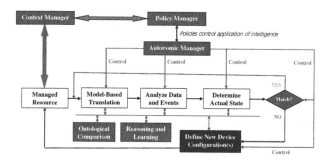

Figure 4 shows an enhanced architecture that uses context-aware policy to control the autonomic manager, which then governs each of the architectural components of the control loop, enabling the different control loop components to change the type of algorithm used, the type of function used, and

**Fig. 4.** Simplified FOCALE Architecture

even the type of data to use as a function of context. This is facilitated by enabling the detection of context changes to change the active policies that are being used at any given time.

The policies used in our project follow a standard event-condition-action model: we monitor events generated when new wireless system data is available, and uses these events to trigger the evaluation of the conditions of one or more policy rules. If the conditions are matched, then one or more policy actions are executed. In our prototype system, we currently use these actions to perform a Causal Analysis, which will classify the reason for the KPI or KQI violation and define action(s) to be taken to fix the problem automatically (or instruct humans what needs to be done).

## 5.6  Machine Learning and Reasoning

The mission of any autonomic system is to adapt to change, according to its underlying business rules. Current systems that use policy (regardless of whether it is part of an autonomic system) use it in a *static* way. Specifically, they assume that the policies that are applied to a system can handle all interactions that the system has. This has many problems, but the three most serious ones are: (1) it is impossible for policies to be defined to anticipate all conditions, (2) management systems are static, in that they are designed to manage known resources and services; if a new resource or service is dynamically composed, how can a management system manage it, and how can pre-defined policies be applicable, and (3) if the underlying context or business objectives change, existing policies may no longer be relevant. Therefore, FOCALE assumes that business objectives, user needs, and environmental conditions may all change dynamically. This is accommodated by varying the functionality of each element in the control loops in Figure 4 according to context.

Machine learning enables the incorporation of new and learned behavior and data. Information modeling facilitates machine learning by providing a general to specific ordering of functionality, as well as details regarding aggregation and connectivity, within the system. A reasoning engine is used to select variables and attributes applicable to the determination of system behavior. Machine learning can be applied to temporal, spatial as well as hierarchical system aspects, allowing for learned behavior about different system "cuts" or cross-sections.

Hypothesis formation is a mapping of the data to be explained into the set of all possible hypotheses rank-ordered by plausibility [22]. We define the hypothesis space by using a combination of the information model, the results of the topology discovery process, and axiomatic knowledge. If the hypothesis space is too large, then falsification techniques can be used to provide a "critic" function [22], which helps reject some hypotheses and reduce the hypothesis space cardinality. Two examples of a critic function are (1) incorporating upper and lower boundary conditions on capacities and qualities directly into the information model to use for comparison purposes, and (2) the use of an ontology by incorporating "never-has-a", "is-not-a-kind-of", and especially "does-not-cause" relationships.

Our knowledge framework operates as follows. A system is loaded with existing business rules that the system must strive to optimize, as well as desired system behavior (e.g., in the form of sets of state machines). The underlying model and ontology can be used to filter data received, matching expected data against the corresponding system model as well as to determine if new data should be added to the model or not. Received data is used to deduce the current state of the system, which is compared to its desired state. If the states don't match, then the control loop uses policy to generate commands to move the system to the desired state. Note that the knowledge framework correlates commands generated to data received. New data can generate new hypotheses and/or change the weight of exisiting hypotheses.

One or more machine learning algorithms may be employed to gain experience from the environment, and to aid the reasoning process. We expand the traditional definition of machine learning [23] to include notions of identifying specific values (statistics), identification of specific attribute-value pairs (traditional "data-mining"), and finally the identification of attributes and processes linked to events (our new definition of "machine learning"). Clearly, techniques such as candidate elimination and decision trees, coupled with notions of positive and negative examples, may be employed to help define those attributes of interest surrounding an anomalous event. However, this tells us nothing about the cause behind this event (how the attributes might be linked), nor what the sequel effects and consequences might be. Furthermore, it conveys no understanding, and serves in identical fashion to clues at a crime scene with no underlying explanation as to how the clues are related.

Our machine learning approach combines modeled data with the knowledge of subject matter experts to define a set of axioms and theories. We use machine learning to maintain and repair established theories, as well as in finding successively minimal descriptions of those theories upon encountering future examples of the behavior described by the theories. This minimization of causal structure ("Occam's Razor") is useful in refining suboptimal behavioral descriptions via the repeated application of parsimony and coverage algorithms.

The edge probabilities in our theory graph are also a target for machine learning. Finite state machines are a way of encoding behavior, and these may be considered a form of causal structure. The transition probabilities between states need to be maintained for any managed entity whose behavior varies with context. Machine learning and statistics are critical not only in refinement of transition probabilities and maintenance/repair/induction activities, but also in finding behavioral cues by linking together state change with stimulus/response pairs that describe behavior.

### 5.7 FOCALE Operation

Sensor data from the Managed Element is analyzed to determine if the current state of the Managed Element is equal to its desired state. If it is, the process repeats. If it isn't, then the autonomic manager examines the sensor data.

If the autonomic manager already understands the data, then it continues to execute the processes that it was performing. Otherwise, the autonomic manager examines the models and ontologies to develop knowledge about the received data (the remaining steps are complex and beyond the scope of this paper; indeed this first step can often be enough). This knowledge is then fed to a set of machine-based learning and reasoning algorithms that reason about the received data. For example, if the data represents a problem, then the algorithms try and determine the root cause of the problem; finding a cause, actions are then issued, which are translated into vendor-specific commands by the model-based translation functions, and applied to the appropriate Managed Elements. Note that this may include Managed Elements that were not the cause of the problem, or were not being monitored. The cycle then repeats itself, except that in general the monitoring points will have changed to ensure that the reconfiguration commands had their desired effect.

## 6  Conclusions

This paper described a management architecture for a multi-technology radio access "system of systems". We described typical measurement techniques and performance measurement construction, and then related these requirements to the design of our FOCALE architecture. FOCALE is a novel type of autonomic network, a special outgrowth of autonomic computing research. We focused on how innovations in context awareness, its relation to policy management, and innovations in machine learning and reasoning were included into FOCALE.

We are currently prototyping FOCALE, with the ultimate goal of using it to test various Seamless Mobility scenarios. Existing results showed marked improvement in various RF optimization scenarios in terms of accuracy of diagnosing problems and recommending appropriate remediation. This is supported by innovative drill-down algorithms coded in a rule-based expert system. Results on RF optimization and performance will be published in a future paper.

# References

1. Lee, J., Miller, L.: CDMA Systems Engineering Handbook, Artech House Publishers: (1998) ISBN 0-89006-990-5
2. Rosenberg Adam, N., Kemp, S.: CDMA Capacity and Quality Optimization. McGraw-Hill, New York (2003) ISBN 0-07139-919-4
3. Ovesjö, F., Dahlman, E., Ojanperä, T., Toskala, A., Klein, A.: FRAMES Multiple Access Mode 2 – Wideband CDMA., PIMRC (1997)
4. Mitola, J.: Cognitive Radio Architecture: The Engineering Foundations of Radio XML, Wiley-Interscience, ISBN 0471742449
5. http://www.motorola.com/content.jsp?globalObjectId=6611-9309
6. Strassner, J., Agoulmine, N., Lehtihet, E.: FOCALE – A Novel Autonomic Networking Architecture, LAACS (2006)
7. OMA-DM WG information and documents
   http://www.openmobilealliance.org/tech/wg_committees/dm.html
8. CarrierIQ product overview, http://www.carrieriq.com/overview.htm
9. Hepsaydir, E., Yates, W.: Performance Analysis Of Positioning Using Existing CDMA Networks, IEEE Position Location and Navigation Systems (1994)
10. TMF Wireless Service Measurements Handbook Approved version 3.0, GB923v3-0_040315.pdf (March 2004)
11. Kreher, R.: UMTS Performance Measurement: A Practical Guide to KPIs for the UTRAN Environment (October 2006) ISBN: 0-470-03487-4
12. Pareto chart definition http://en.wikipedia.org/wiki/Pareto_chart
13. IBM, Autonomic Manifesto www.research.ibm.com/autonomic/manifesto
14. IBM, An Architectural Blueprint for Autonoimc Computing, April 03
15. Kephart, J.O., Chess, D.M., Kephart, J.O., Chess, D.M.: The Vision of Autonomic Computing (January 2003)
16. Strassner, J., Raymer, D., Lehtihet, E., Van der Meer, S.: End-to-end Model-Driven Policy Based Network Management, In: Policy, Conference ( 2006)
17. Strassner, J., Kephart, J.: Autonomic Systems and Networks: Theory and Practice, NOMS, Tutorial ( 2006)
18. Strassner, J., Raymer, D.: Implementing Next Generation Services Using Policy-Based Management and Autonomic Computing Principles, NOMS (2006)
19. Strassner, J.: Seamless Mobility – A Compelling Blend of Ubiquitous Computing and Autonomic Computing. In: Dagstuhl Workshop on Autonomic Networking (January 2006)
20. Wong, A., Ray, P., Parameswaran, N., Strassner, J.: Ontology mapping for the interoperability problem in network management. Journal on Selected Areas in Communications 23(10), 2058–2068 (2005)
21. Strassner, J.: Policy-Based Network Management, September 2003. Morgan Kaufman Publishers, San Francisco (2003) ISBN 1-55860-859-1
22. Josephson, J., Josephson, S.: Abductive Inference: Computation, Philosophy, Technology ch. 7. Cambridge University Press, Cambridge, UK (1996)
23. Mitchell, T.: Machine Learning, McGraw Hill International Editions, New York (1997) ISBN 0-07-042807-7

# A 'Pumping' Model for the Spreading of Computer Viruses

Geoffrey Canright and Kenth Engø-Monsen

Telenor R&I, 1331 Fornebu, Norway
geoffrey.canright@telenor.com

**Abstract.** We present qualitative arguments concerning the probable infection pattern in a directed graph under the (weak or strong) influence of the outside world. This question is relevant for real computer viruses, which spread by following the (logical) directed links formed by address lists. Our arguments build on previous work in two (seemingly unrelated) areas: epidemic spreading on undirected graphs, and eigenvectors of directed graphs as applied to Web page ranking. More specifically, we borrow a recently proven result (used to design a 'sink remedy' for Web link analysis) and use it to argue for a *threshold effect*: that the effects of the outside world will not appear in the pattern of infection until the strength of the influence of the outside world exceeds a finite threshold value. We briefly discuss possible tests of this prediction, and its implications.

## 1 Introduction

For some years now, the phenomena involved in epidemic spreading on networks has received considerable attention, which in turn has given quite interesting results and insights. The problem has obvious practical relevance; two examples are the spreading of diseases over human social networks (such as sexual networks), and the spreading of data viruses among networked computers.

A recent review of this problem may be found in Mark Newman's review article [1]. One of the most striking results is that of Pastor-Satorras and Vespignani [2]. These authors examined a spreading model in which nodes can become Iinfected (I), but then (at some rate) become Susceptible (S) to infection again. (Since all nodes in a "clean" network start in the Susceptible state, this model is called the 'SIS' model.) For this model, one can define an effective spreading rate $\lambda$ that is simply the ratio of the rate for the S$\rightarrow$I transition (over a link) to the rate for the I$\rightarrow$S transition (at an infected node). For such a model, one normally expects that there is a threshold spreading rate $\lambda_c$, such that, for $\lambda > \lambda_c$, the infection spreads to the entire network, while for $\lambda < \lambda_c$, the infection is only very limited in scope. Pastor-Satorras and Vespignani showed however that, for networks with a power-law node degree distribution, $\lambda_c = 0$: an infection with *any* finite probability for propagation will eventually reach the entire network, regardless of how quickly nodes can cure themselves. This rather counterintuitive result revealed starkly the importance of looking at network topology in

A.K. Bandara and M. Burgess (Eds.): AIMS 2007, LNCS 4543, pp. 133–144, 2007.

studying epidemic spreading. It also may have practical relevance for explaining the prevalence of computer viruses, since the Internet has been found (at least at large scale) to have roughly a power-law degree distribution [3].

Our own work [4,5,6] has focused on a simpler model—the so called 'SI' model, in which nodes, once infected, remain so. Obviously, with this SI model, there is no question of the long time state of a network: if it is connected, and infected anywhere, then eventually it is infected everywhere. We have instead focused on understanding how (in 'space' (network) and time) an infection propagates, and how that propagation is affected by the network topology. In other words, rather than look at long-time, whole-graph properties, we have looked at local events in time and space. We have shown that there is a natural and parameter-free way to characterize a network's topology, such that it may be uniquely decomposed into *regions*. These regions are well connected subgraphs, such that infectious spreading is relatively fast and predictable in its course within a region—but slower, and more difficult to predict, between regions.

This work, like those cited above, has assumed that the network's links are undirected—ie, symmetric, so that the probability of propagation is the same in each direction over the link. This assumption is often made, and it simplifies all analysis. However it has been pointed out [7,8] that, in the case of propagating computer viruses, the links should properly be viewed as one-way. That is, most viruses use the email address list of the infected host node to propagate further; and the entries in these lists are one-way pointers, with no guarantee that the pointed-to node points back.

A graph built up of one-way (directed) links is termed a directed graph. The general topology of a directed graph is much less simple than that of an undirected graph, even when each is fully connected. That is, in a directed graph, there can and typically do exist *sources* (subgraphs for which there are paths *out* but no paths *in*), and *sinks* (subgraphs for which there are paths *in* but no paths *out*). This fact clearly has important implications for virus spreading: for example, sinks are likely to be infected, while sources can only be infected from the 'outside world'.

Furthermore, a directed graph may be uniquely decomposed into disjoint subgraphs which are called *strongly connected components* or SCCs. For each pair of nodes $i$ and $j$ in the same SCC, there is a directed path from $i$ to $j$. Thus SCCs are 'somewhat like' undirected connected graphs, in that every node in an SCC is reachable from every other. It follows that any two SCCs $C_1$ and $C_2$ in a directed graph either have no links directly connecting them, or have links running only one way (eg, $C_1 \rightarrow C_2$). Furthermore, source SCCs only have outlinks to other SCCs, and sink SCCs only have inlinks from other SCCs.

The World Wide Web is a fascinating example of an empirical, dynamic (and largely unmanaged) directed graph. Here [9] measurements have shown that the WWW has (roughly) a 'bow-tie' structure, with a 'giant SCC' or GSCC forming the 'knot' at the center of the bow tie, a number of 'In' SCCs which have paths to the GSCC but may not be reached from it, and a number of 'Out' SCCs which are reached from the GSCC but have no path to the GSCC. Newman, Forrest, and Balthrop [8] have empirically measured the directed graph formed from email addresses for around 17000 active users at a university; they find a similar bow-tie structure, with the GSCC holding about 20% of the nodes, and the Out set (the largest) holding about 34%. For simple SI propagation, then, one finds that, once the GSCC is infected, one expects about 54% of the nodes to eventually be infected—which is the 'worst case' for this directed graph.

We are interested in extending our 'topographic' or 'regional' approach to epidemic spreading [4,5,6] to the case when the graph is directed. We are motivated both by the intellectual challenge which is presented by directed graphs, and also by the practical utility that may be gained from such an extension. We note that our regions approach leads very naturally to suggestions for design and/or modification of network topology, towards the goal of hindering spreading [6]. Hence we expect that a successful extension of this approach to directed graphs would bring us closer to the practical goal of protecting computer networks (and mobile phone networks) against viruses.

Our plan for the rest of this paper is as follows. In the next section we briefly review the regions approach for undirected graphs. Then, in Section 3, we describe unpublished work with Mark Burgess [10] on Web link analysis. We will argue that this work gives us insight into the propagation of infection on directed graphs. We will develop this connection in Section 4. A principal result of our reasoning will be the prediction of a *threshold phenomenon* in infective spreading on directed graphs. In Section 5 we illustrate the threshold behavior as it is seen in the weight distribution of the principal eigenvector of a directed graph, using a small directed graph for concreteness. Finally, in Section 6, we will discuss how our new prediction may be tested in simulations, and will also discuss some of the implications of our prediction.

## 2   Centrality and Spreading over Symmetric Networks

The principal idea in our approach to spreading on undirected graphs is that a certain measure of a node's *centrality* is also a good measure of that node's importance in spreading. More specifically: a node's *eigenvector centrality* or EVC is a good measure of its 'spreading power'. (For a detailed exposition of these ideas, along with some mathematical justification, see [5].)

Furthermore, eigenvector centrality is 'smooth': a node's EVC is a linear combination of its neighbors' EVC, hence the EVC does not vary arbitrarily as one moves over the network. This smoothness justifies the definition of *regions*: there are (typically) very few local maxima of the EVC (from smoothness), and each one defines the 'Center' of a region. Our topographic approach (viewing EVC as a 'height') then says that every node finds its Center (hence its region) by following a steepest-ascent path until it terminates at a local maximum.

We then show in [5] that epidemic spreading within each region follows a predictable pattern of evolution: first (statistically) 'uphill', then very fast infection of the rest of the region.

The key idea in our approach is (again) that a measure of node centrality, taken from the principal eigenvector of the graph's adjacency matrix, can play an extremely useful role in understanding and predicting the spread of an infection. We wish to use this same key idea in understanding spreading on directed graphs. To do so, we first briefly review some facts about node centrality and principal eigenvectors of directed graphs.

## 3   Web Search, Link Analysis, and Pumping

Much effort has been directed towards understanding importance in directed graphs via eigenvectors of some the adjacency matrix $A$ (or its transpose $A^T$, or combinations such as $A^T A$, etc). Much of this work is motivated by the utility of this kind of 'link analysis' to estimating the importance or 'authority' of Web pages; pioneers in this line of work are Kleinberg [11] and Brin and Page [12].

Already we see that life is more complicated with directed graphs, where $A \neq A^T$. For example, the four operators $A$, $A^T$, $A^T A$, and $AA^T$ all have distinct principal eigenvectors. Which one are we to use to estimate a node's importance as a Web page? We have studied this problem in [10]. One important problem here is the so-called 'sink problem': unless one takes some corrective measures, the principal eigenvector of either $A$ or $A^T$ will have zero weight at many (even most) of the nodes. Colloquially, one says that 'all the weight goes to the sinks'. The famous PageRank approach [12] (which involves a normalized version of $A^T$) uses a 'random surfer' operator RS to connect all nodes to all nodes (with a small weight $\epsilon$). This makes the resulting graph into a single SCC, and thereby eliminates the sink problem, giving some nonzero weight to every node. Kleinberg's HITS approach is quite different: he uses the non-normalized but compound operators $A^T A$ and $AA^T$ to obtain (respectively) 'authority' and 'hub' scores for each node. Each of these compound operators is symmetric, and so the HITS approach avoids the sink problem in a quite different way.

In our unpublished work with Mark Burgess [10], we have found yet another, equally distinct, sink remedy. Briefly, we find that the statement 'all weight goes to the sinks' contains some germ of the truth, but is too simple. A more precise statement is that all nonzero weight in the principal eigenvector lies in the 'dominant SCC', and in all SCCs which are 'downstream' of this SCC—and nowhere else. (The dominant SCC is that SCC having, in its own spectrum, the largest eigenvalue for the whole graph; also, the notion of 'downstream' is readily given a precise definition, which furthermore corresponds nicely to our intuition for this word.)

We illustrate this result in Figure 1. The proof may be found in [10]. However, the idea is readily grasped (as illustrated in the figure), and may be used to reason further, as follows. We suppose that we wish (in the context of Web link analysis) to obtain meaningful nonzero weights for all nodes in the graph—including those that have zero weight in Figure 1. We focus on the source SCCs (marked with a '+' in Figure 1). Suppose we could arrange that one of the source SCCs had the largest eigenvalue of the entire graph—say, the one at the bottom left of the

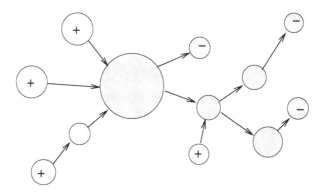

**Fig. 1.** A schematic depiction of the distribution of nonzero weight in the principal eigenvector of a directed graph. The size of each SCC (disc) represents the size of its largest eigenvalue. Only the shaded SCCs have non-zero weight; unshaded SCCs have zero weight. If the sources (marked with a + symbol) could be 'pumped up' to be largest, then the flow could encompass the whole graph.

figure. Then we can get nonzero weight over more of the graph—but still not all of it. What we really need, then, is for *all* of the source SCCs to be dominant. This sounds like a contradiction; but it need not be. Of course, given a general directed graph, one has—without making alterations—no control over which SCC is dominant. However, we can implement a 'sink remedy', not by adding links (as is done with the RS operator), but by 'pumping up' the eigenvalues of *all* the source SCCs in the graph, until they are all (i) equal, and (ii) larger than any other eigenvalue in the graph. Intuitively, then, all the source SCCs will share dominance in this case (and we prove this in [10])—thus giving nonzero weight over the entire graph, and so solving the sink problem. (Note that we do so without making the graph strongly connected.)

Note that we see in Figure 1 a similarity to our picture of infectious spreading on a directed graph: if we simply suppose that the dominant SCC is also the GSCC (a likely assumption), then Figure 1 gives a picture of the likely (after long time) distribution of an infection on a directed graph.

Thus we find—pictorially—a correspondence between, on the one hand, the distribution of weight in the dominant eigenvector of a directed graph, and, on the other hand, the likely distribution of infection on this same graph. This correspondence recalls the 'key idea' (cited at the end of Section 2) of our topographic/regions understanding of spreading on undirected graphs: "that a measure of node centrality, taken from the principal eigenvector of the graph's adjacency matrix, can play an extremely useful role in understanding and predicting the spread of an infection". In the next section we will develop this correspondence, for the case of directed graphs, carrying it to the point of making a concrete and novel prediction.

## 4   'Pumping' and Epidemic Spreading on Directed Graphs

First we recall (as noted explicitly in [8]) that any infection of a finite, uninfected network must come from the 'outside'. This seemingly trivial fact is an important part of the reasoning in this section. Therefore we will develop a model for the system (network + outside world), and study this enlarged system.

We assume that we know nothing about the 'outside world' (that being part of the definition of 'outside'), except that (i) it is infected, (ii) it has links to the nodes in our known, mapped network, and (iii) these links are capable of transmitting the infection from the outside world to the network. Since we know so little about this outside world, we will model it as a single 'World node' W. This node has (given our ignorance) an equal probability of infecting every other node in the known network K. We represent this fact by drawing directed links from W to every node in K. We do not draw links *to* W (even though they also exist) since we assume that W is large; hence its properties—in particular, its likelihood of sending infection to K—will not (by this assumption) be affected by flow of infection into W.

The resulting picture is shown in Figure 2. The symbol $q$ gives the probability (per unit time) of an infection moving from W to any node in K, over each W→K link. This probabilistic rate must be compared with the corresponding probabilities for infection $i \rightarrow j$ between nodes $(i,j)$ in K; for simplicity, we take this rate to be $p$ for all pairs which have a link $i \rightarrow j$ in K. Our arguments will be of such a nature that they should also hold for varying $p_{i \rightarrow j}$; in this case, we can regard $p$ simply as a 'typical' rate for links in K.

We note that the addition of the World node W gives an SCC structure in which the W node is a one-node SCC which is a source; and it is the *only* source in the augmented graph.

Clearly, the progress of the infection depends on the dimensionless ratio $q/p$. Typical simulation studies, such as our own [5] and those in [8], infect a *single*

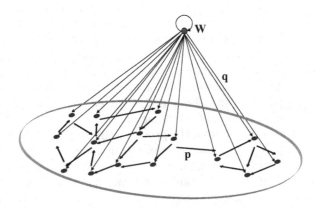

**Fig. 2.** Extended view of infectious spreading over a network, with the outside world modeled by a World node $W$

node in K, and then observe the resulting spread. Clearly, this is the limit $q/p \to 0$; otherwise we might expect further nodes to be 'spontaneously' infected before the infection's course is complete. We know from [8] that one gets, in this limit, a picture of the likely completed infectious state like that in Figure 1.

We can sharpen this assertion slightly. Newman, Forrest and Balthrop (NFB) argue (and find in simulations) that the GSCC is infected, along with Out. The picture in Figure 1 is consistent with this if the GSCC is the dominant SCC. Why should this be the case? We reason as follows. Each SCC $C_\alpha$ has an eigenvalue spectrum which is computed by simply ignoring all links external to $C_\alpha$, and finding the spectrum of the resulting (smaller) adjacency matrix $A_\alpha$. Further, each SCC $C_\alpha$ has a spectral radius $\rho_\alpha$ which is simply the largest eigenvalue from its spectrum. The spectral radius is thus the dominant eigenvalue for the 'little graph' formed by isolating an SCC.

The spectral radius $\rho_\alpha$ is then the rate at which a set of weights, propagating over the links under matrix multiplication, will increase in the long time limit of such propagation. We can also thus call $\rho_\alpha$ the 'gain' of SCC $C_\alpha$.

Perron-Frobenius theory [13] then tells us that the spectrum of the full, many-SCC directed graph is simply the union of the spectra of the SCCs. Thus the dominant SCC for the full graph has an eigenvalue $\Lambda$ in its own spectrum which is equal to the dominant eigenvalue for the entire graph (and of course $\Lambda$ is its spectral radius).

These (well known) facts support our point—that the GSCC likely has $\Lambda$ in its spectrum—because the GSCC (likely) has the largest 'gain'; ie, it (likely) has more nodes, and furthermore (likely) a higher number of nodes with high node degree, than the other SCCs. These two aspects of a graph determine its gain.

It is in fact not necessary for our argument that the GSCC be the dominant SCC; we simply argue that this is quite likely in real networks. Our argument rather rests on the assumption stated previously: that the pattern of weights in the dominant eigenvector of the entire graph has a strong similarity to the probable infection pattern of the graph at long time. This statement is strongly supported by our studies of undirected graphs [5]; so we take it as an assumption here. And it tells us that the long-time infection distribution for the graph in Figure 1 is given by the shaded parts—in the limit $q/p \to 0$. (Note that there is no World node in Figure 1, nor in the analysis [10] leading to this picture.)

The picture is trivially simple in the opposite limit, namely $q/p \to \infty$ (the system administrator's nightmare!). In this limit, infectious flow from the World overwhelms all internal dynamics coming from the topology of the known network K, and the infection probability simply grows uniformly in time and 'space' until the entire network is infected. Thus, in this limit, the value and location (SCC) of the network's spectral radius $\Lambda$ is irrelevant.

How then do we interpolate between these two limits?

To answer this question, we hold fast to our working assumption—that the dominant eigenvector gives the answer. However, now we clarify a small feature of Figure 2 which we have not mentioned before. Note that the World node W has a 'self-loop' in Figure 2. Without this self-loop, W—which we are forced to model as a *single node*—has a gain of zero, and so in fact has *no* effect on the dominant eigenvalue of the graph. Specifically—without the self-loop—under repeated iteration by the adjacency matrix (augmented with a row and column for W), any weight which is present at W before the first iteration is sent into the graph, and W has zero weight thereafter. This clearly poorly models the true action of W—which is in fact a large graph with (presumably) many SCCs, and which remains in a condition to inject infection for all time. Hence we add the self-loop, with some loop strength $s$. We have no idea what this strength can be, other than this: that W is dominant for large $q/p$, and negligible for small $q/p$. Hence we set $s = c(q/p)$, and leave $c$ (with dimensions of a rate) undetermined.

With this self-loop in place, and its dependence on $q/p$ as given, we get the interpolation that we expect: for $q/p \to 0$, the effect of W on the eigenvector (and on the infection pattern) is negligible; while, at some point before $q/p \to \infty$, the gain $s = c(q/p)$ of W becomes the dominant eigenvalue for the entire graph—at which point, the entire graph becomes 'shaded' (infected).

Now we note that, if we follow the distribution of weight in the dominant eigenvector during this interpolation (ie, with increasing $q/p$), we find that the evolution of this distribution is *not smooth* as $q/p$ grows. Specifically (as proven in [10]) the weights in those 'white' SCCs which have zero weight for $q/p = 0$ remain exactly zero for all values of $q/p$, until $c(q/p)$ exceeds $\Lambda$ (the dominant eigenvalue of the graph at $q = 0$). Only then do these weights begin (smoothly) to exceed zero.

Thus—invoking our (hard-)working assumption one more time—we expect that the probable infection pattern also does not evolve smoothly with increasing $q/p$. Instead, we expect the evolution of this probable infection pattern to approximately mimic the evolution of the weight distribution in the dominant eigenvector. More explicitly, our arguments predict that:

- A *threshold effect* should be observed in the infection pattern, as a function of increasing infection rate $q/p$ from the outside World. For $q/p$ less than a threshold value $S$, all nodes upstream of the dominant SCC have very small probability of infection, so that the infection pattern shows little or no change from the picture of Figure 1. However, when $q/p$ exceeds the threshold value $S$, *all* upstream nodes—along with all other nodes—begin to have a finite probability of infection, so that the likely infection pattern starts to become uniform over the graph.
- Furthermore, since the threshold is set by the dominant eigenvalue $\Lambda$ of the dominant SCC of the 'unperturbed' graph, we predict that the threshold World-strength value $S$ should grow linearly with $\Lambda$.

These predictions together constitute the main result of this paper. Our predictions follow from three things: first, our fairly good understanding of the tight relationship between the course of epidemic spreading on undirected graphs and the weight distribution in the graph's dominant eigenvector (ie, the eigenvalue centrality or EVC); second, our understanding of the same weight distribution for a general directed graph (in particular, where one finds zero weight, and why); and thirdly, our novel 'pumping' sink remedy, which tells us how this weight distribution is affected when one 'pumps' one or more source SCCs of the directed graph.

**Fig. 3.** A simple directed graph, with 12 nodes and four SCCs

# 5   A Simple Example

In this section, we illustrate our arguments with a very simple example graph. The graph itself is shown in Figure 3. This graph has four SCCs: {1,2}, {3}, {4–10}, and {11,12}. The first two SCCs are source SCCs (to the left in the figure). The biggest SCC {4–10} (center) is neither source nor sink; it plays the role of the GSCC for this graph. Finally, the SCC {11,12} (to the right) is a sink SCC, and is downstream from the GSCC (while the two source SCCs are upstream from the GSCC).

The theory of [10] tells us that the nodes 1, 2, and 3 get zero weight in the dominant eigenvector of this graph, because they are upstream from the dominant SCC—which is the GSCC. And so we expect that, at very small infection rate from outside, these nodes also have vanishing probability of being infected before the entire rest of the graph gets infected.

Now we add the World node to this picture (this may be pictured by recalling Figure 2). Again our theory tells us that nodes 1, 2, and 3 get zero weight in the eigenvector of the augmented graph—as long as the gain of the W node (ie, the strength of its self-loop) is smaller than the dominant eigenvalue $\Lambda$ of the GSCC (and hence of the entire graph). We find that, for this graph, $\Lambda$ is approximately 1.405.

Now we find (numerically) the weight of node 2 in the dominant eigenvector for the augmented graph (Figure 3 plus World node), for increasing values of the World node gain. (Node 2 is chosen arbitrarily from the set of upstream nodes 1, 2, and 3; all give the same picture.) Figure 4 shows the result.

We see from Figure 4 that—precisely as predicted by Ref. [10]—the weight at node 2 is *exactly* zero until the gain of the 'pumped' source node W exceeds the dominant eigenvalue $\Lambda \approx 1.4$ of the graph. Only then does the weight at node 2 (and at the other upstream nodes) grow. It seems clear from the figure that the initial growth is linear (as a function of the gain) beyond the threshold. This result is not explicitly predicted by the results of [10]. We believe however that this observation (linear growth above the threshold) is likely to be correct.

Figure 4 illustrates graphically the threshold phenomenon (predicted in [10]) for the weight distribution on upstream nodes in the dominant eigenvector of a directed graph. The present paper then predicts that a similar threshold phenomenon will occur in the distribution of *infection probability* at upstream nodes,

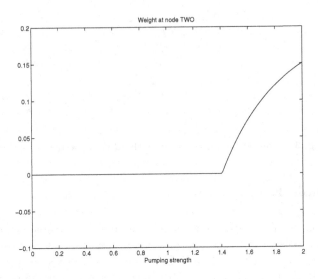

**Fig. 4.** Variation of weight at an 'upstream' node (ie, one in the In set) as we vary the 'pumping' strength from the World node. The threshold effect is clear: the weight at node 2 only begins to grow above zero after the pumping rate exceeds the dominant eigenvalue $\Lambda$ ($\approx 1.4$) of the entire graph.

under increasing 'drizzle rate' from the outside World. We also predict—again analogously to the picture in Figure 4—that the location of the threshold value is determined by the dominant eigenvalue $\Lambda$ of the graph.

## 6   Summary and Discussion

Our prediction of a threshold result is interesting, and merits testing. Our arguments are far from a proof. However, we regard them as sufficiently persuasive that we plan to test our threshold prediction in the immediate future.

We believe that such a test is straightforward. In fact, a realistic topology for testing is even simpler than that of Figure 2—because we can drop the need to represent the World as a subgraph of the whole, and simply let infections drizzle in to each node of a simulated computer network topology with a rate $q$. That is, we remove the World node W and its self-loop (which were added to give us a well defined eigenvector). This removes any need to think about the constant $c$ (which gave the scale of the self-loop). So, in the context of simulating virus propagation, we simply compare the two rates $q$ and $p$ via their dimensionless ratio $q/p$ (which we continue to call $s \equiv q/p$).

Our predictions, obtained from studying the distribution of weights in the eigenvector, may be stated in a language which allows for direct testing via simulations. We simply need to test for two things:

- The effects of the World W, which are negligible as $q/p \to 0$, remain zero or very small until the strength $s$ of the World exceeds a threshold value $S$.

These same effects should then begin to grow significantly at $s = S$, so that quantitative measures of such effects will show a 'kink' there.

- This threshold value $S$ should vary, at least approximately, linearly with the dominant eigenvalue $\Lambda$ of the known network.

Thus we see that we have removed some of the artificiality from Figure 2, without in any way altering the predictions obtained from this figure and the associated analysis and arguments. In short: testing of the predictions of this paper should be extremely straightforward; we plan to carry out such tests in the immediate future.

This brings us to a more difficult question, namely: supposing that our tests give interesting results, how can one apply them to the real world, for which the 'outside world' for any real computer network is highly complicated, and furthermore difficult to map and measure (or unknown)?

We suppose that threshold effects are confirmed by simulations. These same simulations will then give guidelines to the relation between the important threshold 'trickling-in' rate $Q$ (given by $S = Q/p$, with the threshold value $S$ obtained from simulations) and the internal infection rate $p$. We then imagine a system administrator who wishes to know the degree of threat to her network K. She must be able to estimate $p$ (a typical rate for infection over links in K) and also $q$ (the typical likely rate, for each node, of infection arriving from the outside). She then has an estimate of $s = q/p$, which may be compared with the threshold $S$ found from simulations.

In some cases, such analysis may be possible, without such a high degree of uncertainty that they are meaningless. But then the next question arises: is there any point to such analysis?

The answer may be No. That is, perhaps values for the World strength $s$ which are greater than the critical the value $S$, for realistic graphs and a realistic World, do not occur in practice. This possibility of course cannot be ruled out yet.

However, neither can we rule out the possibility that $S$ turns out to be both greater than zero (as we predict), and also less than the actual World strength for a significant number of real networks (each with its own view of the World, ie, its own degree of threat from the outside). In such a case our prediction ceases to be purely theoretical. And then the kinds of action needed to minimize the possible spread of computer viruses, in a given known network K, will indeed depend on whether K finds itself in an above-threshold World or not.

Suppose K is in a World such that $s \ll S$. Then the In component faces a significantly smaller degree of threat than do the GSCC and the Out component. In other words, prevention measures can be concentrated on the latter components. In the opposite case $(s > S)$ all nodes in the network are in equal need of protection.

Practically speaking, and independently of our theory, prevention measures should probably be focused on the GSCC. Our prediction however raises the possibility that, in some cases, there is nothing special about the GSCC, and one must instead regard all the nodes (computers) as equally threatened, and equally in need of protection. We hope in future work to give more quantitative guidelines for when such might be the case.

This work was partially supported by the Future and Emerging Technologies unit of the European Commission through Project DELIS (IST-2002-001907).

# References

1. Newman, M.E.J.: The structure and function of complex networks. SIAM Review 45, 167–256 (2003)
2. Pastor-Satorras, R., Vespignani, A.: Epidemic spreading in scale-free networks. Phys. Rev. Lett. 86, 3200–3203 (2001)
3. Faloutsos, M., Faloutsos, P., Faloutsos, C.: On power-law relationships of the internet topology. In: SIGCOMM '99: Proceedings of the conference on Applications, technologies, architectures, and protocols for computer communication, pp. 251–262. ACM Press, New York, USA (1999)
4. Canright, G., Engø-Monsen, K.: Roles in networks. Science of Computer Programming, pp. 195–214 (2004)
5. Canright, G., Engø-Monsen, K.: Spreading on networks: a topographic view. In: Proceedings, European Conference on Complex Systems (2005)
6. Canright, G., Engø-Monsen, K.: Epidemic spreading over networks: a view from neighbourhoods. Telektronikk 101, 65–85 (2005)
7. Kephart, J.O., White, S.R.: Directed-graph epidemiological models of computer viruses. In: Proceedings of the 1991 IEEE Computer Society Symposium on Research in Security and Privacy, pp. 343–359 (1991)
8. Newman, M.E.J., Forrest, S., Balthrop, J.: Email networks and the spread of computer viruses. Physical Review E 66, 35–101 (2002)
9. Broder, A., Kumar, R., Maghoul, F., Raghavan, P., Rajagopalan, S., Stata, R., Tomkins, A., Wiener, J.: Graph structure in the web. In: Proceedings of the 9th international World Wide Web conference on Computer networks: the international journal of computer and telecommunications networking, pp. 309–320. North-Holland Publishing Co, The Netherlands, Amsterdam (2000)
10. Burgess, M., Canright, G., Engø-Monsen, K.: Mining location importance from the eigenvectors of directed graphs (2006) http://research.iu.hio.no/papers/directed.pdf
11. Kleinberg, J.M.: Authoritative sources in a hyperlinked environment. Journal of the ACM 46(5), 604–632 (1999)
12. Page, L., Brin, S., Motwani, R., Winograd, T.: The pagerank citation ranking: Bringing order to the web. Technical report, Stanford Digital Library Technologies Project (1998)
13. Minc, H.: Non-negative Matrices. Wiley Interscience, New York, (1987)

# Improving Anomaly Detection Event Analysis Using the EventRank Algorithm

Kyrre Begnum and Mark Burgess

Oslo University College, Norway
kyrre@iu.hio.no,mark@iu.hio.no

**Abstract.** We discuss an approach to reducing the number of events accepted by anomaly detection systems, based on alternative schemes for interest-ranking. The basic assumption is that regular and periodic usage of a system will yield patterns of events that can be learned by data-mining. Events that deviate from this pattern can then be filtered out and receive special attention. Our approach compares the anomaly detection framework from Cfengine and the EventRank algorithm for the analysis of the event logs. We show that the EventRank algorithm can be used to successfully prune periodic events from real-life data.

## 1 Introduction

Time series data mining for anomaly detection and event correlation has produced a wealth of approaches and publications. Keogh[1] et. al note what they call an "explosion of interest in mining time series data". They find, to their dismay, that most of the approaches are sensible to different data than what is being used in their respective publications.

In the world of system administration research, we see an effect of Keogh's observation: few published detection algorithms make it into mainstream system administration tools. Several factors might explain this. Firstly, as a systems technician at a site, one needs a certain insight into the deployed detection mechanisms in order to understand the alarms properly. This is simply because no tools are free from the nuisance of false positives and a human usually has to check for the validity of an alarm manually. Secondly, most algorithms require fine-tuning of some chosen parameters in order to work optimally. Finding the correct parameter for a particular context requires further expertise and experiments from the technician.

One of the important philosophical and technical challenges of anomaly detection is the tension between numerical and symbolic data. Importance or interest ranking is generally based on statistical frequency analyses of classified symbolic events, while numerical measures such as load-average and traffic rates have to be digitized and classified into symbols in order to define policies for responding. Like all forms of signal analysis, analogue to digital conversion is balanced against numerical statistics of classed events. We move from numbers to symbols and back again. Methods of ranking go even further down this path, taking sequences of events and ordering them numerically by frequency or by activity.

A.K. Bandara and M. Burgess (Eds.): AIMS 2007, LNCS 4543, pp. 145–155, 2007.
© Springer-Verlag Berlin Heidelberg 2007

Classification of such measurables into categories like high/low or normal/abnormal is supposed to give the system administrator a condensed and more informative view of the system, and inherently includes a policy aspect that defines away fundamental uncertainties.

Anomaly detection systems have been used at the Department of Engineering at Oslo University College for nearly eight years, through the systems management tool cfengine[2]. Cfengine condenses a steady flow of data down to anomalies that are passed to the system administrator. These are based on statistical properties of system variables using two distinct methods. The number of anomalies seen per machine amounts, according to our policies, to between 300 and 800 per week across different Unix hosts. The vast majority of these events are benign system behaviour. Cfengine therefore allows the system administrator to ignore anomalies as a matter of policy. The remainder are assumed to represent noteworthy behaviour.

One of the aims of detecting anomalous events is to identify those anomalies which have been most interesting in some sense. However, this seems to be a subjective judgement fit only for a policy manager to decide. We would like to provide all possible assistance in making this judgement however. Events occur periodically and are part of the normal behaviour of the system variables, within measurement tolerances[3], but there are also events that carry a *surprise* value to this normal picture. These are events that we would like to highlight automatically.

In this paper we apply data mining to a symbolic stream of alarm events from cfengine, and identify events which are more interesting based on a weekly profile of arrivals and the EventRank algorithm[4,5]. This approach reduces the number of events presented to the policy administrator by 65% to 75%. We are testing this in an analysis tool at our university.

The paper is organised as follows: In Section 2 we briefly present the anomaly detection framework of cfengine followed by a description of the EventRank algorithm and compare it to other ranking approaches like principal component analysis (PCA). Section 3 presents our approach and its results. We discuss our findings and suggest future improvements in Section 4.

## 2    Background

### 2.1    Cfengine's Anomaly Detection Framework

Cfengine's current anomaly detection framework, cfenvd, is well documented and discussed elsewhere[3,11]. It uses two statistical methods of analysis on a number of system variables including measures of memory, load, process activity and network counters. Some typical variables monitored by cfenvd include:

- users - The number of logged-in users on the system.
- rootprocs - The number of processes owned by the system administrator.
- otherprocs - The remaining number of processes.
- loadavg - The average load on the system.

- `diskfree` - The percentage of free diskspace on the root partition.
- `ssh_in` - The number of incoming SSH connections.
- `ssh_out` - The number of outgoing SSH connections.
- `www_in` - The number or incoming WWW connections.

All of these counters are presently numerical quantities. Cfenvd extracts statistically significant patterns from the influx of data events and then calculates adaptive measurement scales based on standard deviation from expected values by a process of machine learning. The frequencies of these deviations are also measured and used to determine distributional properties of data[11].

**Two-Dimensional time-series analysis.** The fundamental model for analysis is the two-dimensional time series approach[3] (2DTS) which uses the periodicity observed on computer resources and divides the time series into slices of period $P$ (one week has been determined optimal[12]). An observed data point at time $t$ is described as belonging to the position $\tau$ in the $n$'th iteration of the period P using the relation

$$t = nP + \tau.$$

For all iterations of the period $P$, one can average the points observed at each $\tau$ and calculate the mean and standard deviation. In words, this means that, for every time during a week, cfengine calculates what can be described as a typical state for every variable it observes. The variance observed at each point affects the standard deviation and consequently what can be considered normal behaviour of that variable. A learning profile is considered to be accurate after six to eight weeks[12].

Learning is only useful if certain information is also forgotten. We would like to remember only interesting or important knowledge and forget things that are irrelevant. Relevance is time-sensitive. Knowledge goes out of date eventually. Forgetfulness is therefore introduced into the algorithm so that the recent observations weigh more in the calculations than the older ones. The profile is updated constantly with the new data.

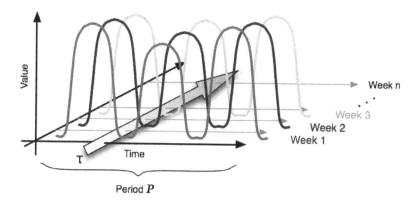

**Fig. 1.** A schematic illustration of the 2DTS profile with period P = 1 week

A detection threshold is policy determined, and we typically use two standard deviations from the observed mean for every $\tau$. If a new observed value is higher than the threshold, an symbolic event is defined by cfengine when the agent runs the next time. The 2DTS is described in detail in [3,11].

**Leap-Detection Test.** The periodic model above gives stable results that are quite insensitive to local variability, once variances have been learned. This spanning of multiple weeks does not allow us to effectively resolve local events on a short time scale however. A second method of analysis is therefore used: a statistical test based on the $\chi^2$ test for the detection of leaps in time series data. The leap-detection test (LDT) for time series data was proposed by Cochran[6] and later pointed out by [7]. The formula of the test is given as:

$$\chi^2 = \frac{(x_1 + x_2 + \ldots + x_i - i * x_{i+1})^2}{i * (i+1) * \overline{x}}$$

where $x_1, x_2, \ldots, x_i$ are previously observed values in the time series and $x_{i+1}$ is the most recent observation. The value of $i$ therefore denotes the size of the *memory*. The mean $\overline{x}$ includes all $i + 1$ values. Basically, what the test addresses is a hypothesis that the latest value is significantly different of the observed population so far. The $\chi^2$ value is compared to a threshold value which is typically chosen in accordance with a confidence policy level, and levels of uncertainty. Cfenvd adjusts this threshold automatically by automatic learning and adaptation. Alternative approaches use tables or let the decision fall on the local system administrator.

The number of measurements one uses to calculate LDT influences the accuracy and the adaptability of the LDT. A shorter memory will increase the *forgetfulness* of the algorithm and make it adapt more quickly to stable changes. A long memory will be prone to false alarms after a leap is detected. The default memory length is 10 intervals. With cfenvd evaluating its data every 2.5 minutes, it makes for a memory that spans 25 minutes.

Both the above methods are used in an independent cause model to trigger events measured in units of standard deviations which can then be either hidden or revealed as a matter of policy. Cfagent, the configuration management part of cfengine, has a programmable behaviour based on the alarm events from cfenvd. Every time cfagent is run, it handles the set of events that have been triggered since last time. Every type of event can only be handled once even if the corresponding alarm has been raised several times since the last time cfagent ran. Also, cfagent does not know of the *order* in which an event arrived.

**Definition 1 (Cluster).** *We define a* cluster *as the current set of events that are active when cfagent runs. We write it as a colon-separated list like the following:*

```
rootprocs_high_dev2 : loadavg_high_ldt : www_in_high_ldt
```

*Each word represents an event in terms of the anomaly detection method used and the variable.*

Cfagent is typically configured to analyze the stream of events every 15 minutes, in our testbed, which is close to the autocorrelation time of the measured variables. During our experiments, all events in the cluster are logged by cfengine to a file which we are then able to analyze off-line.

With these two anomaly detection algorithms, the number of alarms per machine amounts to between 600 to 800 per week for servers, and 300 to 400 per week for workstations if one would allow all possible events to be considered. Many of these events, especially those related the LDT test, are harmless and describe nothing but a normal "burstiness" in certain variables. What is needed is a method to automatically filter the uninteresting events without prior knowledge. We assume, that events would be interesting, i.e carry more information, if they appeared at times in the week when it was not common for them. This is analogous to the 2DTS anomaly detection method, as it also classifies values as unnormal if they are very deviant from what is usual in that time of the week.

## 2.2 EventRank

Several approaches to deciding event importance have been tried in the past. We have previously discussed the use of principal component analysis[8] for understanding the relevance of correlations in alarms around a network. Principal eigenvector approaches have been criticized for taking too static a view of interactions between networked hosts however. The EventRank algorithm[4,5] is a ranking algorithm designed to rank individuals in a social network based on their participation in "collaborative events", such as publishing a paper together or receiving the same emails.

The authors of EventRank assign each individual an amount of *potential* (they all start out with the same amount) based on their record of participation in the network, and also relative to the level of participation of the other individuals. For every time an individual does not participate, it will decrease its potential and the participants will increase theirs. This means, that an active individual will receive alot of potential but will start losing it again if it remains inactive for a longer period. The total amount of potential is conserved.

EventRank terminology conflicts slightly when compared to ours. What the EventRank algorithm would call an "event" is in our case actually the cluster. And each individual or participant is considered an event in our terms. Thus, each of our events, e.g. `rootprocs_high_ldt`, can be a participant in a cluster. Every time one of the events participates it will receive potential.

We denote the potential of event $e \in E$ at time $t_i$ by $R_i(e)$ which takes on values from [0,1]. All events start out with the same potential $\frac{1}{|E|}$ where $|E|$ is the number of events in E. The combined potential will always remain the same, meaning that once an event has potential 0, it cannot "give" any more potential to others. $R_i(e)$ at time $i$ with the current cluster $C_i$ is defined as

$$e \in C_i \;:\; R_{i-1}(e) + \alpha_i \cdot \frac{\overline{R}_{i-1}(e)}{\sum_{d \in C_i} \overline{R}_{i-1}(d)}$$
$$e \notin C_i \;:\; R_{i-1}(e) \cdot (1 - \frac{\alpha_i}{T_{N_{i-1}}})$$

The impact of each cluster is adjusted by $\alpha_i$ where $0 \leq \alpha \leq T_{N_{i-1}}$ and $T_{N_{i-1}}$ is the total amount of potential held by the events not part of the current cluster $C_i$. $\overline{R}_{i-1}(e)$ denotes the reverse of the potential of $e$, i.e $1 - R_{i-1}(e)$. We follow the approach from EventRank own literature and define $\alpha_i$ as

$$\alpha_i = f \cdot T_{N_{i-1}}$$

where $f$ is a constant, in our case 0.4.

One of the key aspects of the EventRank algorithm is that it adapts to the temporal aspects of the data. The probability of an event is not so important compared to whether or not the event has been active lately.

The *information* of an event $e$, as known from information theory[10] and applied in [9], is defined to be $I(e) = -log_{|E|}Prob(e)$ where $E$ is the set of events and $Prob(e)$ is the probability of event $e \in E$ appearing. Its interpretation is that a seldom event carries more information to the system operator. An event which is very active for a short time period will have increased its statistical probability throughout the rest of the data, yet in the EventRank algorithm, it will lose its potential soon after the burst is over. This form of *forgetfulness* will ensure that only data from the immediate past are given weight.

### 2.3    EventRank Versus PCA

The EventRank algorithm is argued by its authors to better make use of temporal aspects in the data compared to other ranking methods for event-based data that base themselves on a graph, like the principal component analysis (PCA) method. Their argument is that instead of analysing the graph as an end-result, one can rather re-calculate the rank from the temporal arrival of events and who has participated lately. Previous experience with the PCA method has shown us that it can be hard to apply on time-series data in certain cases[8]. The use of this alternative approach is therefore interesting as our data strongly fits their event-based approach.

Figure 2 shows this in greater detail. Six clusters of events and six different events make up the example. For each time two events appear in the same cluster, they increase the weight of the edge between them in the graph. The result shows the EventRank algorithm ranking e1 and e6 the highest, based on their very recent appearance. The PCA ranks e4 and e2 the highest. Even though we just saw e6 in two of the last three clusters, it is ranked lowest. The level of information $I(e)$ rank e6, e3 and e5 as carrying the same amount of information. This is obviously because they appear the same amount of time and not related to when or together with what other events they appear.

The EventRank algorithm shows us which events, due to recent activity, are the most usual. But due to their frequency, they become less informative to the system administrator. We follow the philosophy of [9] in that the most interesting events are the events that appear that do *not* have a high potential. A low potential and rank means that the event is unusual and therefore carries more information and surprise. An event has a low potential if it is below its starting point of $\frac{1}{|E|}$. In the example above, that would make below 1/6.

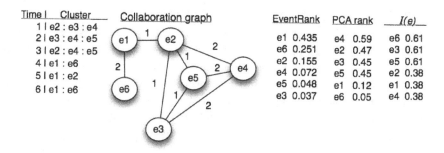

**Fig. 2.** A comparison of the different ranking results using EventRank, PCA and $I(e) = -log_{|E|}Prob(e)$. The rankings differ based on the different types of input they use. The EventRank uses the order of arrival of the event clusters while the PCA method considers the resulting adjacency matrix based on the graph.

Principal Component Analysis (PCA) shows us the most dominant events using connectedness with the other events it has appeared with. The interpretation of a high ranked event in PCA would be an event that has appeared many times together with many other events. PCA considers to a greater extent the relationship between the different events but how should one apply *seldomness* or surprise value in PCA? One problem is that there is no clear threshold like in the EventRank approach. It becomes difficult to classify the events based on a ranking. A hard-coded limit, like the bottom 25%, is also difficult to apply because it is arbitrary and artificial, compared to the EventRank algorithm where in fact all but one event could become low potential. If we were to identify the most frequent event which happened together with other frequent events, then PCA would be more beneficial than EventRank, since a single event appearing alone over several times would get the highest potential. However, since our events signify neither malignant user behaviour nor system faults, we are more interested in filtering away those that appear very often with very many other events.

A further point made by the authors in [4] is that EventRank is attractive because it is fairly understandable. For large numbers of events and many clusters combined with PCA, the resulting graph and matrix may be too complex in order to for a human to get extra support for its findings.

The most convincing argument, however, for EventRank versus PCA in our context is the intrinsic functionality for forgetfulness in the EventRank algorithm. The same could be achieved with PCA through a sliding window and the removal of weight. However the optimal length for this window is an open question we would welcome the investigation into this in a follow-up project.

## 3   EventRank in Offline Analysis of Logs

Event data from two servers and two workstations were collected over a time period of three months. The data were parsed for each machine and divided into a weekly profile in the same way as cfenvd's own approach. All the data up to the last week are considered as a training set, and in the last week we test whether the events have a lower potential than their initial $\frac{1}{|E|}$. The weekly profile is divided into hours, e.g Monday 08:00 - 09:00, Thursday 22:00 - 23:00 and so on to a total 168 time-slots in the profile. All event clusters arrive at a 15 minute interval and are stored in the appropriate slot in the weekly profile.

For the last cluster we compare if any of the events have a low potential. If so, only they are reported to the system administrator. We compare the number of events reported to the original amount. For comparison, we also calculate the level of information, or *surprise*, as used in [9] using $Prob(e) = \frac{count_i e}{clusters_i}$, i.e the number of times the event $e$ was shown in a cluster divided on the total amount of clusters for time-slot $i$. Note, that we calculate the EventRank relative to the time-slot that the cluster is in. This means that each time-slot will have its own rank. This means also, that an event will be considered as interesting only if it appears in a time-slot where it has a low potential.

Two types of potential are recorded for each event: the *transient* potential is the current value of potential for the event and is bound to change for each new cluster that arrives. The *cumulative* potential is the sum of potential earned over time and is in essence the integral of the transient potential. Although the cumulative potential is not used by us to decide on the level of information for each event, it is included in this analysis for eventual further improvement of the approach.

On all four systems, the number of events was reduced to between 1/3 and 1/4 of its original amount. The low potential events were still spread across the time-slots but appeared mostly alone or in pairs.

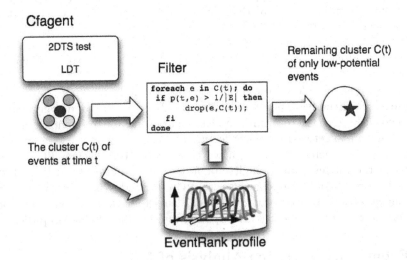

**Fig. 3.** An illustration of the data-mining process. Each cluster of events is evaluated according to their weekly profile and only those events with a low profile will continue on to be analyzed further by the system administrator.

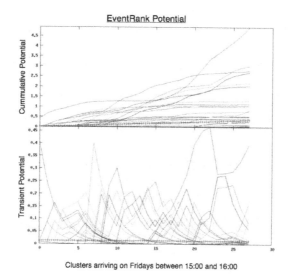

EventRank Potential

Clusters arriving on Fridays between 15:00 and 16:00

**Fig. 4.** A plot showing the cumulative and transient potential from the EventRank algorithm for the events for the time-slot Fridays between 15:00 and 16:00. The transient potential is much more bursty and as a result the ranking changes often.

The EventRank plot (in Figure 4) for the time-slot Fridays between 15:00 and 16:00 shows the transient potential to be unstable. An event will increase its potential quickly but loose it more slowly. This results in the tails on the right side of most peaks. A dotted line of $+$'s shows the threshold of $1/|E|$ that divides between low- and high-potential events. If an event appears in a new cluster while the potential is below that threshold, it will be considered interesting. The cumulative rank shows that some of the events quickly rise above the others and maintain their position over time. A sharp increase of potential over a certain period will make the cumulative potential sharpen its curve. A low potential will result in a near-flat curve.

The type of events that was reported as low potential was predominantly concerned with services, such as `ftp_in_high_ldt` and not so much with the system variables, like `rootprocs_high_ldt` and `loadavg_high_ldt`. Further investigation into the system events that had a high potential revealed to us that they in fact showed up regularly and almost everywhere and therefore contained no surprise or information. In the transient potential plot in Figure 4, we can see that some events rise high quickly but never fall down below the threshold. They produce a jagged line well above the threshold for a long period. These event happen so often in this time-slot that they remain "uninteresting". The events that were reported as low-potential appeared in the event-logs seldom enough to fall back below the threshold. They can be recognized in the transient potential plot as those small peaks which then glide down again. We see this as a successful pruning of the event flow using the EventRank algorithm.

**Table 1.** The reduction of events on the four systems on the Department of Engineering network

| Machine | Last weeks events | Low-profile events | Factor |
|---|---|---|---|
| server1 | 687 | 250 | 0.36 |
| server2 | 800 | 198 | 0.247 |
| workstation1 | 432 | 157 | 0.36 |
| workstation2 | 363 | 105 | 0.29 |

The information ranking for the low potential events using $I(e)$ did not correspond directly to EventRank. Low potential events had usually a mid-range level of information, indicating that they were not completely unknown in the profile.

## 4   Discussion and Conclusions

Anomaly detection is about looking for the unusual amongst the regular and the uninteresting. This is an inherently ambiguous pursuit and it needs some guidance from policy to narrow down its goals. We have to say what we mean by interesting, and we have explored one possible criterion here. Our main goal in this paper was to reduce the workload of the system administrator by eliminating uninteresting events. This makes policy decisions about relevance better informed by analysis.

We should point out that what we attempt here is not the same as the problem of reducing "false positives" in Intrusion Detection Systems (IDS). Such a classification into "real" and "false" events cannot be made in our case. In the case of Intrusion Detection "true" means that an actual intrusion took place, something that can be verified. The task of an anomaly classifier, on the other hand, is less clear than this. It makes no sense to speak of black-and-white true and false positives, there are only shades of grey in deciding how interesting events are. Policy enters into this decision, but we must also try to inform policy with rational analysis. An algorithmic ranking like the ones used here can play an important role in this.

The EventRank algorithm removes common and repetitive events without prior knowledge. There still to be room for improvement here. The main facility to adjust the EventRank algorithm is to choose the level of impact $\alpha_i$ each cluster of events ought to have. Would a different impact lead to different results? A lower value for $f$, say 0.2, would decrease the number of reported events slightly more, but can it be done in a better way? In every anomaly system there is an arbitrary choice that we cannot escape – a part of policy[11].

In ref. [4] several alternative formulae for $\alpha_i$ that are based on prior knowledge of the data are discussed. A specialized $\alpha_i$ that considers a prior classification of the events might improve the ranking further. An example of such would be that clusters that contain events which address critical services have less impact and thereby more likely to fall below the threshold again quickly.

We are developing a data-mining tool that runs in batch-like fashion on data snapshots of from cfengine and which allows the system administrator to see which events are picked out as most interesting. Several other forms of analysis have been included into this tool, such as several ways to plot and visualize the most frequent combinations of events as well as detailed information about the trend of each event.

The InfoMiner[9] project has a noteworthy and similar approach which has inspired us to some extent in this work. It looks for surprising periodic patterns in a sequence of symbolic events. It derives a measure of *surprise* for a pattern by the level of information for each event in the pattern relative to the frequency of the pattern. Although the approach has the same aim, extracting events with a higher information from a noisy event stream, the data used in this reference is a strict sequence of events unlike ours. Furthermore, the patterns, like $(e_1, *, e_4, e_2)$ assume that the events in a certain order are significant and that repetition makes them more interesting while we only have clusters of events and assume that seldomness alone make events interesting.

We shall return to the outstanding issues of anomaly ranking in later work.

This work is supported by the EC IST-EMANICS Network of Excellence (#26854)

# References

1. Keogh, E., Kasetty, S.: On the Need for Time Series Data Mining Benchmarks: A Survey and Empirical Demonstration. In: SIGKKD '02, ACM Press, New York (2002)
2. The CFengine website http://www.cfengine.org
3. Burgess, M.: Two dimensional time-series for anomaly detection and regulation in adaptive systems. In: Feridun, M., Kropf, P.G., Babin, G. (eds.) DSOM 2002. LNCS, vol. 2506, p. 169. Springer, Heidelberg (2002)
4. O'Madahain, J., Smyth, P.: EventRank: A Framework for Ranking Time-Varying Networks. LinkKDD'05. ACM Press, New York (2005)
5. O'Madahain, J., Hutchins, J., Smyth, P.: Prediction and Ranking Aldorithms for Event-Based Network Data. In: SIGKDD Explor. Newsl. 2005, ACM Press, New York (2005)
6. Cochran, W G.: Some Methods for Strengthening the Common $\chi^2$ Tests. Biometrics 10(4), 417–451 (1954), doi:10.2307/3001616
7. Bortz, J., Lienert, G.A.: Kurzgefasste Statistik die klinishe Forschung, 2. Auflage, p. 347. Springer, Heidelberg (2003)
8. Begnum, K., Burgess, M.: Principle components and importance ranking of distributed anomalies. Machine Learning Journal 58, 217–230 (2005)
9. Yang, J., Wang, W., Yu, P.S.: InfoMiner: Mining Surprising Periodic Patterns. In: KDD '01: Proceedings of the seventh ACM SIGKDD international conference on Knowledge discovery and data mining, ACM Press, New York (2001)
10. Cover, T.M., Thomas, J.A.: Book: Elements of Information Theory. J.Wiley & Sons, Chichester (1991)
11. Burgess, M.: Probabilistic anomaly detection in distributed computer networks. Science of Computer Programming 60(1), 1–26 (2006)
12. Burgess, M., Haugerud, H., Reitan, T., Straumsnes, S.: Measuring host normality, ACM Transactions on Computing Systems (2001)

# Modeling and Performance Evaluation of the Network and Service Management Plane

Abdelkader Lahmadi, Laurent Andrey, and Olivier Festor

LORIA - INRIA Lorraine - Nancy Univerists
615 rue du Jardin Botanique
F-54602 Villers-lès-Nancy, France
{Abdelkader.Lahmadi,Laurent.Andrey}@loria.fr

**Abstract.** Today, little is known about the costs associated with the manageability of a system. This lack of knowledge has a deep impact both on the quality and the performance of managed networks and services and even the management system itself. Thus, it becomes crucial to assess this cost and better understand the performance of management systems both with common metrics and performance evaluation methodologies. Based on empirical observations and analytical results, we identify interesting performance behavior of JMX (Java Management eXtension) based-management frameworks.

**Keywords:** JMX, Benchmarking, Management Performance.

## 1  Introduction

The rapid growth of the Internet over the last decade has been startling. However, efforts to manage its services and their underlying networks have often fallen afoul of a poor performance management systems to manage them. The problem is not that management systems and protocols do not exists, but rather that the lack of performance models, tools and benchmarking platforms to assess their cost and well understand their needs on resources consumption are not well studied. Furthermore, studying the performance of the value-added functional plane without taking in consideration the cost of management activities and its impact would lead to inaccurate estimation of the quality of service and might impact the business benefit. Consequently, questions arise like: what is the cost of a management system, its impact on a managed system ? how a management system scales with the growth of a managed system ?

The same problem has arisen in other computer science disciplines (databases, distributed systems, IP networks,etc). An extensive literature exists, and many standards have emerged in these disciplines to assess the performance of the proposed systems and architectures. In the network and services management community however, it was surprising that we did not find any agreement on conventions for evaluating the performance of management systems. Existing performance metrics like response times, throughput, cost, quality and scalability in literature are inconsistent and confusing. As a result, no common foundation has been established to evaluate the performance of management systems so far. One approach to solving the above lacks is to develop

A.K. Bandara and M. Burgess (Eds.): AIMS 2007, LNCS 4543, pp. 156–159, 2007.

benchmarking platforms and collecting measurement data sets to identify and well define the most outstanding performance metrics and their measurement methodology.

The aim of our work is to provide common performance metrics to evaluate the performance and the cost of management frameworks using measurement and analytical techniques for common unrealistic and realistic management scenarios. We have focused our performance evaluation studies on JMX, the *de facto* standard to manage Java based applications.

## 2   Results

The main results of our work are so far:

*Management impact.* As an initial investigation of the performance of management activities, we analysed the impact of JMX activities on the performance of a managed J2EE server[1] [1]. We have built an analytical formulae to quantify this impact that puts in relation three main categories of performance metrics: the throughput of a monitoring system in terms of the number of collected attributes per second, the cost of management activities in terms of resources consumptions (CPU, memory and network bandwidth) and the quality of monitoring operations in terms of their respect to a tolerable delay. The formulae that we did propose has implications on network management like the SNMP one, as well as on services and applications management frameworks. In a second stage, we have extended this initial work to study the impact of instrumentation models as described in [2] on both the performance of the management and an instrumented web server. We did show that the web users perceived performance in terms of the number of HTTP transactions/s and their respective delays are highly affected by the management activity in the boot driver and component models while a daemon integration model limits the management activities impact on the functional plane. However, we showed that under low monitoring rates in the order of 200 requests/second, the three integration models have a small impact on the web server performance.

*Benchmarking platform.* To better understand the performance of management frameworks, we have developed a benchmarking platform [3] dedicated to JMX management paradigms. We selected this framework because it provide inherent manageability to Java technology enabled applications and service, therefore, the impact of management activities is more visible. The JMX framework has not a management information model, instead it offers several types of managed objects (MBeans) to instrument resources and supports many protocols (TCP/RMI, HTTP, SOAP) for the communication between a manager and an agent. Nevertheless, our platform is flexible and modular enough to be extended to other management frameworks as SNMP. We have focused on the manager-agent model with synthetic tests where we have varied the number of managed objects (MBeans), their types, the monitoring rates and the number of agents. Despite the high saleability of benchmarking results [4] which is its key justification, our experience on the benchmarking of the JMX framework, shows us how much this technique is time consuming and error-prone. It also reveals its limited coverage of the

---

[1] We used JBoss as managed server: http://www.jboss.org

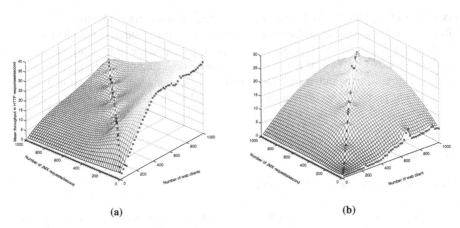

**Fig. 1.** The impact of a driver model of a monitoring agent on a web server performance in terms of (a) throughput and (b) HTTP transactions delays

space of performance factors values. For example, in [5], a complete coverage of all our measurement series to identify the impact of the three integration models of an agent within a managed systems (as depicted in Figure 1) needs 3 months of measurement, or 1 month at best if we parallelize measurements. Thus, we believe that analytical and simulation techniques are more suitable to investigate deeper the performance of management frameworks. However, before doing simulation we need modeling the behaviour of management activities.

*Management delays.* Based on the developed benchmarking platform, we have elaborated in [6], a delay model for the manager-agent model. This model is interesting for simulating the behaviour of JMX based management activities delays. Our finding is that the management delays behaviour closely follows a normal distribution with a small number of agents, and becomes more heavy tailed and approximates a weibull distribution with a considerable number of agents. The delays scaling behaviour is interesting because we can quantify the temporal accuracy of management data collected by a manager to a somewhat *delay tolerance*. This parameter is considered as an upper bound on the delay, any collected attribute from an agent experiences, that holds with high probability and is determined empirically based on the managed environment. Most of our methodology used to model management delays could be applied to other management related performance metrics (number of polled/notified attributes).

*Analytical Modeling.* We have elaborated analytical models for management systems performance evaluation from theoretical concerns regarding queueing models. The developed models are sufficiently general to capture management frameworks , based on the manager-agent pattern, performance and provide a check on measurement results. We have modeled the *manager-agent-managed system* pattern as a closed queuing network. The model parameters and the types of queues are identified from our measurement data sets obtained. The performance factor was the monitoring rate in terms of polled attributed per second. We find that our proposed model captures well the performance of the management system under small monitoring rates, but it becomes inaccurate when monitoring rates are higher.

## 3  Conclusion and Future Works

The aim of our work is to provide a common evaluation methodology and performance assessment of a management framework. We illustrated our work with the manager-agent JMX-based management framework, widely used to manage *J2EE* applications on which several Internet services rely (retailers, banks, government institutes,etc). Our findings show that the management activities have a deep impact on the performance of a managed service. This impact depends on the monitoring rate and the integration model of the agent within the managed system. We also show that high monitoring rates degrade both the performance of management and managed systems, especially delays that become more random and their underlying statistical distribution more heavy-tailed. Thus, we believe that optimizing management activities by minimizing their cost and rates while maximizing their coverage and business benefit needs to be fitted and well defined within solid optimization frameworks.

## References

1. Lahmadi, A., Andrey, L., Festor, O.: On the impact of management on the performance of a managed system: a jmx-based management case study. In: Schönwälder, J., Serrat, J. (eds.) DSOM 2005. LNCS, vol. 3775, pp. 24–37. Springer, Heidelberg (2005)
2. Kreger, H., Harold, W., Willamson, L.: Java and JMX: Building Manageable Systems. Addison-Wesley, London (2003)
3. Andrey, L., Lahmadi, A., Delove, J.: A jmx benchmark. Technical report, Loria-INRIA Lorraine (2005)
4. Jain, R.: The art of Computer Systems Performance Analysis. John Wiley & Sons, Inc, New York (1991), ISBN: 0-471-50336-3
5. Lahmadi, A., Ghitescu, A., Andrey, L., Festor, O.: On the impact of management instrumentation models on web server performance: a jmx case study. In: Bandara, A., Burgess, M. (eds.) Autonomous Infrastructure, Management and Security, AIMS, Oslo, Norway, Springer-Verlag's, Heidelberg (2007)
6. Lahmadi, A., Andrey, L., Festor, O.: On delays in management frameworks: Metrics, models and analysis. In: State, R., van der Meer, S., O'Sullivan, D., Pfeifer, T. (eds.) DSOM 2006. LNCS, vol. 4269, Springer, Heidelberg (2006)

# Abstractions to Support Interactions Between Self-Managed Cells

Alberto Schaeffer-Filho and Emil Lupu

Department of Computing, Imperial College London
180 Queen's Gate, SW7 2AZ, London, England
{aschaeff,e.c.lupu}@doc.ic.ac.uk

**Abstract.** Management of pervasive systems cannot rely on human intervention nor centralised decision-making functions due to their complex and intrinsically mobile nature. In previous work, we proposed the concept of a self-managed cell (SMC) as an architectural pattern for building ubiquitous applications. A SMC consists of hardware and software components that form an autonomous administrative domain. SMCs may be realised at different scales, from body-area networks, to an entire room or larger settings. However, to scale to larger systems it is necessary for SMCs to collaborate with each other, to federate or compose in larger SMC structures. We describe here the main abstractions we have defined and explore future directions towards this goal.

## 1 Introduction

The complexity of pervasive systems inhibits a centralised or manual management approach. Such systems are saturated with technological capabilities that need to be integrated and work seamlessly. Typical pervasive environments consist of mobile devices, which cannot refer to a centralised management application. In addition, the complex and dynamic nature of such environments prevents any attempt of manual configuration. The feasibility of pervasive systems will depend on their ability to autonomously manage themselves, relying on local decision-making and feedback control-loops. In essence, this is the proposition of autonomic computing [1].

In previous work [2], we introduced the concept of a *Self-Managed Cell (SMC)* as an architectural pattern for building ubiquitous applications. A SMC consists of a set of hardware and software components that form an autonomous domain. SMCs monitor events of interest and perform actions when specific conditions occur, thereby adapting their configuration and operation to changes through a policy-driven feedback control-loop. We have used the SMC pattern in several application areas, such as health monitoring, management of autonomous vehicles, and management of large virtual organisations. This paper focuses on health monitoring applications where a body-area SMC of sensors and actuators monitors the medical condition of the patient and reacts to changes in the patient's condition or context. For example, changes in the patient's blood glucose level may trigger the activation of an insulin pump. Similarly, a cardiac

A.K. Bandara and M. Burgess (Eds.): AIMS 2007, LNCS 4543, pp. 160–163, 2007.

monitoring subsystem may trigger adaptations in its thresholds based on input from a physical activity monitoring SMC, trigger the activation of an artificial pacemaker, or contact emergency care if it detects an impending heart-attack.

Our main challenge is to define how SMCs can federate and collaborate with each other with little or no user intervention. Interactions between SMCs must be spontaneous, automated and may take the form of *peer-to-peer* collaborations or *compositions* where SMCs can operate and be managed within the context of a containing SMC. SMCs may represent individual devices, personal area networks, or even larger settings such as smart rooms. SMCs must autonomously decide whether and how to interact with discovered SMCs in their surroundings. These interactions are not limited to invocations between SMCs but must also include exchanges of events and policies between the SMCs in order to enable them to react to each other's behaviour. Due to the complexity of smart environments, SMCs need to compose into larger encapsulated structures, exposing their resources (including internal SMCs) only when they are relevant to surrounding SMCs.

This paper presents the first steps of this research, discussing the main abstractions we have defined to facilitate collaboration between SMCs. Ultimately, the collaboration between SMCs will allow services provided in the environment to be combined in order to achieve higher level goals. This will require goal refinement and planning-based techniques.

Although several studies have proposed frameworks for pervasive spaces [3,4], they tend to share two limitations: they focus on pervasive spaces of a relatively fixed size (e.g. a room) and they fail to cater for dynamic interactions between pervasive spaces. In contrast, we consider the SMC as an architectural pattern applicable at different levels of scale, ranging from small body-area networks, to large-scale virtual organisations. SMCs are expected to dynamically discover and collaborate with other SMCs, whilst most other projects focus on a single-size, single-instance perspective.

## 2   Self-Managed Cells and Their Interactions

A SMC comprises a dynamic set of management services that are integrated through a common publish/subscribe *event bus*, which supplies the basic communication infrastructure between the SMC's components (Figure 1.a). Together, the *event bus*, the *policy service* and the *discovery service* provide the core functionality of a SMC, as they are sufficient to implement a policy-driven feedback control-loop (Figure 1.b) [5]. The discovery of new components or changes of state in the current resources are published on the event bus and trigger the execution of *obligation* policies in the form of *event-condition-action* rules. Such policies define the actions that must be performed in response to events, thereby adapting the SMC to context changes.

However, in ubiquitous environments, where smart entities may range from a body sensor or personal belonging to a room or an entire building, SMCs have to interact and collaborate in different ways. Because such environments are

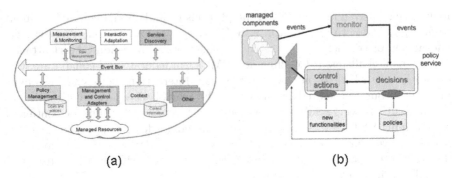

**Fig. 1.** The SMC core services (a) implement a feedback control-loop (b)

saturated with technological capabilities, the ability to encapsulate resources and hide underlying complexity is crucial to their scalability. Therefore, we have investigated how SMCs could *compose* into complex structures whilst preserving the autonomy of their components. A composition interaction encapsulates a SMC (with its own resources) as a managed resource within a containing SMC. Functionality is exposed to external interacting SMCs through *customised interfaces* which are specific to them. For example, a patient SMC would expose access to its sensors to doctors, but hide the sensors from other patients. These customised interfaces also provide the ability to mediate and filter interactions with external SMCs. In pervasive systems, interactions and mediation aspects must be determined at run-time and must change dynamically in order to adapt to new circumstances such as failure of a sensor or discovery of a new one. This presents new challenges when compared to component composition in distributed systems where composition is often statically defined.

In order to perform complex interactions, SMCs can exchange obligation policies with each other. The set of policies that defines the behaviour of an interaction is called a *mission* and it specifies how a remote SMC should behave within the context of the interaction in terms of sending notifications, and reacting to events by invoking actions. For example, upon discovery of a patient SMC, a doctor SMC may load into the former an ECG monitoring mission, containing policies that perform heart beat readings at a specific frequency for a given amount of time, sending partial reports to the doctor's office every six hours and, in the occurrence of abnormal conditions, setting the alarm off in the nurse station. The term mission suggests that collaborations between SMCs can be done in terms of high-level goals. However, the ability to endow SMCs with planning capability on relatively small devices remains part of our future work.

SMCs discover each other at run-time, but policies defining how they should interact with discovered SMCs must be specified beforehand. For example, the doctor should be able to specify the mission in advance, and load it dynamically into the patient SMC when the latter is discovered. We have introduced *roles* as placeholders for remote SMCs yet to be discovered. Roles are associated with the missions and define the set of functions that a SMC of a specific type (e.g. patient) is expected to provide. Thus, roles provide a scope for specifying the policies of a mission. This is somewhat different from the use of roles in Ponder (where there is no notion of expected behaviour from external components) or IETF PCIM (where roles define capabilities of policy targets). When remote SMCs are discovered they are assigned to their respective roles, and missions specified by the discovering SMC are instantiated on these remote SMCs.

## 3  Current Status and Future Work

Our prototype covers the implementation of obligation policies in the policy interpreter, exchange of customised interfaces and deployment of missions. Future work will address collaboration definitions whose enforcement is itself distributed and collaborations based on exchanges of high-level goals. A strategy for goal refinement and planning in a SMC-rich scenario will have to be conceived, in order to provide a complete solution for interactions between SMCs.

## 4  Concluding Remarks

This paper has briefly described a set of key abstractions to facilitate collaborations between SMCs. Allowing SMCs to dynamically compose into more complex structures caters for larger pervasive applications. Customised interfaces allow SMCs to selectively hide their complexity, exposing internal components only when they are relevant to specific partners. Finally, the same event-condition-action rules that provide to the SMC its ability of self-management can be grouped into missions and used across multiple SMCs, extending their local control-loop to involve remote SMCs available in the surroundings. Abstractions such as roles, customised interfaces and policies are not inherently novel, however the ways in which they can be combined and used to support interactions between autonomous SMCs remains a challenging task that requires further work.

## References

1. Kephart, J.O., Chess, D.M.: The vision of autonomic computing. IEEE Computer 36(1), 41–50 (2003)
2. Lupu, E., Dulay, N., Sloman, M., Sventek, J., Heeps, S., Strowes, S., Twidle, K., Keoh, S.L., Schaeffer-Filho, A.: AMUSE: autonomic management of ubiquitous systems for e-health. Special Issues of the Journal of Concurrency and Computation: Practice and Experience, Wiley (to appear)
3. Roman, M., Hess, C., Cerqueira, R., Ranganathan, A., Campbell, R., Nahrstedt, K.: A middleware infrastructure for active spaces. IEEE Pervasive Computing 1(4), 74–83 (2002)
4. Johanson, B., Fox, A., Winograd, T.: The interactive workspaces project: experiences with ubiquitous computing rooms. IEEE Pervasive Computing 1(2), 67–74 (2002)
5. Sloman, M.: Monitoring Distributed Systems. In: Network and Distributed Systems Management, pp. 303–347. Addison-Wesley, Reading (1994)

# Self-management Framework for Unmanned Autonomous Vehicles

Eskindir Asmare and Morris Sloman

Imperial College London, Department of Computing,
180 Queen's Gate, London Sw7 2AZ, UK.
{e.asmare,m.sloman}@doc.ic.ac.uk

**Abstract.** In this paper we identify the challenges in enabling self-management for Unmanned Autonomous Vehicles and briefly outline our policy-based approach for realising a self-management framework. We also present preliminary results.

## 1 Introduction

Unmanned Autonomous Vehicles (UAVs) are often used in missions that are dangerous or otherwise impossible for humans. The challenge in deploying UAVs in real life missions is enabling them to perform self-management. UAVs should configure themselves automatically in accordance with high level mission specifications and seek ways of improving performance. They should detect, diagnose and repair failures as well as protect themselves from attacks. Although there have been various research on robot-control architectures, the focus has largely been in organizing intelligence. We argue that if robots such as UAVs are to be used in real life applications then they should be able to manage their intelligence.

The aim of our research is to develop a UAV self-management framework which is applicable to both individual and teams of UAVs. Our approach is novel for using a policy-based self-management framework to manage robots such as UAVs. In this short paper we present an outline of our approach and briefly report the progress in design and implementation of a mission-management architecture.

## 2 Policy-Based Mission-Management Architecture

We use policy-based management as it provides a powerful and flexible approach to specifying adaptive self-management strategy which can be dynamically modified. We use the Self Managed Cell(SMC) [1] as the general architectural pattern for realising self-management of both individual and team of UAVs. The SMC supports the Ponder2 policy language [2].

So far we have identified three management issues to be addressed in the self-management framework. These are mission, team and communication management. The main issues in mission management are specifying and interpreting the

A.K. Bandara and M. Burgess (Eds.): AIMS 2007, LNCS 4543, pp. 164–167, 2007.
© Springer-Verlag Berlin Heidelberg 2007

mission in a way that facilitates mission adaptation and reassignment, as well as cooperation among UAVs participating in the mission. Forming and maintaining teams of UAVs is necessary to enable cooperation. This requires a team management scheme, and communication management to maintain communication link between team members. This differs from the usual ad-hoc routing in that we aim to control the movement of the UAVs, performing their various tasks, in order to keep within wireless range of other UAVs in order to support network routing.

The main concepts in the mission-management architecture are capabilities, missions and roles. A *capability* is a description, generated and advertised by a UAV, that specifies the inherent functions the UAV can perform with the devices it has and the credentials it provides. A *mission* is a set of sequential or concurrent tasks which must be performed in order to achieve an overall goal. A planning process is needed to generate the tasks from the goal. The planner may generate more than one strategy for achieving a goal or the context may change such that the strategy for achieving the goal has to adapt to the current situation. The implication of this is that the UAV mission-management architecture should allow adaptation of missions. A *role* is a placeholder which provides an interface for the purpose of specifying the mission of a UAV. The mission of a UAV, which is a sub-mission of an overall-mission, is specified in the form of policies whose events and actions are a subset of the interface of a role the UAV is assigned to. When a UAV is discovered by another UAV, it is assigned to a role, by matching its offered capabilities with those required by the role. If necessary, the role-missions will be downloaded to the UAV. This defines the tasks it performs and how it interacts with other roles in terms of services offered or used, events received or generated etc.

A group of UAVs form a Mission-SMC to cooperate to accomplish a mission with each UAV being assigned to one or more roles within the Mission-SMC. A *Mission-SMC* is an SMC formed by a group of UAVs as a result of interpreting a mission-SMC specification(overall-mission specification). The Mission-SMC specification contains the types of roles required to perform the mission, and a shared knowledge base which might contain certificates, overall-mission constraints etc. For each role type, role assignment, mission and authorisation policies are specified. We specify a Mission-SMC in terms of roles using policies in order to facilitate mission adaptation by reconfiguring the Mission-SMC or changing the mission of UAVs assigned to roles.

## 2.1 Mission Scenario

Our approach for mission management is illustrated using a simple reconnaissance scenario where the objective is to collect data regarding the layout and contents of a house. In the following, the possible roles in the scenario are described and a role definition is shown for one of the roles.

*Commander*: this is a manned vehicle, with a range of communications equipment, responsible for managing the mission. *Surveyors*: send video images from the house to the aggregator which it relays to the commander. *Aggregator*:

produces a map of the whole space and distributes it back to the surveyors so that they can use it for the remaining reconnaissance. It will also send all the aggregated information to the command centre.

Figure 1 shows the definition for the Surveyor role which comprises a description of the required capabilities to perform this role(used in role assignment decisions) and the role interface. The mission and authorisation policies which are related to the surveyor role are also shown.

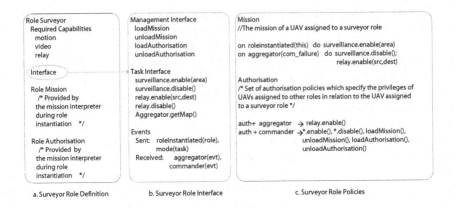

a. Surveyor Role Definition    b. Surveyor Role Interface    c. Surveyor Role Policies

**Fig. 1.** Surveyor Role

The policies shown in Figure 2 specify how a newly discovered UAV can be assigned to the appropriate role, after the credentials have been successfully verified, based on the UAV's capabilities. Encoding the role assignment as policies enables us to change the strategy of this assignment during the mission without interrupting its functioning.

```
1.oblig on discovered ( uxv, credentials, resources)
   do /smc/roles/commander.assign(uxv)
   when authenticate (credentials) and resources.comms = "longRange"
2. oblig on discovered ( uxv, credentials, resources)
   do /smc/roles/surveyor.assign(uxv)
   when authenticate (credentials) and hasCapabilities(motion, video, relay)
3. oblig on discovered (uxv, credentials, resources)
   do /smc/roles/aggregator.assign (uxv)
   when authenticate (credentials) and capabilities.processor > medium
```

**Fig. 2.** Role Assignment Policies

## 2.2   Preliminary Results

So far we have been developing schemes for role-definition, mission-specification and capability-description. We have also started designing and implementing

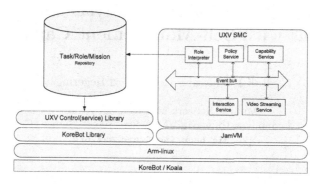

**Fig. 3.** Architecture of UAV Mission Management

the policy-based UAV mission-management architecture. The implementation extends the core SMC implementation developed in the AMUSE project [1] to realise UAV Self Managed Cells(UAV-SMCs). A teleo-reactive [3] based wall-following robot task is implemented as a way towards implementing a surveillance mission which we intend to use for testing the self-management framework. Figure 3 shows the architecture of our prototype design and implementation.

Our research environment is comprised of three Koala [1] robots. The Koala robot is a mobile robot which has 16 infrared proximity sensors, around the body of the robot, and a camera. It has a Motorola 68331, 22MHz onboard processor, a 1Mb ROM and 1Mb RAM. The robot is extensible in that various modules can be added. It has a KoreBot[1] module which has an ARM PXA255 400MHz processor, 64Mb SDRAM, 32Mb Flash and a Wi-Fi card. The KoreBot runs Linux.

# References

1. Lupu, E., Dulay, N., Sventek, J., Heeps, S., Strowes, S., Twidle, K., Keoh, S.L., Schaffer-Filho, A.: Amuse: Autonomic management of ubiquitous e-Health systems. To be published in Concurrency and Computation: Practice and Experience (2007)
2. Keoh, S.L., Twidle, K., Pryce, N., Schaeffer-Filho, A., Lupu, E., Dulay, N., Sloman, M., Heeps, S., Strowes, S., Sventek, J., Katsiri, E.: Policy-based management for body-sensor networks. In: Proceedings of the 4th International Workshop on Wearable and Implantable Body Sensor Networks (BSN07), pp. 92–98. Springer-Verlag, Heidelberg (2007)
3. Nilsson, N.J.: Teleo-reactive programs for agent control. Journal of Artificial Intelligence Research 1, 139–158 (1994)

---

[1] http://www.k-team.com

# Towards a Toolkit for the Analysis and Design of Systems with Self-Management Capabilities

Ralf Koenig and Heinz-Gerd Hegering

Munich Network Management Team
Ludwig-Maximilians-Universität München, 80638 Munich, Germany
{koenig,hegering}@mnm-team.org

**Abstract.** Systems with more and more sophisticated self-management capabilities are introduced in many application domains, such as robotics, the military, aerospace, ground vehicles, IT network and systems management. So far, descriptions of such systems are neither decomposed into common modules nor aligned to a common reference model. For this reason, it is hard to compare them regarding common cross-domain properties of systems with self-management capabilities (SwSMC). It is also hard to transfer design knowledge from one application domain to another. A review of related work reveals few publications with guidance to analytical decomposition into functional modules and the identification of patterns specific to the structure and behavior as well as design and use of self-management capabilities.

To approach this problem, by using cross-domain evaluation criteria and identification of common patterns we can achieve uniformly structured system descriptions. The approach will be implemented by a common system model of SwSMC, an evaluation sheet for such systems, an evaluation results repository, a pattern catalogue and a set of recommendations how to apply the patterns during the design of such systems and keeping an eye on effectiveness and efficiency. So far, a system model and the evaluation sheet have been created, and some evaluations of research prototypes have been carried out. Despite the low number of evaluations so far, first patterns stand out.

## 1 Introduction

Self-managing systems are expected to have desirable features such as model-based automation, autonomic operations according to policies, robustness, scalability, and resilience to errors by human operators, all of which promise lower operational costs. Marketing efforts by hardware, software and solutions vendors stimulate business and therefore scientific interest in current and future "self-managing" products and services.

At the same time however, limited predictability of emergent behavior, lack of transparency and service guarantees, neglected security requirements, and a general lack of control are properties which are also currently associated with self-managing systems, leading to a slow adoption of such systems in productive environments of service providers.

A.K. Bandara and M. Burgess (Eds.): AIMS 2007, LNCS 4543, pp. 168–171, 2007.

Current "self-managing" systems are not completely self-managed, instead they are managed systems equipped with certain self-management mechanisms that deal with certain operational aspects. Depending on both the importance of these self-managed aspects for the functionality of the whole system and the maturity of the used self-management mechanisms, the systems can be associated with some level of autonomy, between complete dependence on and obedience to external control and complete autonomy. Therefore in this article, the term "systems with self-management capabilities" (abbreviated as "SwSMC") is used.

## 2    The Research Problem

Most publications on new SwSMC focus on the design and use of the particular system from a point of view specific to one intended application domain. Typically, the application-specific benefit is demonstrated well but the decomposition into building blocks, or the design decisions that would also be of use for other application domains are neglected.

The problem therefore is in a) coming up with a simple yet sufficient common system architecture model, that many SwSMC can be aligned to and b) identifying a cross-domain set of evaluation criteria that captures the specific aspects of self-management capabilities, c) to identify common building blocks and patterns in such systems and d) to give better guidance when to apply which patterns.

## 3    The Chosen Approach

The description of an autonomic element as defined by IBM in [1] was chosen as a a basis for the system architecture model. The system to be analyzed first needs to be decomposed into such autonomic elements. So far, systems typically are composed of very few *types* of such autonomic elements, often just one only. For each autonomic element, an evaluation sheet needs to be filled in, that covers two parts: a black-box evaluation and a white-box evaluation.

The *black-box evaluation* covers the system functionality (offered service), service guarantees and metrics, the implementation of the sensor-effector interfaces to the managed resource and to higher-level managers, and the communication via these interfaces. This includes all communication with external human managers, other autonomic elements, and the managed resources.

The *white-box evaluation* covers the interior of the Autonomic Element: internal static and dynamic system structure, variables and internal state, SASO (stability, accuracy, settling time, overshoot) [2] properties of internal control loops, the implementation of the MAPE-K (monitor, analyze, plan, execute based on knowledge) [1] components, the interfaces between the MAPE-K components and the internal communication bus, and internal fault handling. Evaluations of the MAPE-K components also cover system design decisions: requirements, the candidate technologies that were taken into account, the assessment of the individual alternatives, and the final decision.

## 4    First Results

Based on the results of the system evaluations, first results have been achieved.

*Identification of functional components in SwSMC.* Steps (and techniques) in a feedback loop: *monitoring* (duplicate detection and removal, plausibility checks, translation); *analysis* (problem determination, event correlation, clustering, searching, prediction, (constraint) solver, filtering, classification, expert system) with methods such as pattern matching, heuristics, neuronal networks, Bayesian networks, linear programming; *planning* (short term, long term, strategic planning, scheduler, calender/plan); *execution* (serialization, translation, transaction handling); *knowledge management* and *machine learning*.

Components that interface to (human) managers in a feedback loop: configurator (also called wizard), solution adviser, decision maker, effects forecaster, explainer.

Standard uses of a feedback loop: closed loop: stabilizer, optimizer, load balancer; open loop: notifier, watchdog.

*Reasons for adding self-management capabilities.* Most of the time, SwSMC have been designed to improve efficiency: SwSMC are built to automate operational tasks that are typically simple, repeated very often, have a low number of decision alternatives, need constant monitoring and very quick response. Only in few cases, SwSMC are designed with the goal to improve effectiveness, i.e. results that would not be achievable without self-management capabilities.

## 5    Competitive Approaches Including Comparison with Selected Approach

In a literature review in the major conferences on autonomic computing in the last four years, the paper abstracts were skimmed to find related work on a) a proposal for an evaluation scheme and b) common building blocks or design patterns that make out the self-management capabilities in SwSMC.

[3] introduces patterns of self-management, such as: resource reallocation, corruption resiliency, user authorization, model comparator, progress measurement. The origin of these patterns and their use are not visibly derived from system evaluations, while in our case we will link actual products/research prototypes with evaluation results. [4] describe the evaluation of seven black-box properties of SwSMC and work to group many existing systems into categories. They do not base their observations on a common evaluation scheme nor give advice how to use the patterns. [5] lists autonomic elements behavioral modes, patterns in the interaction of autonomic elements, and design patterns. In contrast to the approach in this paper, the results are not based on a standardized evaluation scheme but are abstracted from dealing with two prototype SwSMC.

[6] describe a translation and system access layer to coordinate using multiple autonomic managers on the same resources. A functional decomposition of the autonomic managers to be coordinated is not performed. [7] describes some

requirements and expected difficulties when benchmarking SwSMC. The paper concentrates on comparisons on the performance and autonomy level, but does not propose to explain benchmarking results with the details of the system structure. [8] applies the Viable Systems Model and the Soft Systems Methodology to the analysis of SwSMC. However, the authors do not present an evaluation sheet nor a common structure for system descriptions.

All in all, from the review of related work, while there are some publications on evaluation matters and a few patterns, none of them takes the approach to present a common evaluation scheme and to derive patterns from the results, as well as guidance on their use.

## 6    Future Work

Future work includes the evaluation of SwSMC, mostly based on publicly available system descriptions in natural language. We will reformat selected articles on SwSMC into the format by semantic tagging. By demonstrating the original articles and the results next to each other, the value of a common structure should become more apparent. The results of the evaluations will be collected in a repository. This repository will then be examined for patterns. We look for patterns in the system design, the system structure, the use of the system and the level of autonomy. An important part will be to correlate system properties with certain features in the system design and system implementation. In addition, development kits for SwSMC (such as the IBM Autonomic Computing Toolkit and IBM Agent Building and Learning Environment) shall be examined to see what kind of support they offer in the implementation of the building blocks mentioned before.

## References

1. IBM: An architectural blueprint for autonomic computing (4th edn.) (2006)
2. Hellerstein, J.L., Diao, Y., Parekh, S., Tilbury, D.M.: Feedback Control of Computing Systems. John Wiley & Sons, Chichester (2004)
3. Wile, D.S.: Patterns of self-management. In: Proc. of the 1st ACM SIGSOFT workshop on Self-managed systems (WOSS'04), pp. 110–114 (2004)
4. Huebscher, M., McCann, J.: Evaluation issues in autonomic computing. In: Jin, H., Pan, Y., Xiao, N., Sun, J. (eds.) GCC 2004. LNCS, vol. 3251, p. 597. Springer, Heidelberg (2004)
5. White, S.R., et al.: An architectural approach to autonomic computing. In: Proc. of the 1st Intl. Conf. on Autonomic Computing (ICAC'04), pp. 2–9 (2004)
6. Cheng, S.W., et al.: An architecture for coordinating multiple self-management systems. In: Proc. of the 4th Working Conference on Software Architecture (WICSA'04), pp. 243–254 (2004)
7. Brown, A.B., et al.: Benchmarking autonomic capabilities: Promises and pitfalls. In: Proc. of the 1st Intl. Conf. on Autonomic Computing (ICAC'04), pp. 266–267 (2004)
8. Bustard, D., et al.: Towards a systemic approach to autonomic systems engineering. In: Proc. of the 12th Intl. Conf. and Workshops on the Engineering of Computer-Based Systems (ECBS'05), pp. 465–472 (2005)

# Estimating Local Cardinalities
# in a Multidimensional Multiset

Patrick Truong and Fabrice Guillemin

France Telecom R&D, 2, avenue Pierre Marzin, F-22307 Lannion
{patrick.truong,fabrice.guillemin}@orange-ftgroup.com

**Abstract.** In connection with port scan and worm propagation in the Internet, we address in this paper the problem of estimating the ber of destinations communicating with a given source. We propose a computational and memory-efficient technique of finding the top-talker sources. The proposed algorithm is tested against actual data (NetFlow records from the interconnection IP backbone network of France Telecom).

**Keywords:** Cardinality, Local Cardinality, Multiset, Top-talkers, Real-time data mining, Network monitoring and security.

## 1 Introduction

The ever growing capacities of transmission links in today's telecommunication networks together with huge addressing spaces make monitoring and supervision extremely difficult for network operators. With regard to security (e.g., anomaly detection), the analysis of huge amounts of data is all the more critical as this task has to be almost real time in order to quickly react to unexpected behaviors by customers and to preserve the grade of service of the network. While anomaly detection in IP networks has been studied extensively in the technical literature, less attention has been paid to the following problem: for a given source, estimate the number of distinct destinations that are in communication with this source. This problem, that we refer to as *local cardinalities* problem, is specifically related to port scans or worm propagation where a malicious host initiates a large number of flows with a wide range of destination addresses in order to compromise end user terminals.

Counting cardinality of a multiset is a well studied topic in the domain of algorithm analysis, see for instance the pioneering work by Flajolet and Martin on probabilistic counting [1]. However, to the best of our knowledge, only a few papers address the estimation of local cardinalities [5,6]. Venkataraman *et al.* [5] propose two approaches to this problem by using hash-based flow sampling, which can be very greedy in terms of storage capacity. Moreover, sampling elements that appear several times may decrease estimation accuracy. In [6], the authors use a Bloom filter, but their bitmap method may suffer from collision.

In this paper, we develop a new algorithm to estimate local cardinalities using constant small memory. The basic ingredients are the Loglog counting algorithm

A.K. Bandara and M. Burgess (Eds.): AIMS 2007, LNCS 4543, pp. 172–175, 2007.
© Springer-Verlag Berlin Heidelberg 2007

developed by Durand and Flajolet [2] together with Bloom filters. In Section 2, we give our theoretical description of the problem. In Section 3, the proposed algorithm is described and is tested in Section 4 against real network data.

## 2   Problem Formulation

A multiset is a set where each element can appear several times; the cardinality of the multiset is the number of distinct elements. Let us consider in the rest of the paper a multidimensional multiset $\mathcal{M} = \{(x_1, y_1), (x_2, y_2), \ldots, (x_N, y_N)\}$, where the elements $x_i, y_i$ belong to an alphabet $\mathcal{A}$ (e.g. the IP addressing space) and $N$ is the size of the multiset (i.e., the total number of elements with possible repetitions). In practice, the cardinal of the alphabet $\mathcal{A}$ and the value of $N$ are very large. Let $\mathbb{1}_{\mathcal{M}} \colon \mathcal{A} \times \mathcal{A} \mapsto \{0, 1\}$ be the indicator function such that $\mathbb{1}_{\mathcal{M}}(x, y)$ is equal to one if $(x, y) \in \mathcal{M}$ and otherwise equal to 0.

The *local cardinality* problem can then be formulated as follows: given any $x \in \mathcal{A}$, find the number of distinct $y$'s that are paired with $x$ in the multiset. In other words, we have to estimate the quantity $d_x = \sum_{y \in \mathcal{A}} \mathbb{1}_{\mathcal{M}}(x, y)$, which is referred to as the *local cardinality* of $x$. Moreover, the element $x$ is called a *top-talker* if his local cardinality is larger than $\phi n$, where $n$ denotes the cardinality of the multiset $\mathcal{M}$ and $\phi$ is some constant in $(0, 1)$.

## 3   Algorithm Description

Let us first recall that the Loglog counting algorithm [2] relies on the use of a hash function $f$ that transforms elements of the multiset $\mathcal{M}$ into sufficiently long binary strings in such a way that bits composing the hashed value appear as random numbers with equal probabilities of taking the values 0 and 1. For $z \in \mathcal{M}$, let $\rho(z)$ be the position of the first 1-bit of $f(z)$. The probability that $\rho(z) = k$ is $1/2^k$. So, we expect the maximum $R = \max_{z \in \mathcal{M}} \rho(z)$ to be a rough estimate of $\log_2(n)$. To improve the accuracy of the estimate, the stochastic averaging procedure can be used and consists of simulating $m = 2^k$ independent experiments over the multiset by taking the first $k$ bits of a hash value to identify the index $j$ of the experiment and updating the maximum $R_j$ with $\rho(z)$ computed from the rest of the bit string. The authors of [2] show that the cardinality of the multiset $\mathcal{M}$ is estimated by

$$\xi = \alpha_m m 2^{\frac{1}{m} \sum_{j=1}^{m} R_j}, \qquad (1)$$

where $\alpha_m = \left(\Gamma(-1/m)(1 - 2^{1/m})/\log 2\right)^{-m}$. This estimator is asymptotically unbiased and the standard error is approximately $1.30/\sqrt{m}$. For $m \geq 64$, $\alpha_m$ can be replaced by $\alpha_\infty = e^{-\gamma}\sqrt{2}/2 = 0.39701$ with $\gamma$ denoting Euler's constant.

The shortcoming of the Loglog counting is that hashing induces information loss about elements of the multiset. Hence, our idea is to use Bloom filters in combination with Loglog counting for local cardinalities estimation. Our algorithm consists then of maintaining a three-dimensional array $T[u][v][j]$ with width $U$, length $V$ and depth $m = 2^k$. Each entry of the array is initially set to zero. We also have $U$ hash functions chosen uniformly at random from a pairwise-independent family $h_u \colon \mathcal{A} \mapsto [\![0, V-1]\!]$, $u = 0, \ldots, U-1$, and one hash function $f$ as in the Loglog counting algorithm described above. The first two dimensions of the array $T$ can be viewed as a Bloom filter or a multistage filter as in the paper by Estan and Varghese [4].

When an element $(x, y)$ of the multiset $\mathcal{M}$ arrives, we first compute the hashed value $f(x, y)$. The first $k$ bits of $f(x, y)$ are used to identify the index $j$ among the $m$ buckets, and we determine $\rho(x, y)$ as the position of the first 1-bit of $f(x, y)$ deprived of its first $k$ bits. Then, we update the array $T$ as follows:

$$\forall \, 0 \le u \le U - 1, \; T[u][h_u(x)][j] = \max \left( T[u][h_u(x)][j], \rho(x, y) \right)$$

We can estimate at any time the local cardinality of any element $x$ by using Equation (1) with $R_j$ evaluated as in [4] by

$$R_j = \min_{0 \le u \le U-1} T[u][h_u(x)][j]. \tag{2}$$

To overcome the problem of over-estimating small cardinalities, we define the ratio of empty buckets as $\tau = m \cdot \ln \frac{m}{empty}$ [3], where $empty$ is the number of $R_j = 0$. The local cardinality of $x$ is then estimated as follows:

$$\text{if } \tau > 3.5m, \; \tilde{d}_x = \alpha_\infty m 2^{\frac{1}{m} \sum_{j=1}^{m} R_j} = \xi$$

$$\text{if } 2.5m < \tau \le 3.5m, \; \tilde{d}_x = (1 - \frac{\tau - 2.5m}{m})\tau + \frac{\tau - 2.5m}{m}\xi$$

$$\text{if } \tau \le 2.5m, \; \tilde{d}_x = \tau$$

In addition, we can find the top-talkers by keeping a heap as in [7]. More precisely, upon the arrival of an element $(x, y)$, we update our data structure $T$, and immediately after, we estimate both the local cardinality $\tilde{d}_x$ and the global cardinality $\tilde{n}$: if $x$ is already in the heap, we update its count; else if $\tilde{d}_x \ge \phi\tilde{n}$, we add $x$ to the heap. We also delete the element with lowest count from the heap if its count is smaller than $\phi\tilde{n}$. Similarly, we can find the top $K$ of the local cardinalities by maintaining a heap.

## 4   Evaluation

We evaluate our algorithm by using a trace of NetFlow records [8] captured on the interconnection IP backbone of France Telecom. The trace represents an average of 60,000 records per second. Each NetFlow record contains statistics about an IP flow. We test our algorithm with the following parameters for the array $T[u][v][j]$: $U = 7$, $V = 3000$ and we choose $m = 4096$. (Experiments show that the accuracy is better when $m$ increases.) The length of the observation window is set to one minute. There are exactly 2,543,978 distinct pairs of source and destination addresses, and 1,497,964 distinct source addresses. We observe that there are many small local cardinalities, but there are also source addresses involved in a large number of flows as depicted in Figure 1(a). In this figure, we have plotted the estimated local cardinalities as a function of the exact local cardinalities as well as the relative error ($\pm 2\%$). These experimental data show that the value $m = 4096$ yields very good results with an error smaller than $\pm 2\%$. Figure 1(b) illustrates small local cardinalities for $m = 4096$.

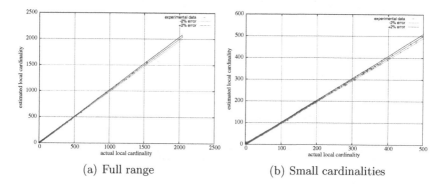

(a) Full range                    (b) Small cardinalities

**Fig. 1.** Actual vs. estimated local cardinalities for m=4096

Our algorithm works online, using constant small memory, so we expect to find real network applications like tracking port scans or spread of worms.

# References

1. Flajolet, P., Martin, G.N.: Probabilistic counting. In: Proceedings of the 24th Annual Symposium on Foundations of Computer Science (1983)
2. Durand, M., Flajolet, P.: Loglog counting of large cardinalities. In: Proceedings of the 11th Annual European Symposium on Algorithms (September 2003)
3. Whang, K.Y., Vander-Zanden, B.T., Taylor, H.M.: A linear-time probabilistic counting algorithm for database applications. In: IEEE transaction of Database Systems (June 1990)
4. Estan, C., Varghese, G.: New directions in traffic measurement and accounting: focusing on the elephants, ignoring the mice. In: Proceedings of ACM Transactions on Database Systems (August 2003)
5. Venkataraman, S., Song, D., Gibbons, P.B., Blum, A.: New streaming algorithms for fast detection of superspreaders. In: Proceedings of the 12th Annual Network & Distributed System Security Symposium (February 2005)
6. Zhao, Q., Kumar, A., Xu, J.: Joint data streaming and sampling techniques for detection of super sources and destinations. In: Proceedings of ACM Internet Measurement Conference (October 2005)
7. Charikar, M., Chen, K., Farach-Colton, M.: Finding frequent items in data streams. In: Widmayer, P., Triguero, F., Morales, R., Hennessy, M., Eidenbenz, S., Conejo, R. (eds.) ICALP 2002. LNCS, vol. 2380, Springer, Heidelberg (2002)
8. Introduction to Cisco IOS NetFlow. http://www.cisco.com/application/pdf/en/us/guest/products/ps6601/c1244/cdccont_0900aecd80406232.pdf

# Harnessing Models for Policy Conflict Analysis

Steven Davy and Brendan Jennings

Telecommunications Software & Systems Group,
Waterford Institute of Technology, Cork Road, Waterford, Ireland
{sdavy,bjennings}@tssg.org

**Abstract.** Policy conflict analysis processes based solely on the examination of policy language constructs can not readily discern the semantics associated with the managed system for which the policies are being defined. However, by developing analysis processes that can link the constructs of a policy language to the entities of an information model, we can harness knowledge relating to relationships and associations, constraint information, behavioural specifications codified by finite state machines, and extensive semantic information expressed via ontologies to provide powerful policy analysis processes.

## 1 Research Problem

Existing approaches to policy conflict detection are primarily concerned with analysing the information contained within individual policies defined for a specific managed system. However, this approach, in general, does not take into account application specific semantics. This semantic information can be represented using information models and ontologies relating to a specific managed system. By tightly coupling a policy language to a rich information model policy conflict analysis processes can begin to harness this information and use it to detect potential policy conflicts, in particular application specific conflicts.

Much research on policy conflict detection has dealt with domain independent policy conflict, which is concerned with the modality of policies, most notably by Lupu and Sloman in [1]. Dunlop et al. [2] detect possible occurrences of domain independent conflict between the modality of policies; taking into account the detection of conflict based on overlapping events to predict runtime conflict. This PhD programme is concerned not only with conflict analysis for domain independent conflict but also analysis for application specific conflict. Bandara et al. [3] propose a policy conflict analysis approach for domain independent and application specific conflicts. However, their method of application specific conflict detection is based on constraints only and the policy language is not tied directly to an explicit information model. Instead, they translate the policies into a logic program based on event calculus, and examine this to detect conflict.

Application specific conflicts that arise solely due to the behaviour of the managed system have been examined in [4, 5], where the implicit behaviour is how IP packets are processed by network interfaces for both firewalls and IPsec encapsulation and conflict is detected through examination of the individual IP rules by dedicated algorithms. In [6] Chomicki et al. describe the use of action-constraints over policy

A.K. Bandara and M. Burgess (Eds.): AIMS 2007, LNCS 4543, pp. 176–179, 2007.

actions to explicitly detect occurrences of conflicting actions at runtime. Their approach focuses on action cancellation and event cancellation where the actions are ordered by priority within a constraint, so that lower priority actions are prevented from being executed. This work was further extended by Bertino et al. [7], who present methods of incorporating user specified preferences for prioritisation of conflicting actions. However, this approach relies on the explicitly relating policy actions together; in contrast, we propose to automate the creation of these relationships by leveraging the information model.

The challenge is to develop algorithms and processes that take full advantage of this source of rich information to aid in the discovery and detection of conflicting policies. Four approaches will be taken in this work, where they can be used exclusively or in combination with each other to achieve the desired goal. However all algorithms developed will fit into an overarching generic process detailing the phases of policy analysis.

## 2  Approach

In order to tightly couple a policy language to an information model, we developed a process that enables the generation of an integrated suite of languages and tools for policy specification, analysis and deployment [8]. Basing the process on MDA (Model Driven Architecture), the information model described in UML formed the starting point for generating the policy language and related analysis tools. The tools generated can query over both the policy language, and information model thus

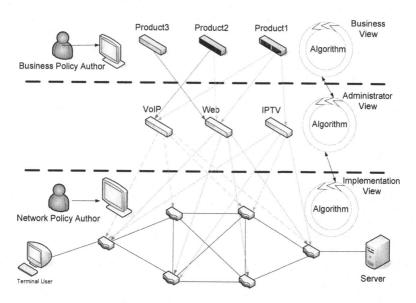

**Fig. 1.** Policy Refinement and Analysis

enhancing policy specification, analysis and deployment. We believe that the refinement of policies must be closely aligned with the conflict analysis of policies.

The scenario our policies are based on details the provision of various internet service products to subscribing customers [8]. There are three views of the managed system: the business view, the administrator view and the implementation view. As illustrated in Figure 1 policies at the business view are transformed to policies at the implementation view. The following lists various ways in which the information model can be harnessed to provide effective policy analysis:

- *Association and Relationships*
  A customer referenced in a policy specification can be stored as an identifier within a database, where we can access the database using the identifier to get information about the customer. However this information will not describe the customer's relationship to other entities in the system. For example, an association between classes in an information model can indicate that a customer can be associated with a set of purchased products. This information can then be used to ascertain if a given customer is related to a given product. A conflict may arise when the result of a policy causes the deactivation of a product at the implementation view, where this conflicts with the provision of that product to a customer at the business view. An approach based exclusively on analysing the constructs of the policy language may not be able to explicitly make the connection between implementation view policies, and business view policies.

- *Model Constraints*
  Another method of leveraging the information model is to analyse constraints defined over the properties of modelled elements and associations, so that we can detect if these constraint are breached by deploying a policy. For example, a constraint over the associations between ethernet interfaces in the information model can specify that the bandwidth of provisioned services that use these interfaces be limited to 80% of link capacity. By making this constraint available to the policy analysis component, we can detect a constraint breach, and thus a policy conflict when an existing customer upgrades their policy and subsequently too much bandwidth is provisioned on the associated ethernet interfaces. In [9] we demonstrated that by examining information model based constraints, that specific form of policy conflict can be prevented by further refining the specific policies to only be applicable in cases where constraints are never breached.

- *Ontologies*
  An information model ontology provides richer semantics than can be achieved with associations, and constraints. Ontologies can represent relationships between concepts, and individuals, and provides reasoning capabilities over these. When the information model is enhanced with ontological concepts, more in-depth restrictions on policy can be enforced and reasoned over for the purpose of policy analysis. For example, a high priority voice service may be assigned a PHB (per hop behaviour) of AF31 (assured forwarding), however in case this service cannot be classed as AF31 due to network restrictions we can class it to an "equivalent class" such as AF32, and re-deploy the policy. Relationships as equivalence and disjoint can be easily represented in an ontology, but not in a UML based information model. In [8], we describe how to build a base system ontology that can be enhanced to describe more extensive system semantics.

- *Finite State Machines*
  Finite state machines (FSMs) are used to describe the behaviour of an entity using input events to states causing state transitions. Using FSMs we can associate behaviour to managed entities. Future research will investigate how to best take advantage of FSMs to detect occurrences of unwanted behaviour. For example, as policy is being deployed it affects the relevant states of managed entities; the enumeration of state across the system is a snapshot of current behaviour. Since we know from the FSMs the potential next states we can devise algorithms to discover combinations of unwanted states.

## 3  Future Work

The usefulness of combining the above mentioned approaches to exploit information models of a managed system will be investigated, specifically combining finite state machines with ontologies. One aim is to introduce a tiered FSM where lower levels of the machine describe the behaviour of individual managed entities and higher levels of the machine describe the interaction of the system as a whole. Therefore mis-behaviour at the lower levels due to mis-configuration or policy conflict will propagate to upper levels, and the relevant policies can be flagged for analysis.

## References

1. Lupu, E.C., Sloman, M.: Conflict in Policy Based Distributed Systems Management. IEEE Transactions on Software Engineering 25(6), 852–869 (1999)
2. Dunlop, N., Indulska, J., Raymond, K.: Dynamic Conflict Detection in Policy-Based Management Systems, In: Enterprise Distributed Object Computing Conference, pp. 15–26 (2002)
3. Bandara, A.K., Lupu, E.C., Russo, A.: Using Event Calculus to formalize policy specification and analysis. In: 4th IEEE Workshop on Policies for Distributed Systems and Networks (2003)
4. Cholvy, L., Cuppens, F.: Analyzing Consistency of Security Policies. IEEE Symposium on Security and Privacy, pp. 103–112 (1997)
5. Bandara, A.K., Kakas, A., Lupu, E.C., Russo, A.: Using Argumentation Logic for Firewall Policy Specification and Analysis. In: State, R., van der Meer, S., O'Sullivan, D., Pfeifer, T. (eds.) DSOM 2006. LNCS, vol. 4269, pp. 185–196. Springer, Heidelberg (2006)
6. Chomicki, J., Lobo, J., Naqvi, S.: Conflict Resolution Using Logic Programming. IEEE Trans. Knowl. Data Eng. 15(1), 244–249 (2003)
7. Bertino, E., Mileo, A., Provetti, A.: PDL with Preferences. In: 6th IEEE International Workshop on Policies for Distributed Systems and Networks (POLICY 2005), pp. 213–222 (2005)
8. Barrett, K., Davy, S., Jennings, B., van der Meer, S., Strassner, J.: Model Based Generation of Integrated Suites of Languages and Tools for Policy Specification, Analysis and Deployment, submitted to IEEE Workshop on Policies for Distributed Systems and Networks (2007)
9. Davy, S., Jennings, B., Strassner, J.: Policy Conflict Prevention via Model-driven Policy Refinement. In: Proc 17th IFIP/IEEE Distributed Systems: Operations and Management (DSOM), pp. 209–220 (2006)

# Distributed End-to-End QoS Contract Negotiation

Hélia Pouyllau and Stefan Haar

IRISA/INRIA, Campus de Beaulieu F-35042 Rennes cedex, France

## 1 Negotiation for X-Domain Provisioning

The Internet is based on an X-Domain topology: interconnected domains are managed by independent actors (Fig.1). Deploying critical services (e.g. VPN, video-conference etc.) over such a topology requires to be able to guarantee *end-to-end QoS*. For this, and to guarantee privacy, *Service Level Agreements (SLAs)*, also called *QoS contracts*, are committed pairwise between domains. While local QoS control issues *inside* on each participating domain can be considered solved [4], open problems persist in the field of end-to-end QoS provisioning and monitoring for *multi-domain services*. The key factors to be taken into account are the heterogeneity, independence and privacy requirements of the individual domains.

Before establishing a service, a *negotiation* has to occur: it consists in selecting a chain of pair-wise commitments that satisfies the end-to-end QoS requirements, given that global QoS is subject to cumulation effects: for instance, delays on each domain *sum up* along a path. We use the term of *QoS budget* (borrowed from [8]) to reflect how the customer's tolerance (w.r.t to end-to-end delay, jitter, etc.) is *consumed* by the actual services on each component, leaving a reduced margin for the rest of the chain. Once a contract chain is selected by the negotiation, QoS contracts are *reserved* and the service is established. Each domain *monitors* the QoS contract agreed on with its neighbor in the path, and also its local QoS provisioning. If the domain observes repeated contract violations by its neighbor, it can activate a *re-negotiation* process to select another partner in the path and thus changing the sub-path of the contract chain.

So, the problem addressed is to satisfy a QoS budget by a contract chain taking into account *i*) cumulative effect of QoS parameters; *ii*) domain independence and contract privacy, which forbid any centralized solution, and *iii*) a global cost function; this cost function can capture different optimization criteria (e.g. the sum of contract prices). We address different cost optimization problems under QoS budget constraints. They have been identified as Integer Linear Programming (ILP) problems and reduce to the general assignment problem, which is NP-Hard [6]. If they can be solved using centralized ILP techniques in principle, domain independence and contract privacy constrain us to design *fully distributed* solutions based on the *Dynamic Programming* (DP) principles. We develop also self-repairing mechanisms in case of negotiation failures and contract violations (re-negotiation).

A.K. Bandara and M. Burgess (Eds.): AIMS 2007, LNCS 4543, pp. 180–183, 2007.

**Intra-domain assumptions.** Although the internal architecture of the participating domains may be different (e.g. DiffServ, ATM), we assume a set of QoS classes is defined by each domain w.r.t. common service level, types, and ressource requirements. A QoS class aggregates several QoS properties (e.g. delay, bandwidth etc.). This QoS class configuration problem is considered solved [4,7]; so, we consider that for each domain, the available QoS classes are known. We proposed a Web Service architecture in [5,1] for intra-domain service management in a heterogeneous environment.

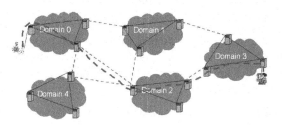

**Fig. 1.** X-domain provisioning

**X-domain provisioning.** Fig. 1 represents communication links between domains. We consider provisioning of X-domain services along routes established by a BGP-like protocol and available in the local routing tables on each domain: $i)$ for each pair (source, target) a route is ranked (primary, secondary etc.) using shortest path techniques; $ii)$ a domain knows only the next neighbors on each such route given by the target domain, but no full path. In the present stage, our negotiation procedure explore the primary path to establish a contract chain, see Fig. 1: when end-users of a domain $d^0$ want to access, e.g. by video-conference, domain $d^N$, they select a level of QoS. Negotiation finds, using DP, a distribution of this initial QoS budget, over all domains, from $d^1$ (in contract with $d^0$) to $d^N$ (in contract with $d^{N-1}$), and selects the "cheapest" chain of contracts that is feasible within this budget. Contracts are agreed on between adjacent domains, in a *nested* way: each domain $i$ is responsible for the composed contract that commits $i$ and all domains $i+1, ..., N$ until the target $N$.

### 1.1   Negotiation Problems

**Single request negotiation.** The first step consists in the negotiation of an individual service request crossing several domains, that is in selecting the optimal path of QoS contracts between a source and a target such that the cumulative QoS satisfies the QoS budget along the path of domains. Our solution uses a distributed algorithm, presented in [3], based on *DP*, whose sub-problem decomposition naturally fits to this problem.

**Multi-request negotiation.** Consider now the satisfaction of *several* QoS budget requests. Assume service $s_1$, corresponding to request $r_1$, is running according to commitments from a previous negotiation, and that another request $r_2$ (corresponding to a service $s_2$) arrives, whose service path would cross $s_1$'s path at domain $d^i$. If $s_1$ creates a heavy load on domain $d^i$, it may become impossible to satisfy $r_2$. Rebalancing the QoS contracts along $s_1$'s path may reduce the load on domain $d^i$, allowing it to accept $s_2$. Thus, we have to take local resource capacity constraints of the individual domains into account. We solve this optimization problem using a distributed *Forward-Backward DP* [2] algorithm: it breaks the problem into local ones solvable by ILP methods. Note that *concurrent* contract rebalancing in a chain has to be controlled; thus we design a token protocol to allow only one modification per chain at any time. However, such a protocol could be subject to *distributed deadlock* in case of cycles; its prevention is the subject of future work.

**Self-repair mechanism, negotiation failure.** The negotiation process may fail if all cumulative budgets found along the intended chain of contracts exceed the requested budget. The domain detecting the failure launches the negotiation process on an alternative route, i.e. secondary, tertiary etc in the routing table.

**Self-repair mechanism, re-negotiation.** Moreover, the monitoring infrastructure may detect runtime violation of some middle-to-end contracts. If local compensation is impossible, self-repair can be achieved by switching to an *alternative* middle-to-end chain. For this, a *re-negotiation* process is launched: alternative routes are explored in order, until a new middle-to-end chain is found; only then is the old chain canceled.

**Negotiation in a general graph.** In the previous problem, the route explored to find contract chains is the primary route in routing tables. Since nothing guarantees the best QoS is found on the shortest path, we currently aim instead of finding the optimal QoS path exploring all possible routes, i.e. at *end-to-end QoS routing*.

## 1.2   Results and Future Work

We have implemented the DP solution for the single and multi-request problems using Web Services (WS) technology, thus ensuring interoperability [1]. Fig. 2 illustrates performances of the Forward-Backward algorithm implemented in WS. The benchmark consists in evaluating a negotiation request crossing 4 domains. The Y axis represents negotiation time in ms, the X axis the number of contracts per domain. Execution time was tested for 2, 4, 6 and 8 SLOs (note that the number of SLOs is the dimensionality of budget and contract vectors). The second diagram shows results for fewer than 12 contracts per domain; each request takes less than 3 seconds, which is a good time in a realistic context. We are also currently developing a benchmark (implemented in Matlab) in order to evaluate performances of different optimization algorithms, centralized and distributed. The first results indicate the performances of our distributed algorithms are comparable to (and sometimes better than) the centralized ones. Besides enriching the benchmark, we plan to test our algorithms on the following extensions:

**Negotiation of "pipes".** Consider a pair of domains for which many X-domains are requested. It is, rather than negotiating individual requests one

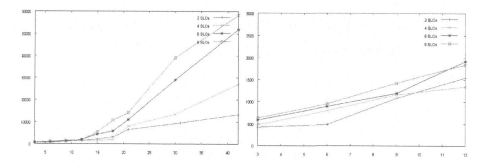

**Fig. 2.** Performances for a request crossing 4 domains

by one and in real time, to negotiate offline a *pipe*, i.e. a *set* of contract chains together with a mechanism that allocates chains to incoming requests. This selection can then implement a policy which balances the load between chains of the pipe. In this context, load-balancing is of greater importance than performance of the negotiation process.

**Negotiation in a large-scale system.** Our negotiation process is adapted to a set of selected domains known to be cooperative; in a more realistic, large-scale open-world setting we will have, in addition, requests from outside the cooperative world that perturb our system; thus several negotiation processes have to be integrated: *i*) solving consumption and budget constraints for non-cooperative domain requests, and *ii*) selecting optimized contract chains for cooperative domain requests.

# References

1. Aghasaryan, A., Piekarec, S., Pouyllau, H., Haar, S., Fabre, E., Ciarletta, L., Mbarek, N., Moreau, E.: Multi-domain self aware management: Negotiation and monitoring. In: IEEE International Conference on Telecommunications (2006)
2. Baum, L.E.: An inequality and associated maximization technique in statistical estimation for probabilistic functions of Markov processes. In: Inequalities III (1972)
3. Pouyllau, H., Ciarletta, L., Aghasaryan, A., Haar, S.: X-domain QoS budget negotiation using dynamic programming. In: IEEE Advanced International Conference on Telecommunications (2006)
4. Lima, S., Carvalho, P., Freitas, V.: Self-adaptive distributed management of QoS and SLSs in multiservice networks. In: IEEE/IFIP International Symposium on Integrated Network Management (2005)
5. Self-Aware ManagemeNt (SWAN) Research project. Decision number 035481 -. RNRT (2006), http://swan.elibel.tm.fr
6. Martello, S., Toth, P.: Knapsack problems: algorithms and computer implementations. John Wiley & Sons, Inc, New York (1990)
7. Nguyen, T.M.T., Boukhatem, N., Pujolle, G.: COPS-SLS usage for dynamic policy-based QoS management over heterogeneous IP networks. IEEE Network (2003)
8. TIPHON project. Part3: Signalling and Control of end-to-end QoS. ETSI (2002)

# Distributed and Heuristic Policy-Based Resource Management System for Large-Scale Grids

Edgar Magaña and Joan Serrat

Universitat Politècnica de Catalunya
Jordi Girona 1-3, Barcelona, Spain
{emagana,serrat}@nmg.upc.edu

**Abstract.** This paper presents a distributed and heuristic policy-based system for resource management in large-scale Grids. This approach involves three phases: resource discovery, scheduling and allocation. The resource discovery phase is supported by the SNMP-based Balanced Load Monitoring Agents for Resource Scheduling (SBLOMARS). In this approach, network and computational resources are monitored by autonomous monitoring agents, offering a pure decentralized monitoring system. The resource scheduling phase is supported by the Balanced Load Multi-Constrained Resource Scheduler (BLOMERS). It is a heuristic resource scheduler, which includes an implementation of a Genetic Algorithm (GA), as an alternative to solve the inherent NP-hard problem for resource scheduling in large-scale Grids. Allocation phase is supported by means of a Policy-based Grid Management Architecture (PbGMA). This architecture integrates different sources of service necessities such as requirements demanded by customers, applications requirements and network conditions. It interfaces with Globus middleware to allocate services into the selected resources with certain levels of QoS.

## 1 Introduction – The Research Problem

Grid Computing is defined as a heterogeneous, distributed and shared system where applications are solved in dynamic, multi-institutional virtual organizations (VOs). This key concept involves the inherent ability to negotiate resource-sharing arrangements among a set of participating parties (providers and costumers) and then to use the resulting resource pool for some purpose. Basically, Grids should integrate and coordinate resources and users that live within different control domains. Besides, it is built from multi-purpose protocols and interfaces that address such fundamental issues as scheduling, security, resource discovery, and resource allocation. Finally, Grid allows its constituent resources to be used in a coordinated fashion to deliver various qualities of service, relating for example to response time, throughput, availability, and security, and/or co-allocation of multiple resource types to meet complex user demands, so that the utility of the combined system is significantly greater than that of the sum of its parts.

Large-scale Grids are formed by thousands of nodes sharing multiples kind of resources (computational, network, applications, instruments, etc) and therefore, the total amount of shared resources become millions of individual entities that most be adequately integrated and coordinated for solving multi-disciplinarian problems. In

A.K. Bandara and M. Burgess (Eds.): AIMS 2007, LNCS 4543, pp. 184–187, 2007.

this dynamic, heterogeneous and geographically dispersed environment, Resource Management (RM) is regarded as a vital component of the Grid Infrastructure. The ability to coordinate efficiently and share multiple kinds of resources in these systems introduces inherent challenging management problems. We would like to highlight the following ones: Grid Resource Management Systems must fulfill at least three sources of requirements which are respectively requirements demanded by customers, applications requirements and network conditions. Resource Management process should be reliable, efficient and minimal time consuming as well as imperceptible for its hosting nodes. Finally, these systems must offer certain level of Quality of Service per application to manage. These factors make highly challenging the resource management process, mainly when the amount of entities to manage is quite significant, resources appear and disappear without any control and there is not a determinate patter of resource availability, as normally happen in large-scale Grids.

## 2  Thesis Objectives

We propose an alternative solution to the state of the art in terms of Grid Resource Management, by means of splitting and distributing the resource management process in three main phases. The first one is Resource Discovery, which generates a list of potential resources. The second one is Resource Selection, which searches and matches job's requirements with resources availability. The last one is Job Allocation, which includes files staging and cleanup. We face the Resource Discovery phase by introducing our SBLOMARS architecture that stands for SNMP-based Balanced Load Monitoring Agents for Resource Scheduling. It is a set of autonomous, distributed and SNMP-based monitoring agents, which are in charge of to generate real-time and statistical resource availability information for every resource and entity forming the Grid. So far, SBLOMARS is able to monitor processor, memory, network (interface level), memory, storage, applications and network (end-to-end networking traffic) for different architectures such Unix-based systems, Solaris, Microsoft-based and even Macintosh systems. It is also self-extensible to multi-processor platforms as well as storage cluster systems. Its design is based on SNMP technology to improve the generality and heterogeneity problem and also based on autonomous distributed agents to improve the scalability problem in large-scale Grids.

The Resource Selection phase searches and matches job's requirements with resource availability. In other words, it involves determining which resources are the best ones for executing a specific job, application, service, etc. Our approach covers this phase by introducing the Balanced Load Multi-Constrain Resource Scheduler (BLOMERS). This scheduler makes use of the real-time and statistical resource availability information generated by SBLOMARS monitoring agents. BLOMERS implements a heuristic approach in order to improve the scalability problem and by means of statistical resource availability information, it schedules in a network and resource load-balanced way.

Jobs allocation phase is solved by a Policy-based Grid Management Architecture (PbGMA) [1]. We have extended the dynamic components and interfaces (Policy Decision Point – PDP and Policy Enforcement Point - PEP) of this approach to be compatible with Globus Architecture to allocate Grid Services along of large-scale

Grid Infrastructures. This architecture deals with three different sources of resource requirements. The users QoS necessities, resource provider's availability (i.e. amount of resources free to execute new services) and services specifications according to Open Grid Services Architecture (OGSA).

## 3 Thesis Contributions

SBLOMARS monitoring agents [2] consist in a set of distribute resource monitoring agents which are constantly capturing end-to-end network and computational resources performance. SBLOMARS improves the scalability problem by the distribution of the monitoring system into a set of sub-monitoring instances which are specific per each kind of computational resource to monitor. This approach reaches a high level of generality by means of the integration of Simple Network Management Protocol (SNMP) and thus, it offers a wide ability to handle heterogeneous operating platforms. SBLOMARS has been designed as a full independent and autonomic system. It could be re-configured by itself based on the performance load in their hosting nodes. SBLOMARS also introduces the concept of vectorial software structures, which are used to monitor from simple personal computers to complex multiprocessor systems or clusters with multiple hard disk partitions. These couple of features makes our approach novel compare with similar monitoring systems such as Ganglia [4]. In contrast to current monitoring approaches, SBLOMARS integrates an end-to-end network-level monitoring technology. The CISCO IOS® IP Service Level Agreements allows users to monitor end-to-end network-level performance between routers or from either remote IP network device.

BLOMERS scheduler [3] deals with several conditions. Basically, it selects a set of candidates' resources from a poll, keeping individual resource performance comparatively balanced in all nodes of the Grid. This condition has been added in order to satisfy the computational resource load balancing. In BLOMERS approach, we propose to find a sub-optimal solution to the problem of scheduling computational resources. It is based on a Genetic Algorithm (GA), in charge of resource selection, as a part of the resource manager system. So far, BLOMERS is already implemented and running in a local test-bed. It has been compared from quantitative and qualitative points of view in the following paper [3]. We will also execute some schedules in the Grid5000 test-bed as a complementary activity for this research.

The PbGMA [1] was initially designed for active networks but we have extended its essential components to be functional for Grids. This architecture is characterized by a reliable and autonomous deployment, activation and management of Grid Services. This architecture follows the implied conditions by the Open Grid Services Architecture standard. Although applicable to any user profiles, our system is essentially intended for non-massive resource owners accessing large amounts of computing, software, memory and storage resources. Unlike similar architectures, it is able to manage service requirements demanded by users, providers and services themselves. This architecture is also able to manage computational resources in order to fulfill QoS requirements, based on a balanced scheduling of resources exploitation. It is flexible by extending itself the management components and policies interpreters needed to control multiple infrastructures regardless operative platform or network technology.

# 4 Conclusions and Future Work

We have presented SBLOMARS, an open source monitoring approach, whose distinguishing aspect is that it is a full autonomic and distributed monitoring system for computational resource availability and end-to-end network performance in large-scale Grids. This monitored information is used by BLOMERS, which based on a genetic algorithm, produces faster scheduling times without compromising the system scalability and getting resource load balanced all over the Grid. Both systems are embedded into a PbGMA, which close the loop for Grid Services management. We have individually tested, the monitoring agents and the heuristic resource scheduling algorithm, obtaining very promising results. We have shown that the implemented algorithm performs better than a purely random selection mechanism and we expect that the ongoing work will show soon the comparison results with other scheduling approaches [3]. We have performed several evaluation tests to SBLOMARS monitoring agents. On one hand, we have demonstrated that our distributed agents are not consuming significant computational resources in their hosting nodes. On the other hand, we have collected resource availability information from several computer systems with Linux, Solaris and Windows platforms for a twenty-four hours period. At the end of the day, SBLOMARS agents keep running and working perfectly with similar performance values such those that have been shown in this paper [2].

The novelty and advantages in our approach are obtained by the synergy of these systems. We have improved machine utilization, resource scheduling time and user satisfaction. The integration of these three systems would facilitate resource owners the provisioning of facilities for turnaround-assured work. Currently, we are executing performance evaluations in real, geographically distributed test-beds, such as Grid5000 [5]. We are also including network delays when our genetic algorithm generates new populations (resource candidates) to allocate requested Grid Services.

## Acknowledgments

This paper is supported by the IST-EMANICS Network of Excellence (#26854). It is also supported by the Ministerio de Educación y Ciencia project TSI2005-06413.

## References

1. Magaña, E., Lefevre, L., Serrat. J.: Autonomic Management Architecture for Flexible Grid Services Deployment Based on Policies. ARCS'07, Zurich, Switzerland (2007)
2. Magaña, E., Lefevre, L., Serrat, J.: SBLOMARS: SNMP-based Balanced Load Monitoring Agents for Resource Scheduling in Large-scale Grids. In: The 8th IEEE/ACM Conference in Grid Computing, Austin, Texas, USA. (Submitted) (September 19-21st 2007)
3. Magaña, E., Lefevre, L., Serrat, J.: BLOMERS: Balanced Load Multi-Constrained Resource Scheduler. ICNS 2007. Athens, Greece. (June 19-25th, 2007)
4. Massie, M., Chun, B., Culler, D.: The Ganglia Distributed Monitoring System: Design, Implementation, and Experience. Parallel Computing, vol. 30(7), (July 2004)
5. The Grid'5000 Web page: https://www.grid5000.fr/

# Risk Based Authorisation for Mobile Ad Hoc Networks

Nilufer Tuptuk and Emil Lupu

Department of Computing, Imperial College, 180 Queen's Gate, London SW7 2AZ, UK
{nt102,e.c.lupu}@doc.ic.ac.uk

**Abstract.** Mobile ad hoc networks (MANETs) do not share the properties of traditional wired networks, as mobile nodes are more vulnerable to security attacks. Detection of selfish, malicious or faulty nodes presents security challenges that are not encountered traditionally in wired networks. The nodes in the network need to identify, and take the necessary security measures to protect their resources against these malicious nodes. We propose a risk-based authorisation model to help build ad-hoc trust relationships, capturing the dynamic behaviour of the entities with time, and ensuring the sharing of trust information through recommendations.

**Keywords:** Authorisation, Trust, Mobile Ad Hoc Network, and Bayesian Belief Networks.

## 1 Introduction

MANETs are more vulnerable to intrusions than traditional wired networks. Wired networks are able to perform monitoring for malicious traffic at the perimeter, but this is harder to achieve with spontaneous networks such as MANETs as there is no single point for collecting audit data for the entire network.

Rescue scenarios in disaster areas (e.g. flood, hurricanes, or large scale industrial incidents) where the infrastructure is (partially) destroyed are typical usage scenarios for MANETs. The primary task of a rescue network may involve setting up a response task force to evacuate the inhabitants, provide medical help, establish shelters, control damage as well as provide information to the public and the media. Entities in the rescue network may involve members from local and national organisations such as the army, Red Cross, police, fire, emergency management advisors and volunteer rescue teams. Each of these entities controls how their resources are shared according to their own internal policies. Members of the network need to protect their resources from unauthorised entities. For example members of the army and the police may communicate confidential information they do not want to share with other members, such as the media. The aim of this research is to create a decentralised risk-based authorisation model, which uses risk to determine the level of trust needed to access the resources, without the need for pre-configured roles and permissions. Based on the contextual environment, the tolerated risk may be increased or relaxed.

A.K. Bandara and M. Burgess (Eds.): AIMS 2007, LNCS 4543, pp. 188–191, 2007.

## 1.1  Related Work

Similar frameworks providing trust based access control are presented in [2], [3] and [4]. However, these models rely on static access control rules and require an administrator to manage changes, as they do not automatically identify and isolate the misbehaving nodes based on their past behaviour. Recent trust and reputation based models [6] make use of centralised servers to provide reputations, which is not possible in MANETs as there may not always be access to these servers. Although there is ongoing work in areas such as entity authentication, key distribution and secure routing for MANETs, few studies aim to realise a self-evolving risk-based authorisation that does not rely on being entirely pre-configured or on manual adaptation and centralised management.

## 2  Risk Based Authorisation Model

Authorisation decisions in mobile ad-hoc network depend on pre-authorisation checks (e.g. authentication), the environment, and the behaviour history of the nodes. The environment influences the authorisation decision. In situations such as rescue operations, nodes may be willing to provide their resources and cooperate with other nodes, as the benefit may be high. As illustrated in the Fig. 1 both *Authentication Trust* and *Reliability Trust* are used to make the authorisation decisions. Authentication is a pre-condition for authorisation decision. Authentication tokens (such as attributes, memberships) need to be verified. However in MANETs nodes may not have access to all the information they needed in order to verify them such as online certificate revocation lists. Thus, *Authentication Trust $(AT_{tv})$* indicates the confidence in the authentication established. In contrast, *Reliability Trust $(RT_{tv})$* refers to trust evaluated based on the past behaviour of the nodes. The trust value that a node computes for another node is based on both direct past experience (direct trust), or recommendations obtained from trusted peers (indirect trust).

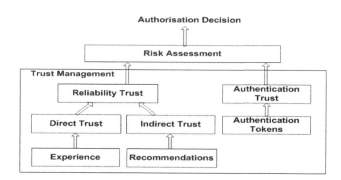

**Fig. 1.** Implementation of Risk Based Authorisation System

Risk is becoming an effective tool used for decision-making in information security [5]. We consider risk as the possible loss due to security violations caused by misbehaving nodes. We make use of the risk related to a specific context to determine the minimum trust level that nodes need to have to permit access. For authorisation to take place both $AT_{tv}$ and $RT_{tv}$ need to exceed the risk threshold ($R_t$) where $R_t$ is computed based on the node's context. Both the trust values ($AT_{tv}$ and $RT_{tv}$) and the risk threshold ($R_t$) are expressed as a probability value between [0,1]. The risk threshold is dynamic and depends on the current context. For example when a node goes into an emergency situation, such as a rescue scenario it could reduce its thresholds. For now, we assume that the function evaluating the risk threshold as a function of the context is given.

## 2.1  Authentication Trust

We propose using Bayesian Belief Networks (BBN) to determine authentication trust by explicitly representing the conditional dependencies between different variables. Traditional rule-based systems are not as flexible as BBN when reasoning under uncertainty as the dependencies between variables may change with the new knowledge. BBNs provide effective decision-support for problems involving uncertainty and probabilistic reasoning. After training the BBN, the network can perform probabilistic inference. Fig. 2 depicts a possible set of dependencies to determine the authentication trust for an attribute certificate. Trust in an authentication token may depend on the confidence in validating token attributes, third parties' trust (general confidence of the public on the authentication protocol), and the trust in the issuer of the token. The trust in the issuer depends on the confidence (i.e., the belief) that the issuer has handled the pre-authentication procedures adequately before issuing the token, and their reputation.

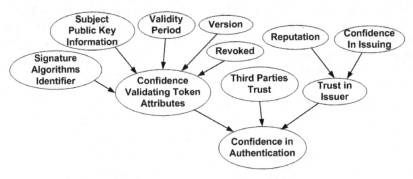

**Fig. 2.** Computing Authentication Trust using Bayesian Belief Network

## 2.2  Reliability Trust

Reliability trust is defined based on direct experience and recommendations. Each node monitors the behaviour of other nodes by analysing the data found in requests and logs. If for example, a node is sending too many requests in a given time $t$, then the behaviour may be considered malicious. There are three types of messages to share information between nodes:

1. *Recommendation Request (RequestID, RequesterID, NodeID)* can be used by a node *(RequesterID)* to request trust information about another node *(NodeID)*.
2. *Recommendation Reply (RequestID, RecommenderID, TrustValue)* allows the node to reply to the *Recommendation Request*. A trusted peer needs to have a certain level of trust to recommend. Otherwise, their recommendations are ignored.
3. *Recommendation Alert (RecommenderID, NodeID, TrustValue)* is used when a node detects first hand misbehaviour, and alerts other nodes. How trustworthy the alert is based on the source *(RecommenderID)* of the alert.

We are proposing using a Bayesian models to combine trust information, experience and recommendations. The updated (posterior) trust value (based on experience and recommendation) is computed by combining the previous (priori) trust value with the new value. Beliefs about the variables can be specified using experience counts, and the impact of prior knowledge can be faded away using fading factors. In the past beta density functions were used to predict the trust probabilities in the interval 0-1. Based on these approaches we are investigating both binomial and multinomial probability distribution functions to combine result of direct trust with indirect trust, to predict the trustworthiness of the entities, and to cope with changes in a principled way.

## 3  Conclusion and Future Work

We have proposed the basic concepts towards providing a risk-based authorisation model for MANET environments to make access control decisions without relying on pre-configuration and centralised management. By capturing nodes behaviour and allowing trusted nodes to share information we can detect and isolate misbehaving nodes. Without risk-based authorisation, nodes will have to provide access to successfully authenticated regardless of the circumstances and their past behaviour. We are currently working on simulations and a prototype this model.

## References

1. Mui, L., et al.: Ratings in Distributed Systems: A Bayesian Approach. Workshop on Information Technologies and Systems (2001)
2. Cahill, V., et al.: Using Trust for Secure Collaboration in Uncertain Environments. IEEE Pervasive Computing (2003)
3. Blaze, M., Feigenbaum, J., Ioannidis, J., Keromytis, A.: The KeyNote trust-management system Version 2. Internet RFC 2704 (1999)
4. Josang, A., Ismail, R.: The Beta Reputation System. In: Proceedings of the 15th Bled Conference on Electronic Commerce (2002)
5. Gordon, L., Loeb, M.: The economics of information security investment, ACM Transactions on Information and System Security (2002)
6. Jøsang, A., Haller, J.: Dirichlet Reputation Systems. In: Proceedings of the Second International Conference on Availability, Reliability and Security (2007)

# Malware Models for Network and Service Management

Jérôme François, Radu State, and Olivier Festor

MADYNES - INRIA Lorraine, CNRS, Nancy, France
{jerome.francois,radu.state,olivier.festor}@loria.fr

**Abstract.** Different kinds of malware like the botnets and the worms are a main threat on Internet for the current and future. Their effectiveness to control systems is proved and we are investigating the malware mechanisms that can be adapted to get an efficient and scalable management plane. Our work consists in modelling malware based network management and assessing its performance.

## 1 Introduction

The network and service management is a major component in order to provide value added services. Due to the multiplication of services and the third-party management delegation, the management boundaries are not clear and the management operations are faced with several problems: more and more devices to manage, an hostile environment due to security appliances (firewalls or intrusion detection systems), the distance between the manager and the devices to manage... However the creators of malware faced the same problems and today the effectiveness of malware is well known. Our work is motivated by their results and we propose a malware based network management plane.

The section 2 will introduce the botnets and the worms. The section 3 presents the motivation of a management framework based on malware. A formal model will be presented in 4. A brief overview of related works is given in 5. Finally, we conclude and plan future works.

## 2 Malware Effectiveness

A botnet is a network of a compromised machines which are usually called zombies or bots, these machines wait for instructions from the master (the hacker) and perform operations on behalf of the latter. IRC networks are a well-known way to send a command on a channel to all the bots. We are very interesting in the botnets using IRC networks for three main reasons. Firstly, the exchange of commands is simple and multiple operations are possible (denial of service attacks or personal data retrieving). So an application can be easily adapted to use an IRC network. Secondly, IRC networks are very resilient [2]. Finally, the botnets have already proven their effectiveness. In [4] some statistics about botnets are presented showing that it is possible to control 400 000 bots.

A.K. Bandara and M. Burgess (Eds.): AIMS 2007, LNCS 4543, pp. 192–195, 2007.

The worms are a main threat for Internet due to the propagation speed [7] and their ability to bypass security equipments. The authors in [7] have shown that little worm can infect a large population 1 000 000 hosts in 2 generations. Moreover the worms are not limited to only propagate themselves. A hacker can lead computers thanks to the P2P network built by the slapper worm [1].

## 3    Malware Benefits

In [8], we propose a novel malware based management framework. We will focus on two kinds of malware introduced in the previous section. Our research is motivated by two main facts. Firstly, a huge number of hosts could be managed without specific and different configurations. Secondly, the management applications are various because the command or propagation mechanisms are totally unlinked with the applications.

However, even though there are a lot of studies about the power of botnets or worms we have to define a precise model to evaluate the efficiency of a malware management based and above all the scalability. There are some important questions to answer like: what is the probability to reach 90% of the hosts ? How much time is needed to have 99% of reached hosts with a probability of 0.99 ? Another aim is to optimize the malware communication scheme to have the best performances.

## 4    Botnet Model

In order to establish a mathematical botnet model, we have to model an IRC network. The servers where the clients are connected are organized as a spanning tree. In [6], the author considers a recursive random tree i.e. each node has a number and the nodes are linked successively to a previous node. In fact the node $j$ has the probability $\frac{1}{j-1}$ to be connected to a given node among nodes $1, 2, ..., j-1$. Indeed, the probability that the distance between node $i$ and node $j$ is $d$ with $i < j$ is:

$$P(i,j,d) = \frac{1}{j-1}[P(1,i,d-1) + P(2,i,d-1) + ... + P(j-1,i,d-1)]$$

We propose to extend this model by finding a formula to determine the probability to have a distance less or equal to $d$ between a given origin node $o$ and a set $N$ of other nodes between a total of $n$ nodes of the tree: $P(o,d,N,n)$. By summing the probabilities for the different sets, we have the global probability independent from $N$.

The formula is recursive. At the beginning we have to determine how many nodes of N we want to connect to the origin node directly (distance $= 1$). There are $|N|$ possibilities: $i \in [1, |N|]$. Then we have to choose the combination of these i nodes which is $CHOICE =< c_1, ..., c_i >\subseteq N$. $REMAINDER = N - CHOICE =< r_1, ..., r_p >$ represents the nodes to be connected directly or not at the next hop nodes previously chosen. So we define a permutation with repetitions of the elements of $SUITE < s1, .., sp >$ with $\forall k$, $s_k \in CHOICE$. The probability of having a node $c_j$ linked to the node $o$ is independant from the probability to have a subtree beginning by $c_j$ and containing all $r_k$ as $s_k = c_j$ within a distance decreased by one. Indeed, we obtain the following formula :

$$P(o, d, N, n) = \sum_{i=1..n \; et \; <c_1,...,c_i>} [\prod_{c_j=[c_1,c_i]} P_1(o, c_j) \times P(c_j, d-1, SET, n)]$$

with $SET = \{r_k\} \setminus s_k = c_j$ and $P_1(o, c_j)$ which is the probability to have the node $c_j$ linked to $o$.

In our case, we assume that a node is connected to a previous at random and thus:

$$P_1(o, c_j) = distribution\_function(o, c_i) = \frac{1}{max(o, c_i) - 1}$$

This description gives a clear idea of how we can compute the probabilities but the formula we used for our experiments is more complex and integrates the fact that a recursive tree implies an order in the node. For example it is impossible to have node 1 connected to node 3 and node 3 connected to node 2. Because we want precise probabilities, we need to have the probability for an exact set $N$ and not a set containing $N$

Figure 1(b) shows that we are able to determine the probability to reach a given number of nodes at a maximal given distance. For instance, we can see that the probability to reach three nodes at a distance less or equal to two is about 0.2. The node are the servers of the IRC network, so we can deduce from this value the probability to reach a certain number $b$ if there are randomly connected to server by multiplying this value by $\frac{b}{n}$. If we want to optimize the number of reached node, we can compare the probability with the different origin node as in 1(a).

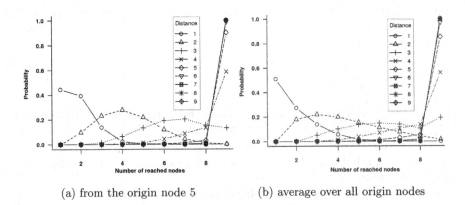

(a) from the origin node 5          (b) average over all origin nodes

**Fig. 1.** The probability to reach a certain number of nodes at a defined distance in tree with a total number of 10 nodes

# 5  Related Works

The classical management frameworks have shown their limits related to the scalability and several authors proposed solutions to deal with this problem. In [3] a decentralized management is proposed where a query is transformed into different subqueries and where the results are aggregated of each one. The idea to use malware for management was proposed in [5] where a worm patrols on different hosts to detect malfunctioning. However the framework is not modeled and the experiments were very limited. Multiple articles or books about what botnets or worms can do and how they are effective can be found in [2] and [7].

# 6  Conclusion and Future Works

The effectiveness of botnets and worms have been proven in the past. We are convinced that a benign usage can be obtained for addressing scalability in the network management plane. It implies to know exactly what we are able to do with them. Thus the model aims to prove the efficiency of this new framework. We attend to extend the model with more parameters and metrics related to the performance of the management plane. A second activity will consist in optimizing the management plane with respect to the previously mentioned metrics and evaluating if a botnet based management framework is possible or not. Finally a realistic testbed implementation will be performed.

**Acknowledgment.** This paper was supported in part by the EC IST-EMANICS Network of Excellence (#26854).

# References

1. Arce, I., Levy, E.: An analysis of the slapper worm. In: IEEE Security and Privacy vol. 1(1), pp. 82–87 (2003)
2. Cooke, E., Jahanian, F., Mcpherson, D.: The zombie roundup: Understanding, detecting, and disrupting botnets. pp. 39–44, (June 2005)
3. Lim, K.-S., Stadler, R.: Real-time views of network traffic using decentralized management. Integrated Network Management. In: 9th IFIP/IEEE International Symposium on (2005)
4. McLaughlin, L.: Bot software spreads, causes new worries. IEEE Distributed Systems Online, vol. 5(6) (2004)
5. Ohno, H., Shimizu, A.: Improved network management using nmw (network management worm) system. In: Proceedings of INET'95: Honolulu, Hawaii (1995)
6. Sachkov, V. N.: Probabilistic methods in combinatorial analysis, chapter 6 - Random Graphs and Random Mappings. Cambridge University Press (1997)
7. Staniford, S., Moore, D., Paxson, V., Weaver, N.: The top speed of flash worms. In: WORM '04: Proceedings of the 2004 ACM workshop on Rapid malcode, pp. 33–42. ACM Press, New York, USA (2004)
8. State, R., Festor, O.: Malware: a future framework for device, network and service management, 2006. In: Journal in Computer Virology, Springer vol. 3(1) pp. 51–60, (2007)

# A Survey of the High-Speed Self-learning Intrusion Detection Research Area

Anna Sperotto and Remco van de Meent

University of Twente, The Netherlands
{a.sperotto,r.vandemeent}@utwente.nl

**Abstract.** Intrusion detection for IP networks has been a research theme for a number of years already. One of the challenges is to keep up with the ever increasing Internet usage and network link speeds, as more and more data has to be scanned for intrusions. Another challenge is that it is hardly feasible to adapt the scanning configuration to new threats manually in a timely fashion, because of the possible rapid spread of new threats. This paper is the result of the first three months of a PhD research project in high speed, self-learning network intrusion detection systems. Here, we give an overview of the state of the art in this field, highlighting at the same time the major open issues.

## 1 Introduction

The continuously increasing number of users, as well as the growing popularity of online services, makes the Internet a common place for attacks and misuses. As a consequence, security in 'cyberspace' has become a high priority issue, to protect the end-users from malicious behavior and to provide a safer service. Network Intrusion Detection Systems (NIDSes) have become in the last years a useful way to monitor network traffic to detect signals of attacks. The spread of 1-10Gbps networks technology, the large amount of data and the increasing size of networks present new challenges to NIDS researchers, looking for adaptive and high speed solutions. This paper presents an overview of the state of the art in Intrusion Detection for high speed networks, with reference to the problem of adaptability and self-management. The paper is organized as follows: Section 2 and 3 describe the major trends in High Speed Networks IDSes and the adaptive approaches to the problem, respectively. Section 4, in the end, presents our conclusions and outlines some ideas for future work.

## 2 State of the Art in High Speed NIDSes

Quickly and thoroughly detecting malicious activity in a network has always been a major aim of NIDSes. This is still true now that gigabit networks are commonly used, with backbone networks of even far more bandwidth capacity. The number of end-users is still increasing, as well as the amount of on-line services. All this is attracting attackers and speeding up worms spread — the consequences result in an always growing damage. Research in this area — as will be described later — shows a great effort in developing high speed (scalable) solutions to the problem of detecting intruders and

A.K. Bandara and M. Burgess (Eds.): AIMS 2007, LNCS 4543, pp. 196–199, 2007.

anomalous activities in backbone networks. Monitoring the network behavior instead of a single host's behavior allows to have a less expensive solution and a more powerful detection: it deals with the state of a set of hosts and not a single machine.

The aim of scalability towards high speed solutions leads to the necessity of having fast systems of detection. According to [8], most NIDSes can currently keep pace only with network traffic of 100-200 Mbps. [5] gives stricter evaluation of Snort (with Bro one of the best-known NIDSes), asserting that it can handle no more than 100Mbps under normal traffic and it has worst performance with heavy traffic (with consequently packet dropping). [1] studies the performance of Snort and Bro in Gbps environments: Snort quickly consumes all the available CPU, while Bro uses all the available memory. The results of these studies indicate that it is no longer possible to have a stateful or even stateless analysis of all the packets that are monitored by a NIDS. Hence, there is the necessity to reduce the amount of data to be processed, for instance by sampling only one out of every $n$ packets, or aggregating packets into flows. Plainly, this drastically changes the type and amount of available data for intrusion detection. This also means that the traditional techniques, i.e. signature based engines, may be less powerful (if usable at all). Furthermore, the attack definitions have to be rewritten according to the new type of data. For example, [9] uses sampled packets to develop a method that statistically estimates the super sources and destinations, i.e., the sources (and destinations) that have an unexpectedly large fan-out (fan-in, respectively; the number of peer hosts) in a small time interval. The identification of super sources and destinations can be useful to detect port scanning and Denial-of-Service (DoS) attacks. The proposed solution aims to memorize the minimally required information to characterize a super source or destination, and combines filtering and sampling techniques to achieve better results. At the same time, [9] provides detection solutions only for a subset of all possible attacks, i.e. attack categories that can be statistically distinguished.

Another approach is the one proposed in [4]. In this case, the data reduction is obtained by, instead of assessing individual packets, looking at trains of packets, i.e., flows (such as TCP connections); the proposed method works directly on flow-level data. The authors propose an Internet backbone monitoring and traffic analysis framework, called UPFrame, that uses NetFlow data exported by routers in a backbone network. The framework is presented as a general purpose platform for Internet monitoring, with possible applications in security. In line with other works by the same authors, e.g., [3], [4] uses UPFrame to detect the propagation of Internet worms in a backbone network, as well as to classify host behavior and to measure a host's activity. Contrary to sampling, flows offer aggregated information about the traffic in a network, moving the analysis towards metadata. These approaches change the nature of data to be analyzed, and, consequently, the analysis methods and the detectable attack types: the amount of analyzed traffic is reduced, but the problem of system accuracy, which may be worse than with systems that take all (raw) data into account, is still open.

## 3   State of the Art in Self-learning Systems

As argued earlier, new threats on the Internet, for instance computer viruses, may spread quickly. It is therefore important that network defense systems are able to cope with new threats fast. This motivates the need for adaptive solutions for NIDSes: defense systems that adapt themselves when the environment changes. Adaptive NIDSes have several advantages. First, an adaptive system may recognize attacks that have never been seen before. Second, the adaptability also entails that less human interaction is needed to update and tune the system.

An approach to adaptive NIDSes is self-learning and, as it has emerged from literature, it can play many roles in Intrusion Detection. Self-learning techniques have been applied in anomaly-based detection engines, i.e., systems in which an event is considered malicious if it deviates from the expected behavior. Recently, the work of [6] presented a statistical model to detect flow-level intrusions, which is suitable for high speed networks. The authors have developed an intrusion detection tool called HiFIND (High-speed Flow-level Intrusion Detection system). The anomaly detection engine of HiFIND is based on the error between the expected value for some analyzed metric and the measured value for the same metric. A deviation suggests the presence of an anomaly in the traffic. HiFIND statistically characterizes the traffic according to the measures the system is required to monitor. For example, it is possible to detect TCP SYN flooding DoS attacks by tracing the difference between the number of SYN and SYN/ACK packets for each triplet source IP, destination IP and destination port. The metric, with respect to the set of monitored hosts, gives a clear indication of the distribution of packets over time. A sharp variation points out a DoS attack.

As HiFIND adds adaptability to the detection engine, self-learning methods also are a useful way to improve high level organization between subsystems in distributed environments (i.e., where various NIDSes are working together, exchanging information about threats etc.). An example of this technique is presented in [2], in which the authors describe a distributed architecture based on the concept of autonomous cooperating systems. Each system has the capability of detecting attacks, combining flow-based statistics and packet payload infomation. At the same time, the subsystem can also share its current knowledge with other systems, improving the total detecting ability (self-optimization).

Finally, the scientific community has considered another problem that is common to all kinds of IDSes, in both gigabit-speed and megabit-speed networks: alert management. An IDS can easily produce hundreds of alerts each hour, each of them may be false positive. Hence, there is a clear need to find a way to reduce the amount of alerts to be analyzed by hand — improving the system's accuracy by both achieving false positive reduction and aggregating correlated alerts into attack scenarios [7].

## 4   Concluding Remarks

The huge spread of high-speed (say 1 Gbps and up) networks and the always increasing number of attacks and network abuses, motivate the interest of both the academic as well as the network operations world in NIDSes. The common goal of NIDS researchers is to improve the system performance, aiming to keep pace with the speed of current networks. At the same time, the NIDS research community seems to show an increasing interest also into adaptive systems, in which less human interaction is required to keep the system running and accurate.

In our research project, we aim to build a high performance NIDS that can cope with speeds of 1Gbps or more. The system, to be competitive, should also achieve the aims of completeness (few failures to detect an intrusion) and accuracy (small number of false positives and negatives). Moreover, the wish to provide secure services to end-users implies that such a system should work in real-time on actual backbones.

The present literature study is the first step in our research. It outlines the current major trends in high-speed network intrusion detection and has shown that there still are many open issues. As argued in this paper, the first problem is keeping up with speed and massive traffic. Therefore, we are considering metadata (flows) as the most suitable solution for achieve data-reduction: indeed, the computational overhead required by a complete analysis of all packets can not be managed anymore in high speed environments. At the same time, we are looking to integrate flows with the information provided by sampled packets: in our opinion the payload of sampled packets may still be useful to characterize the traffic.

The second goal in this research project is to enhance the system with adaptive mechanisms. The use of metadata itself suggests an anomaly based approach: this would permit the system to perceive new traffic patterns and to react to changes in the environment. Furthermore, adaptability can also lead to system self-optimization and self-reconfiguration, reducing the required human interaction.

Finally, in our project we intend to test and validate the system on real networks.

# References

1. Dreger, H., Feldmann, A., Paxson, V., Sommer, R.: Operational experiences with high-volume network intrusion detection. In: SIGSAC: 11th ACM Conference on Computer and Communications Security (CSS'04), pp. 2–11 (2004)
2. Dressler, F., Münz, G., Carle, G.: CATS - cooperating autonomous detection systems. In: 1st IFIP International Workshop on Autonomic Communication (WAC 2004) (October 2004)
3. Dübendorfer, T., Plattner, B.: Host behaviour based early detection of worm outbreaks in internet backbones. In: Enabling Technologies: Infrastructure for Collaborative Enterprise, 2005. 14th IEEE International Workshops on (WETICE'05), pp. 166–171. IEEE Computer Society Press, Los Alamitos (2005)
4. Dübendorfer, T., Wagner, A., Plattner, B.: A framework for real-time worm attack detection and backbone monitoring. In: Critical Infrastructure Protection, First IEEE International Workshop on (IWCIP'05) (November 2005)
5. Gao, M., Zhang, K., Lu, J.: Efficient packet matching for gigabit network intrusion detection using TCAMs. In: Advanced Information Networking and Applications, 20th International Conferece on (AINA'06), pp. 249–254. IEEE Computer Society Press, Los Alamitos (2006)
6. Gao, Y., Li, Z., Chen, Y.: A DoS resilient flow-level intrusion detection approach for high-speed networks. In: Distributed Computing Systems, 2006. ICDCS 2006. 26th IEEE International Conference on, pp. 39–46. IEEE Computer Society Press, Los Alamitos (2006)
7. Kruegel, C., Valeur, F., Vigna, G.: Intrusion Detection and Correlation: Challenges and Solutions. Springer, Heidelberg (2004)
8. Lai, H., Cai, S., Huang, H., Xie, J., Li, H.: A parallel intrusion detection system for high-speed networks. In: ACNS 2004. LNCS, vol. 3089, pp. 439–451. Springer, Heidelberg (2004)
9. Zhao, Q., Xu, J., Kumar, A.: Detection of super sources and destinations in high-speed networks: Algorithms, analysis and evaluation. Selected Areas in Communications, IEEE Journal on, 24, 1840–1852 (October 2006)

# Distributed Case-Based Reasoning
# for Fault Management

Ha Manh Tran and Jürgen Schönwälder

Computer Science, Jacobs University Bremen, Germany
{h.tran,j.schoenwaelder}@iu-bremen.de

**Abstract.** We outline a distributed case-based reasoning system that
exploits various online knowledge sources and reasoning capabilities in
a decentralized, self-organizing platform provided by peer-to-peer technologies. The goal of the system is to assist operators in finding solutions
for faults. We present the research motivation and issues in this paper.

**Keywords:** Case-based Reasoning (CBR), Peer-to-Peer (P2P), Fault
Management, Semantic Search.

## 1   Introduction

The resolution of faults in communication networks and distributed systems is to
a large extend a human driven process. Automated monitoring and event correlation systems [1] usually produce fault reports that are forwarded to operators
for resolution. Support systems such as trouble ticket systems [2] are frequently
used to organize the work-flows.

Case-based reasoning (CBR) [3] has been proposed in the early 1990s to assist
operators in the resolution of faults by providing mechanisms to correlate an
observed fault with previously solved similar cases (faults) [2]. CBR systems are
typically linked to trouble ticket systems since the data maintained in trouble
ticket systems can be used to populate the case database. Existing CBR systems
for fault management usually operate only on a local case database and can not
easily share and exploit knowledge about faults and their resolution present
at other sites. This restriction to local knowledge especially becomes an issue
in environments where software components and offered services change very
dynamically and the case database is thus frequently outdated.

With the success of general purpose search engines like Google, it has become
common practice for operators to "google" for error messages and to search for
problem resolutions in indexed public archives. Experience tells us that quite
often problems can be resolved quickly after "googling" long enough. Solutions
are typically found in indexed discussion forums, bug tracking and trouble ticket
systems, or vendor provided knowledge bases. While some of these data sources
maintain some structured information (e.g., bug tracking and trouble ticket systems), this information can not be exploited due to the usage of a generic search
engine, which does not understand the meta information readily available.

A.K. Bandara and M. Burgess (Eds.): AIMS 2007, LNCS 4543, pp. 200–203, 2007.
© Springer-Verlag Berlin Heidelberg 2007

The focus of our project is on an efficient approach to support fault management for large-scale, diverse information systems of high importance. More specifically, when a serious fault occurs in such systems, what are methods to find reliable solutions for the fault with reasonable time and cost? The proposed approach is based on distributed case-based reasoning which exploits problem solving experience on fault knowledge sources in a distributed environment.

## 2    Research Issues

The goal of our project is to develop a distributed case-based reasoning system to assist operators in resolving faults by finding relevant cases more easily and effectively. The system thus involves several research issues: *i. How to exploit various fault knowledge sources in a distributed environment to discover similar faults? ii. How to represent faults to better retrieve similar faults and their corresponding solutions from knowledge sources? iii. How to reason on the retrieved solutions to propose new solutions adapting to the circumstances of new faults?*

The system will take advantage of peer-to-peer (P2P) technologies to achieve some degree of self-organization and to avoid centralized servers. Peers in the proposed distributed CBR system perform several tasks, such as processing cases and queries, operating CBR engines, communication with operators, report systems and peers. The processing and communication capabilities of peers are thus a main factor influencing the structure of the proper system. By choosing powerful peers, the system likely achieves some promising advantages compared to other systems such as the high availability of resources, the low communication overhead of heterogeneous peers, and the capability of using semantics-based search mechanisms. In particular, we plan to develop and integrate semantics-based search mechanisms that can take advantage of the semi structured data that can be retrieved from the network and integrated into the system. We currently study the architecture of super-peers to support CBR engines (see Fig. 1).

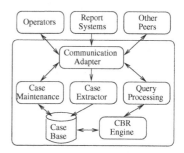

**Fig. 1.** Architecture of a super-peer with a CBR engine

Effective case retrieval requires to represent cases most suitable for search. The heterogeneity of case descriptions leads to difficulties in representing cases. In particular, network faults comprise various data including problem types, error messages, measuring parameters and textual explanations. Our method classifies fault data into *feature* and *semantic* vectors to take advantage of features, semantics, and specific parameters. Evaluating cases requires different evaluation functions to measure the corresponding vectors and an aggregation function to combine the results.

Collaboration among CBR systems is a mechanism to augment their individual reasoning capabilities. The current focus is on exploiting the reasoning capability independently on each engine. Thus, several engines with different capabilities propose solutions for a problem and we assume that reasoning engines work on homogeneous case representations from multiple case databases. A more efficient method employs interactions among CBR reasoning engines to exploit collaborative reasoning capabilities for "ensemble" solutions.

## 3   Related Work

*Structured P2P systems* distribute resources at locations determined by the overlay network topology, facilitating efficient resource search and peer lookup. Typical systems such as CAN or Chord [4] employ hash functions to locate peers and resources on the network. Conversely, *unstructured P2P systems* let the network topology grow randomly with flexible rules; therefore, resources are freely replicating on many peers. Typical unstructured P2P systems such as Gnutella or Freenet [4] achieve better performance with heuristics-based search [4] than with flooding-based search. Both systems support semantic search with some limitation. More recent research has introduced super-peer systems that combine the characteristics of P2P systems with centralized client-server systems to address the problem of heterogeneous peers. *Super-peer systems* manage several clusters; each cluster contains at least one super-peer and peers typically connect to the super-peers in their clusters. With sufficient bandwidth and processing power, a super-peer is more suitable for semantics-based search, as shown in Bibster [5].

   CBR systems basically contain four processes: *case retrieval, case reuse, case revision* and *case retaining*. The first process concerns case representation and case similarity evaluation, whereas the rest are more related to case adaptation and case maintenance. A *case representation* method expresses a case in a formal format to reveal hidden properties and to facilitate case evaluation in case retrieval. Among several representation methods proposed for various domains, few proposals [2,6] in fault management have explored the attribute-value pairs of trouble tickets to present faults. A *similarity evaluation* method measures case properties to calculate the degree of similarity between cases. There exist some widely used methods for evaluating cases represented in attribute-value pairs, such as the global similarity method [7], or the logical match method [8]. Attributes used in these methods are binary, numeric or symbolic values. The *case adaptation* task applies cases obtained from case retrieval to the new situation of a problem to obtain a new solutions; e.g., a retrieved case is first distinguished from the problem, then modified following the differences. Instructions from operators take vital roles in proposing solutions, thus improving the self-adapting capability is the major challenge of case reasoning. After a new solution has been confirmed, the updating task commits changes on the retrieved cases to the case database. This task works closely with the *case maintenance* task, which is responsible for updating the case database, integrating new cases and removing obsolete ones.

Resources and queries in *semantic search* are expressed in formal formats semantically understandable to search engines. P2P systems describe resources in semantic vectors and evaluate the similarity between vectors using similarity functions. Existing systems have employed different methods including the Latent Semantic Indexing (LSI) method [9] for resources described textually and the schema-based method [5] for resources related to structured, domain-specific data. The former brings the essential abstract concepts of the document or query to semantic vectors using single value decomposition (SVD) [9]; whereas, the latter maps the pre-defined features of the document or query into feature vectors using schemas. These vectors are used to locate resources on peers as well as to evaluate the similarity between the query and resources for information retrieval.

## 4 Conclusion

We present the motivation for, the research issues of, and the brief outline of a distributed CBR system that uses P2P technologies and semantics-based search techniques to assist operators in finding solutions for faults. We plan to develop and evaluate the system by running it on the PlanetLab infrastructure [10].

**Acknowledgement.** The work reported in this paper is supported by the EC IST-EMANICS Network of Excellence (#26854).

## References

1. Kätker, S., Paterok, M.: Fault Isolation and Event Correlation for Integrated Fault Management. In: Proc. 5th International Symposium on Integrated Network Management V, pp. 583–596. Chapman & Hall, Ltd, London, UK (1997)
2. Lewis, L.M.: A Case-Based Reasoning Approach to the Resolution of Faults in Communication Networks. In: Proc. 3rd IFIP TC6/WG6.6, pp. 671–682 (1993)
3. Aamodt, A., Plaza, E.: Case-based Reasoning: Foundational Issues, Methodological Variations, and System Approaches. AI Communications 7(1), 39–59 (1994)
4. Androutsellis-Theotokis, S., Spinellis, D.: A Survey of Peer-to-Peer Content Distribution Technologies. ACM Computing Surveys 36(4), 335–371 (December 2004)
5. Haase, P., Broekstra, J., Ehrig, M., Menken, M., Mika, P., Plechawski, M., Pyszlak, P., Schnizler, B., Siebes, R., Staab, S., Tempich, C.: Bibster — A Semantics-Based Bibliographic Peer-to-Peer System. In: Proc. 3rd ISWC '04 (2004)
6. Melchiors, C., Tarouco, L.: Fault Management in Computer Networks Using Case Based Reasoning: Dumbo System. In: Proc. ICCBR '99, pp. 510–524 (1999)
7. Montaner, M., López, B., de la Rosa, J. L.: Improving Case Representation and Case Base Maintenance in Recommender Agents. In: Proc. 6th European Conference on Advances in CBR, London, UK, pp. 234–248. Springer, Heidelberg (2002)
8. Tatarinov, I., Ives, Z., Madhavan, J., Halevy, A., Suciu, D., Dalvi, N., Dong, X., Kadiyska, Y., Miklau, G., Mork, P.: The Piazza Peer Data Management Project. SIGMOD Rec. 32(3), 47–52 (2003)
9. Deerwester, S., Dumais, S.T., Landauer, T.K., Furnas, G.W., Harshman, R.A.: Indexing by Latent Semantic Analysis. JASIS 41(6), 391–407 (1990)
10. PlanetLab Infrastructure. URL: http://www.planet-lab.org/

# Understanding Promise Theory Using Rewriting Logic

Kyrre Begnum and Mark Burgess

Oslo University College, Norway
kyrre@iu.hio.no,mark@iu.hio.no

**Abstract.** We describe our effort to evaluate the syntax and constraints of Promise Theory using a tool developed in the Maude framework. Through the development of a Maude module we are able to do searches and queries in all possible syntactically valid Promise expressions of an arbitrary initial state of participants and constraints. We use this approach to improve the set of grammatical rules that is already available.

## 1  Introduction and Background

Promise Theory is a modeling approach based on the description relationships between entities such as agents, hosts or applications. Its general form allows it to be applied in many scenarios, in example as a high level model of a smart mall[1] or as part of a self-configuring group of web-servers[2]. The three basic promises are:

- Host $n_1$ makes a promise of constraint $\pi$ to host $n_2$: $n_1 \xrightarrow{\pi} n_2$
- A conditional promise: Host $n_1$ makes a promise of constraint $\pi$ to host $n_2$ if someone would promise $n_1$ the constraint $c$: $n_1 \xrightarrow{\pi/c} n_2$
- This promise is a special case in that it promises the usage of constraint $c$ towards the host that made the promise. $n_2 \xrightarrow{U(\pi)} n_1$

Promise theory is still being developed and a refinement of the notation follows as promise theory grows into its desired shape. By changing language features we run the risk of allowing undesired expressions to be formed. To prevent this some semantic "traffic rules" have already been formulated:

- The same promise cannot be present twice.
- A regular promise and a conditional promise between two hosts with the same constraint cannot exist at the same time.
- A usage promise can only be present if there is a promise that offers the constraint to be used.

Are these rules sufficient to avoid meaningless expressions? There will always be a difference in languages between what is syntactically correct and what carries semantic meaning. In the case of Promise Theory as a modeling tool, there is the danger that unsound but valid expressions can hinder proper analysis

A.K. Bandara and M. Burgess (Eds.): AIMS 2007, LNCS 4543, pp. 204–207, 2007.

and representation of the real world. Our aim is therefore to explore the realm of the syntax and beliefs which is provided at present for Promise Theory and use our findings to improve the semantic soundness of the notation.

Maude[3] is a tool for execution and analysis of formal models using rewriting logic. It consists of its own specification language and the possibility to do searches in the execution space of a specified model. Specializations of Maude exist for scenarios in distributed systems such as RealTime Maude[4] and Mobile Maude[5]. Maude has been used previously at the University College of Oslo to evaluate a voluntary RPC protocol as part of the cfengine configuration framework[6].

In this work we apply rewriting logic to the Promise Theory framework in order to analyze how semantics and syntax are in harmony. Model checking in the form of term rewriting is a more exploratory exercise than automated reasoning approaches. With Promise Theory at its current young age, we feel that a tool which would present us with randomized scenarios will help us think "outside the box". Some properties of correct Promise Theory models can be proven with rewriting logic using searches. We emphasize that the main goal of this work is not to validate the theory through software, but to utilize software to help us reflect and improve its design. Our approach is to build a Maude module which will create all syntactically valid promise expressions given a certain initial state. We are also able to apply specific searches in the space of the valid expressions in order to identify expressions which we are interested in.

## 2  A Maude Model for Promise Theory

We first introduce a Maude module called PROMISE which has a concept of a host and a constraint. The constraint is the essence of the promise. We let strings be subclasses of hosts and constraints so that we may use the notation "n1" for a host.

In this module, we do not present the theory that would establish semantic meaning to a promise expression, rather we only provide the building-blocks out of which we will construct a theory in the next module. We define the operators that bind hosts, constraints and promises together:

```
op _-_->_ : Host Constraint Host -> Promise .
```

This is the definition of an operator that takes three arguments (at the position of each underscore). The sorts of the three arguments are defined after the colon. The return sort is specified after the arrow. The result is that this term: n1 - c -> n2 would be a valid Promise. Further, the two other types of promises need extra operators:

```
op _/_ : Constraint Constraint -> Constraint .
op U : Constraint -> Constraint .
```

These two now enable us to write terms for the other Promises too, namely: n1 - pi / c -> n2 and n2 - U(c) -> n1.

A Promise expression is an associative and commutative list of promises. The $\oplus$ concatenator of two promises is used as follows:

$$n_1 \xrightarrow{\pi} n_2 \oplus n_1 \xrightarrow{\pi'} n_2$$

A binary operator _+_ is defined which provides us with the same kind of promise lists in Maude.

## 3   Execution and Search

A Maude specification is executable in that Maude may choose every possible execution path from a given initial state. This means that Maude tries to apply the available rules to the given term. Some times several rules could apply and even the same rule could apply in several places on the given term. This creates branches in the execution path and we are left with a tree structure of possible outcomes.

A new Maude module, TERMINATING-PROMISETHEORY, creates a terminating execution space given an initial state of hosts and constraints. The fact that the specification is terminating is important since it will guarantee that we will be able to search the entire resulting space in finite time. Its algorithm is to recursively create permutations of the combinations of promises that adhere to the traffic rules described above. This allows us to analyze arbitrary scenarios without re-writing the simulation algorithm from scratch. Clearly, the combinatorial space of large scenarios may be so large that waiting for Maude to search through its entirety can become impractical. Starting the searches with some promises already defined will limit the number of resulting permutations.

A simple rewrite command will chose a "random" path in the execution tree. Here is an example where we ask for an execution of 10 rewrite steps:

```
frew [10] hosts: "n1" :: "n2" constraints: "web" :: "db" promiseList: empty .
frewrite [10] in TERMINATING-PROMISETHEORY : hosts: "n1" :: "n2" constraints:
    "db" :: "web" promiseList: empty .
rewrites: 1606 in 0ms cpu (54ms real) (~ rewrites/second)
result PromiseTheory: hosts: "n1" :: "n2" constraints: "db" :: "web"
    promiseList: ("n1" - "db" -> "n2") + "n1" - "web" / "db" -> "n2"
```

Notice the resulting list: $n_1 \xrightarrow{db} n_2 \oplus n_1 \xrightarrow{web/db} n_2$. This situation does not seem to make much sense since $n_1$ both promises $db$ to another host and at the same time indicates that it needs it in order to provide $web$. This is an example of the usefulness of our approach. In order to remove these situations, we could add another assumption to the Promise Theory:

– A host cannot promise a constraint and at the same time indicate the need for the same constraint in a conditional promise.

Deeper analysis is typically based on searches for particular states we are interested in. The basic search is a breadth first search so we will typically find the first instance of what we are looking for. Here we search for a single result where one of the promises is a usage promise.

```
search [1] in TERMINATING-PROMISETHEORY : hosts: "n1" :: "n2" :: "n3"
    constraints: "db" :: "web" promiseList: empty =>! hosts: HL:StringList
    constraints: CL promiseList: PL + H:Host - U(C) -> H':Host .
Solution 1 (state 3898)
states: 19777  rewrites: 72474609 in 22402ms cpu (22400ms real) (3235098
    rewrites/second)
HL:StringList --> "n1" :: "n2" :: "n3"
CL --> "db" :: "web"
PL --> ("n1" - "db" -> "n2") + "n2" - "web" / "db" -> "n1"
H:Host --> "n2"
C --> "db"
H':Host --> "n1"
```

Although there are three hosts available we see that the result here is only between two hosts: $n_1 \xrightarrow{db} n_2 \oplus n_2 \xrightarrow{web/db} n_1 \oplus n_2 \xrightarrow{U(db)} n_1$ The relationship can be described as a "quid pro quo" between "n1" and "n2". "n1" promises "db" to "n2" if someone would provide "web". "n2" promises "n1" what it wants in order to make the conditional come true. This is only one interpretation. Another one could be that "n1" enjoys the "db" promise so much from "n2" that it makes an offer of "web" if it would keep promising "db". "n2" accepts this payment as an incentive to keep the initial promise. Since Promise Theory assumes no order in the promises, multiple interpretations are possible. In either case it is an interesting result which shows the current state of this research.

## 4  Summary

Using Maude we are able to identify surprising and illogical promise expressions. This sort of analysis will perhaps never be exhaustive enough to cover every aspect of the language but that was not our initial goal. In fact, since Promise Theory is still being developed, we consider the Maude specification to be a continuous support tool as new uses for promise theory are explored. This work is supported by the EC IST-EMANICS Network of Excellence (#26854)

## References

1. Burgess, M., Fagernes, S.: Pervasive Computer Management: A Smart Mall Scenario Using Promise Theory. In: Proceedings of MACE, Multicon Lecture Notes, p. 133, (2006)
2. Begnum, K., Burgess, M., Sechrest, J.: Adaptive provisioning using virtual machines and autonomous role-based management, ICAS'06 - SELF workshop - Self-adaptability and self-management of context-aware systems, IEEE (2006)
3. The Maude Homepage, http://maude.cs.uiuc.edu/
4. Ölveczky, P.C., Meseguer, J.: Specification and Analysis of Real-Time Systems Using Real-Time Maude. In: Fundamental Approaches to software Engineering (FASE), 2004. Lecure Notes in Computer Science, vol. 2984, Springer, Heidelberg (2004)
5. Durán, F., Verdejo, A.: A Conference Reviewing System in Mobile Maude. In: Proceedings Fourth International Workshop on Rewriting Logic and its Applications, WRLA 2002, Pisa, Italy, pp. 19–21. Elsevier, North-Holland, Amsterdam (2002)
6. Burgess, M., Begnum, K.: Voluntary cooperation in pervasive computing services. In: Proceedings of the Nineteenth Systems Administration Conference (LISA XIX) (USENIX Association: Berkeley, CA), p.143 (2005)

# Graph Models of Critical Infrastructure Interdependencies

Nils Kalstad Svendsen[1] and Stephen D. Wolthusen[1,2]

[1] Norwegian Information Security Laboratory, Gjøvik University College,
P.O. Box 191, N-2802 Gjøvik, Norway
[2] Information Security Group, Department of Mathematics, Royal Holloway,
University of London, Egham Hill, Egham TW20 0EX, UK

**Abstract.** Critical infrastructures are interconnected on multiple levels, and due to their size models with acceptable computational complexity and adequate modeling capacities must be developed. This paper presents the skeleton of a graph based model and sketches its capabilities.

## 1  Introduction

Critical infrastructures, including primarily the energy, financial services, health care, public services, and transportation sectors [1,2], are interconnected and interdependent on multiple levels. This leads to a number of questions which must be answered satisfactorily to protect the well-being of the population, functioning of government, and economic capabilities. Questions may include what cascading effects a regional failure of one critical infrastructure (such as the recent November 2006 failure of the electric power grid throughout much of continental Europe [3] and the August 2003 power outages in the northeastern U.S. and Canada [4]) may have on other infrastructure components, or to elaborate how adding small and hence cost-effective amounts of redundancy can significantly enhance the overall robustness of this interconnected network of infrastructure services.

While elaborate models exist for many individual infrastructures, it is desirable to also investigate larger-scale interactions among multiple infrastructure sectors. Research questions include the conditions for cascading effects resulting from isolated and coordinated infrastructure component failures, together with circular and transitive effects that might inhibit or at least severely impede the resumption of regular infrastructure services. This requires the development of models of acceptable computational complexity providing adequate modeling capabilities. The level of detail which can be incorporated in such models is limited compared to sector-specific models; however, in many cases the basic identification of interdependencies and critical dependency paths between infrastructure components already provides valuable information.

We describe a general graph-theoretical modeling and analysis framework based on multigraphs which can be used to analyze simple connectivity models, but which is also extensible to characterize particular types and interdependencies in more detail. The graph-theoretical model provides a set of efficient and

A.K. Bandara and M. Burgess (Eds.): AIMS 2007, LNCS 4543, pp. 208–211, 2007.

well-understood formalisms also amenable to algorithmic investigation that a less rigorously formulated approach (e.g. agent-based simulations) cannot provide. Examples of possible model extensions include domain-specific abstract models which take the properties of certain types of infrastructures (e.g. for the electric power grid, pipelines, or even command and control structures) into account and use this family of models to analyze interdependencies among multiple types of infrastructures. Of particular interest to our research are issues involving transitive and circular interdependencies which may not be immediately obvious, may incorporate feedback and amplification, or even ringing and time-dependencies within the infrastructure network. Results from such analysis can e.g. help to devise more robust critical infrastructure networks or, in case of emergencies and disasters, help to prioritize resources to maintain minimum levels of service or to prevent the collapse of infrastructure webs.

## 2   Model Overview

This section gives an overview of our proposed model. For further details and discussions on its interrelationship with other models we refer to [5,6,7].

Interactions among infrastructure components and infrastructure users are modeled in the form of directed multigraphs, further augmented by response functions defining interactions between components. In the model, the vertices $V = \{v_1, \ldots, v_k\}$ are interpreted as producers and consumers of $m$ different types of services or dependency types chosen from the set $D = \{d_1, \ldots, d_m\}$. It is assumed that all nodes $v_a$ have a buffer of volume $V_a^j$ for all dependency types $d_j$. Each node also has a capacity limit $N_{\text{Max}}(v_a, d_j)$ in terms of the amount of resource $d_j$ that can be stored in the node. The dependency types can be classified as ephemeral ($V_a^j = 0$ for all nodes $v_a$, and it follows that $N_{\text{Max}}(v_a, d_j) = 0$), storeable and incompressible ($N_{\text{Max}}(v_a, d_j) = \rho V_a$, $\rho$ is the density of the resource), or storeable and compressible ($N_{\text{Max}}(v_a, d_j) = P_{\text{Max}}(v_a, d_j) V_a$, $P_{\text{Max}}(v_a, d_j)$ is the maximum pressure supported in the storage of resource $d_j$ in the node $v_a$). Pairwise dependencies between nodes are represented with directed edges, where the head node is dependent on the tail node. The edges of a given infrastructure are defined by a subset $\mathcal{E}$ of $\mathcal{E} = \{e_1^1, e_2^1, \ldots, e_{n_1}^1, e_1^2, \ldots, e_{n_m}^m\}$, where $n_1, \ldots, n_m$ respectively are the numbers of dependencies of type $d_1, \ldots, d_m$, and $e_i^j$ is the edge number $i$ of dependency type $j$ in the network. A given dependency between two nodes $v_a$ and $v_b$ is uniquely determined by $e_i^j(v_a, v_b)$. Further, two predicates $C_{\text{Max}}(e_i^j(v_a, v_b)) \in \mathbb{N}_0$ and $C_{\text{Min}}(e_i^j(v_a, v_b)) \in \mathbb{N}_0$ are defined for each edge. These values respectively represent the maximum capacity of the edge $e_i^j(v_a, v_b)$ and the lower threshold for flow through the edge. Hence, two $k \times m$ matrices $C_{\text{Max}}$ and $C_{\text{Min}}$ are sufficient to summarize this information. Let $r_a^j(t)$ be the amount of a resource of dependency type $j$ produced in node $v_a$ at time $t$. We define $D(t)$ to be a $k \times m$ matrix over $\mathbb{Z}$ describing the amount of resources of dependency type $j$ available at the node $v_a$ at time $t$. It follows that the initial state of $D$ is given by $D_{aj}(0) = r_a^j(0)$. For every edge in $\mathcal{E}$ a response function

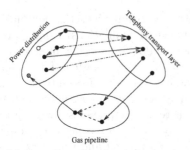

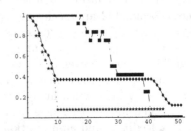

(a) Interdependencies between infrastructures. Continuous lines represent direct dependencies, dashed lines indirect dependencies, and mixed lines bidirectional dependencies

(b) Fraction of functional nodes in the power distribution network (diamond), telephony transport layer (star), and gas pipeline (block) as a function of time.

**Fig. 1.** Figure 1(b) shows the cascading effect of a fatal failure of the gray node of Figure 1(a) at time 0

$R_i^j(v_a, v_b) : D_{aj} \times V_a^j \times N_a^j \times N_{\text{Max}}(v_a, j) \times C_{\text{Max}} \times C_{\text{Min}} \to \mathbb{N}_0$ that determines the $i$-th flow of type $j$ between the nodes $v_a$ and $v_b$ is defined. Given the responses at time $t$, the amount of resource $j$ available in any node $v_a$ at time $t+1$ is given by the sum of the internally generated resources, amount resource in storage, and incoming resources to the node at time $t$. A node $v_a$ is said to be functional at time $t$ if it receives or generates a sufficient amount of resources to satisfy its internal needs. A metric for the level of functionality of an infrastructure is given by the sum of the functionality of the infrastructure components divided by the number of components.

Figure 1 shows the critical interdependencies between a power distribution network, a telephony transport network and a gas pipe. At time 0 in Figure 1(b) the gray power node fails. There is an immediate effect on the telecommunication and power distribution network, while the gas pipe seems to remain functional. After 25 iterations the first gas reservoirs are deprecated, and after 50 iterations the functionality of the gas pipeline drops to zero, leading to series of cascading failures in the power distribution and telecommunication networks.

## 3  Conclusion

The presented model provides a natural progression from the initial studies of large complex networks which concentrated on evaluating the robustness of attacks towards the infrastructure based on static failures [8,9]. The flexible framework for modeling infrastructures and their interdependencies we first reported in [5], and the graph-theoretical model augmented with a set of response functions that can model both unbuffered and particularly buffered resources along with their production and consumption in a network of infrastructure components presented in [6] defines the baseline of our research. The model allows consideration of multiple concurrent types of interdependencies such as may arise in the provision of further infrastructure services along with simple prioritization mechanisms as may be necessary in case of some elements of the infrastructure network becomes unavailable or owing to a partitioning of the interdependency graph.

Our ongoing research focuses on one hand on extending the model to include component reliability [7] and improve time granulation, on the other hand identification of graph-theoretical and combinatorial optimization techniques (particularly as applicable to large-scale graphs) for both the identification of critical interdependencies and efficient mechanisms for increasing the robustness of such interdependent graphs. Future work includes further extensions of the model in which the response function can accommodate multiple resources being provided by each individual vertex in both discrete and continuous variables, resulting in a web of interdependencies.

# References

1. Marsh, R.T., (ed.): Critical Infrastructures: Protecting America's Infrastructures. United States Government Printing Office, Washington D.C., USA, Report of the President s Commission on Critical Infrastructure Protection (1997)
2. Brömmelhörster, J., Fabry, S., Wirtz, N., (eds.): Internationale Aktivitäten zum Schutz Kritischer Infrastrukturen. Bundesamt für Sicherheit in der Informationstechnik, Bonn, Germany (2004)
3. ON Netz GmbH, E.: Bericht über den Stand der Untersuchungen zu Hergang und Ursachen der Störung des kontinentaleuropäischen Stromnetzes am Samstag, 4. November 2006 nach 22:10 Uhr. Technical report, E.ON Netz GmbH, Bayreuth, Germany (November 2006)
4. Hilt, D.: Technical Analysis of the August 14, 2003, Blackout. Technical report, North American Electric Reliability Council, Princeton, NJ, USA (July 2004)
5. Svendsen, N.K., Wolthusen, S.D.: Multigraph Dependency Models for Heterogeneous Critical Infrastructures. In: First Annual IFIP Working Group 11.10 International Conference on Critical Infrastructure Protection, Hanover, NH, USA, IFIP, (In press) Springer, Heidelberg, (March 2007)
6. Svendsen, N.K., Wolthusen, S.D.: Connectivity Models of Interdependency in Mixed-Type Critical Infrastructure Networks. Inform. Sec. Tech. Rep. 12 (In press) (March 2007)
7. Svendsen, N.K., Wolthusen, S.D.: Analysis and Statistical Properties of Critical Infrastructure Interdependency Multiflow Models. Submitted for publication (March 2007)
8. Cohen, R., Erez, K., ben-Avraham, D., Havlin, S.: Resilience of the Internet to Random Breakdowns. Physical Review Letters 85(21), 4626–4628 (2000)
9. Callaway, D.S., Newman, M.E.J., Strogatz, S.H., Watts, D.J.: Network Robustness and Fragility: Percolation on Random Graphs. Physical Review Letters 85(25), 5468–5471 (2000)

# Self-management of Lambda-Connections in Optical Networks

Tiago Fioreze and Aiko Pras

University of Twente
Design and Analysis of Communication Systems (DACS)
Enschede, The Netherlands

**Abstract.** This paper presents a new idea for the management of lambda-connections in optical networks. The idea consists of making multi-service optical switches responsible for automatically detecting IP flows at the packet-level, creating lambda-connections for them, and moving them to the optical-level. In addition to that, they are also in charge of tearing down the connections when no longer needed. This new idea is the result of 1 year of research work at the University of Twente (UT) and it is aimed at resulting in a Ph.D. thesis by the end of 4 years of Ph.D. research.

## 1 Introduction

Optical networks can send vast amounts of data (IP flows) through lambda-connections. These connections are established through multi-service optical switches, which have the capability to perform forwarding decisions at different levels in the protocol stack. As a result, long and big IP flows (elephant flows) could be moved from the packet-level to the optical-level. This move could result in a better QoS for both elephant flows and remaining IP flows: the former would have no jitter and plenty of bandwidth at the optical-level; the latter would be better served due to the off-load of elephant flows.

The detection of IP flows and the management of lambda-connections are important tasks to achieve the desired move. Two approaches are currently used for that [1]: conventional management and GMPLS signaling. The former is characterized by a centralized management entity (e.g., human manager or an automated management process) that is in charge of establishing lambda-connections and deciding which IP flows should be moved to the optical-level. In contrast, the latter is characterized by the fact that optical switches coordinate the creation of lambda-connections among themselves. The decision which IP flows will be moved to the optical level however should be taken by a centralized management entity, or by the entities responsible for the generation of the data flow.

However, there are several problems using these approaches. Both approaches require human interaction to detect flows and manage lambda-connections. This interaction may be slow, since humans need time to perform those tasks, and it is also error prone. For instance, IP flows eligible to lambda-connections may not be detected by network managers.

A.K. Bandara and M. Burgess (Eds.): AIMS 2007, LNCS 4543, pp. 212–215, 2007.

It is interesting to mention that the research work presented in this paper has been developed within the context of the SURFnet GigaPort Next Generation (Gigaport-NG) Research on Networking (RoN) project [2]. This work has also the support of the EMANICS community [3], more specifically the collaboration of the INRIA Lorraine institute [4].

The remaining of this paper is structured as follows. Section 2 introduces our idea on self-management of lambda-connections in optical networks. Then the research questions and the approaches to answer those questions are introduced in section 3. Finally, conclusions and future plans are drawn in section 4.

## 2  Proposed Idea

This section introduces what self-management of lambda-connections stands for. Self-management of lambda-connections consists of an automatic cooperation between the IP and optical domain in order to create lambda-connections for IP flows. The network domain is in charge of detecting IP flows to be transferred over lambda-connections and signalizing the optical domain about the existence of these IP flows. On its turn, the optical domain is in charge of creating lambda-connections for IP flows and releasing them when no longer needed. Figure 1 depicts how our proposed idea would look like.

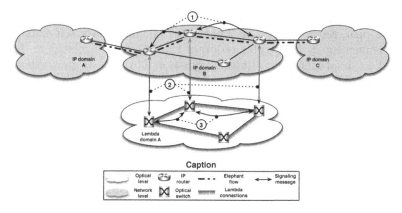

**Fig. 1.** Self-management of lambda-connection in optical networks

In Figure 1 IP routers located at IP domain B detect one elephant flow transiting between IP domains A and C. They start then talking to one another in order to confirm the existence of the detected elephant flow (step 1). When confirmed the existence, the IP routers signalize the optical switches in lambda domain A (step 2). The optical switches coordinate among themselves in order to create a dedicated lambda-connection to the detected elephant IP flow (step 3). From that point on, the elephant flow is switched at the optical level.

Further information about our idea on self-management can be found at [5].

## 3   Research Questions and Proposed Approaches

Since self-management of lambda-connections does not exist in current optical networks, it has to be designed. However, before a self-management architecture is designed, solutions for several research questions should be found. The source of these questions is the introduction of our new idea for managing optical networks. The following questions should therefore be considered and answered:

1. *What are the pros & cons of self-management of lambda-connections compared to current approaches?*
2. *How can self-management be implemented?*
   This question can better be refined into a number of subquestions:
   (a) *What are the requirements to a flow being eligible to a lambda-connection?*
   (b) *How can optical switches automatically detect IP flows?*
   (c) *How can the establishment of lambda-connections be?*
   (d) *How can IP flows be monitored over lambda-connections?*
   (e) *How can the releasing of lambda-connections be?*

Research question 1 aims at comparing our idea with the current management approaches: conventional management and GMPLS signaling. The approach to be taken to answer this question consists of finding out the proper criteria for this comparison. In order to do that, study of the literature and interview with professionals in the network management area will be done.

On its turn, research question 2 envisages explaining how self-management can be implemented. Each subquestion of this question is related to different stages of our implementation. Research question 2.(a) aims at presenting which requirements a IP flow should satisfy to be transferred over a lambda-connection. Some requirements have already been found due to the research work performed in the GigaPort-NG RoN project (see at [6]). The requirements are related to the duration and size of a flow, and as well network policies (that can be different at different network domains). A flow should therefore last more than the time to a lambda-connection is established, have the minimum size for a lambda-connection, and satisfy network policies. Further requirements will be investigated by using different optical networks (e.g., SURFnet6) as case study and by studying the literature as well.

Research question 2.(b) will show how the optical switches should cooperate to detect flows at the packet-level. Inter- and intra-domains will be considered in this question. The approach will consist of creating evaluation scenarios where the number of optical switches in charge of detecting IP flows will vary according to their location in the network domain. The scenarios will consider optical switches located at the edge, core or everywhere in the domain. The evaluation will likely be done by means of simulation tools (e.g., NS2 [7]) or by mathematical theory (e.g., Stochastic Petri nets).

Research question 2.(d) will investigate how IP flows can be monitored when carried over lambda-connections. Two initial ideas are considered: monitoring at optical-level or monitoring at packet-level. The former requires a literature study to check if there are technologies available for monitoring traffic at the optical-level. The latter can be done by monitoring the traffic at the end-points of the optical connections at the packet-level. In this case an evaluation will be performed to check if both end-points are required to monitor IP flows or only one of them. This evaluation will probable be done by using simulation tools.

Last but not least, research questions 2.(c) and 2.(e) aim at showing how the establishment and releasing of lambda-connections can be performed. The approach to answer these questions will focus on the study of the literature. It is worth to point out that some technologies existing in the Generalized Multiprotocol Label Switching (GMPLS) architecture [8] already do that, and they can therefore be considered strong candidates to be used in our research work.

Some of the results obtained so far in our research can be found at [9].

## 4    Conclusions

This paper presented the long-term goal that is intended to be achieved after a Ph.D. period of 4 years. It also showed the investigated problem, the research questions and approaches to be used to answer those questions. The next short-term goal of this research work is going to be the definition of our self-management architecture, where the involved components and their interaction are going to be defined. We would like to thank SURFnet for allowing us to perform measurements on their network. This paper was supported in part by the EC IST-EMANICS Network of Excellence (#26854).

## References

1. Bernstein, G., Rajagopalan, B., Saha, D.: Optical Network Control: Architecture, Protocols, and Standards. Addison Wesley Publishers, London, UK (2003)
2. GigaPort: GigaPort homepage, Available in (2007),
   http://www.surfnet.nl/info/en
3. EMANICS: European Network of Excellence for the Management of Internet Technologies and Complex Services (EMANICS) (2007) Available in:
   http://www.emanics.org/
4. INRIA-Lorraine: INRIA Lorraine Research Unit (2007) Available in:
   http://www.inria.fr/inria/organigramme/fiche_ur-lor.en.html
5. Fioreze, T., Pras, A.: Using self-management for establishing light paths in optical networks: an overview. In: Poster session proceedings of the 12th EUNICE Open European Summer School 2006 (EUNICE 2006) 17–20 ( 2006)
6. Fioreze, T.: D1.1.2 Requirements for lambda-connection management. Internal report GigaPort-NG RoN project (2006) Available in :
   http://wwwhome.cs.utwente.nl/~fiorezet/ron/Deliverable1.1.2(2006).pdf
7. The Network Simulator ns-2: The Network Simulator ns-2 homepage (2007) Available in: http://www.isi.edu/nsnam/ns/
8. Mannie, E.: Generalized Multi-Protocol Label Switching (GMPLS) Architecture Request for Comments: 3495 (RFC 3495) (2004)
9. Fioreze, T., Wolbers, M.O., Meent, R., Pras, A.: Finding elephant flows for optical networks. In: Application session proceedings of the 10th IFIP/IEEE International Symposium on Integrated Network Management (to appear) (IM 2007)

# A Distributed Architecture for IP Traffic Analysis

Cristian Morariu and Burkhard Stiller

Department of Informatics, University of Zürich CH-8050, Zürich, Switzerland
{morariu,stiller}@ifi.unizh.ch

**Abstract.** Current high-speed links become a challenge to traditional real-time analysis of IP traffic. Major research was done in finding sampling methods for IP packets and IP flows in order to reduce the amount of data that needs to be processed while keeping a high level of result accuracy. Although sampling proves to be a promising approach, there may be application sce-narios foreseen, in which decisions may not be based on sampled data, *e.g.,* usage based charging or intrusion detection systems. This paper proposes a distributed architecture for collecting, analysing and storing of IP traffic data. This approach aims to provide a high level of automation, self-configuration, and self-healing so that new nodes may be easily added or removed to/from the analysis network. The proposed solution makes use of unused processing power existing in the network (such as customer's PCs of an ISP) to achieve real-time analysis of IP traffic for high-speed network links.

## 1 Introduction, Motivation and Goals

Traditional centralized approaches to traffic analysis cannot scale with the increase of bandwidth advances mainly due to their memory and computational requirements [1]. Major research was done in the field of packet sampling and flow sampling [2] in order to significantly reduce the amount of data that needs to be processed, while keeping the error of the sampling estimations within low limits. Although they alleviate the compu-tational requirements problems for high-speed packet processing, sampling mecha-nisms are not very accurate in some scenarios where complete information is required (such as IDS systems or usage-based charging systems). Distributed architectures have already been proposed for dedicated network monitoring tasks. The authors of [3] pro-pose an approach in which a packet is processed either by a single router, either by all the routers on the packet's path. However, this solution does not provide any guarantees that a packet will always reach a router responsible with the flow it belongs to. A dis-tributed monitoring architecture for web traffic is proposed in [4]. Although the processing of IP packets is distributed to several nodes, the background storage is cen-tralized, thus making it inefficient in many cases. In [5] a similar approach is presented, but in this case not targeted to web traffic. The main problem with this approach is the limited degree of work distribution (only used for packet capturing nodes). A large de-gree of distribution can be found in [6] where all the involved tasks (packet capturing, flow

A.K. Bandara and M. Burgess (Eds.): AIMS 2007, LNCS 4543, pp. 216–220, 2007.

generation, flow storage, traffic analysing) are distributed. A drawback that can be identified in all related work is the inflexibility of the presented architectures. Any change in the distributed processing network requires reconfiguration of all other processing nodes which raises scalability concerns related to the configuration over-head if this process is not automated. Besides this issue, proper load balancing mechanisms are missing. Round/robin approaches for capturing/processing nodes are not the most fortunate choice, as efficient flow processing requires that all packets within a flow to be captured/processed by the same nodes. Also distributing the work based on flow identifiers (flow ID—all possible values for flow IDs define a flow ID space) does not guarantee that some nodes will not become overloaded (while other may still be un-used) due to an overpopulation of a small flow ID subspace. Moreover, none of the work investigated considered a P2P approach in order to benefit from the scalability and load balance the P2P paradigm inherently supports.

The goal of this work is to design a distributed architecture for real-time analysis of IP traffic on high-speed links. Such an analysis platform forms the basis for applications like flow accounting, flow path monitoring, or distributed Intrusion Detection Systems (IDS). This will determine the basis for alternative mechanisms to traffic analysis by using idle processing power within the network and adapting processing power to the network link load. This approach will lead to a better efficiency of core network proc-esses (such as routing or switching) by removing the burden of packet inspection, and will lead to better analysis results by using more processing power than the one existing in a typical router, thus minimizing the sampling rate required for flow accounting.

## 2  Proposed Approach

The approach proposed is based on the distribution of packet processing to different nodes. Each IP flow will be assigned an identifier (a numeric value between 0 and $2^{64}$) by applying a hash function to the IP packet header. This identifier will be called a flow ID. The flow ID space contains all the values a flow ID may take $(0 \ldots 2^{64})$. A flow ID subspace is defined as a continuous subinterval of this flow ID space. Besides providing more computational resources to the task of packet analysis, this proposal also reduces the flow lookup time within a processing node by splitting up the whole flow ID space and assigning different flow ID subspaces to each processing node.

In order to motivate this work and provide basic requirements the following assump-tions are made:

- Flow accounting in high-speed networks is very expensive (in terms of resource usage) to be operated in a router. Although sampling mechanisms can be used, there will always be a trade-off between routing performance and accuracy.
- Using 10% of the total bandwidth of an ISP for traffic analysis operations is feasible. As this proposal aims into using any available processing resource in the network (such as customer PCs) for flow processing, some of this customer bandwidth will be used for this purpose. Incentive mechanisms will be investigated for having ISP customers run traffic monitoring tools on their PCs.

- Nodes providing the processing resource might not be reliable, but not due to maliciousness. It is assumed that individual nodes may not alter the processing of data they receive or the processing results they report.

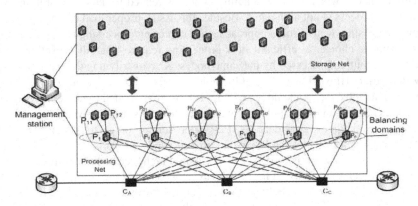

**Fig. 1.** Distributed Analysis Network

The first assumption is a fact proved in several research papers [1], [5], [6]. It is the basis for looking into alternative flow accounting mechanisms for high-speed links. Using 10% of the bandwidth for traffic monitoring purposes is not considered as a drawback, since other monitoring mechanisms also create overhead within the network. The anal-ysis module running on different nodes may be seen as a closed system and the com-munication to/from it will be protected by means of cryptography. The only way anal-ysis results may be interfered with is by detaching a node from the analysis network.

The architecture proposed defines three main components being required for capturing, processing, and storing of monitored data: packet sniffer, packet processing network, and storage network. When the term analysis network is used, all three components are assumed. Figure 1 depicts the architecture proposed for the network monitoring infra-structure. Although the figure only shows monitoring a single link, the same system shall be used to monitor multiple links within an administrative domain. As it can be seen in Figure 1, the three components shall be interpreted as three stages:

- a packet capturing stage (*Figure 1: $C_A$, $C_B$, $C_C$*)
- a packet processing stage (*Figure 1: Processing Net*)
- a data storage stage (*Figure 1: Storage Net*)

The first layer (packet capturing stage) deals with capturing useful packet data from the wire. Since processing packets at wire-line speed is not feasible for a single capturing device, multiple collectors will be able to work together and distribute the capturing task among themselves. Moreover, adding or removing a capturing device will be au-tomatically detected by the capturing stage and the work redistribution will be automatically triggered, when the new processing resources are detected. A special focus will be laid on finding simple and efficient algorithms, easy to be implemented in dedicated capturing hardware. The whole capturing stage will be able to synchronize different capturing parameters (sample rate, flow masks, capture policies). The capturing devices will perform minimal processing, such as deciding whether a packet is sampled or not or what is the next processing node for that packet. The second stage (packet processing stage) will be organized as an overlay network. Each node in the processing stage will be responsible with processing packets belonging to a specific flow ID subspace of the whole flow ID space. Different logical topologies (such as hierarchical overlays, structured and unstructured P2P overlays) for processing network will be analysed for find-ing the best candidate for distributing and balancing workload. The example in Figure 1 shows a hierarchical topology, in which each processing node may delegate intervals from the flow ID subspace, for which it is responsible, to other processing nodes. *E.g.*, assume in Figure 1 that node $P_1$ is responsible for flow ID subspace $[2^{10}-2^{15}]$; it may delegate flow ID subspace $[2^{12}-2^{13}]$ to node $P_{11}$ and flow ID subspace $[2^{14}-2^{15}]$ to node $P_{12}$. As processing capabilities of each single node influence the amount of work each node may perform, statistics will be gathered by reflecting the processing performance of each node. The whole processing network will balance processing power in such a way that:

- no node shall become overloaded, while there is unused processing capacity in the network. The system shall achieve a maximum sampling rate with the given processing power.
- approximately the same sampling rate shall be used over the whole flow ID space

so that no flow ID subspace will be oversasmpled. The third stage, *Storage Net*, will provide storage space for IP flow records. The flow record storage component will be able to retrieve and aggregate flow records quickly.

## 3 Concluding Remarks

Although distributed architectures have already been proposed for IP flow monitoring, their lack in flexibility and scalability prevented them from offering a real solution to high-speed flow accounting. By looking into P2P architectures to process IP traffic, the approach presented here investigates into a new direction of IP traffic analysis. By em-ploying P2P mechanisms it is expected that an efficient, scalable, and accurate IP flow analysis framework will be designed and implemented eventually.

## References

[1] Estan, C., Varghese, G.: New directions in traffic measurement and accounting, ACM SIGCOMM Internet Measurement Workshop, San Francisco, U.S.A. pp. 75–80 (November 2001)
[2] Szeby, T.: Statistical Sampling for Non-Intrusive Measurements in IP Networks, Ph. D. Thesis, Technische Universität Berlin, Universitätsbibliothek (Diss.-Stelle), Fakultät IV–Elektrotechnik und Informatik (2005)

# Iterative Key Based Routing for Web Services Addressing and Discovery

Marco Milanesio and Giancarlo Ruffo

Dept. of Computer Science, University of Turin, Italy
{milane,ruffo}@di.unito.it

**Abstract.** As the nodes and the resources in a structured peer-to-peer network are indexed with unique identifiers, and as the identifiers are assigned to nodes whose nodeId (i.e., the identifier of the peer) is closest (by some metrics) to the identifier, at an application level it is an issue to know the unique identifier a resource is indexed with, to route a message to the node that is responsible for the identifier and thus to retrieve the resource itself. We are studying a way to exploit the features of structured peer-to-peer networks in web services addressing and discovery.

## 1 Introduction and Related Works

As our works is based on structured peer-to-peer networks and web services, we briefly explain here the major features of these environments, focusing on their major drawbacks.

### 1.1 Distributed Hash Tables

Distributed hash tables (e.g., [1,2]) are a class of distributed algorithms that partition the ownership of a set of keys among participating nodes, and can efficiently route messages to the unique owner of any given key. DHTs are typically designed to scale to large numbers of nodes and to handle continual node arrivals and failures.

A DHT provides primitives only for building a mapping between resources (e.g., files, nodes, etc) in terms of a list of pairs `<key, value>`: all those primitives can be summarized by the function `lookup(key)` that returns the identifier of the node responsible for the `key`.

In all the DHTs, nodes and objects are assigned random identifiers (called nodeIds and keys, respectively) from a large id space. Given a message and a key, the DHT routes the message to the node with the nodeId that is numerically closest to the key in a logarithmic number of hops wrt the size of the network. This node is known as the *key's root* in Pastry [8], or the *key's successor* in Chord [1].

In order to route a message, each node maintains a local routing table organized in some way (e.g., a Pastry node maintains a leaf set, a routing table and a neighborhood set): the routing table contains information on a logarithmic

A.K. Bandara and M. Burgess (Eds.): AIMS 2007, LNCS 4543, pp. 221–224, 2007.

subset of the entire system, granting scalability to the structured peer-to-peer system.

Even if DHTs offer a very good level of scalability and robustness to common attacks, they suffer also from various aspects. Consistency, for example, is one of the problem. Every information is replicated and cached in the system, to improve reliability and performance: this leads to the problem of balancing the trade-off between consistency and communication overhead between peers that need to update their cache. In [4], authors point out the difference between key consistency and data consistency: it's true that only one node must be responsible for a certain key, but it's also true, due to the desired performance, that data have to be replicated and cached in some way.

As underlined before, the key based routing, is one of the most problematic aspect: it is simple when keys are known in advance, but this cannot be always assumed at the application level. So, distributed applications based on structured peer-to-peer overlay networks have to set up an interface to communicate with the peer-to-peer network providing the keys used for both routing messages and searching resources. As a consequence, many solutions have been proposed: from the insertion of meta-information and meta-keys to the parsification of the query string (such as in *eMule* with Kademlia support).

The *impoverished query language* due to the key based routing (i.e., the lack of possibility to send complex queries to the system) is the object in [5]: authors try to give a entity-relational view to the peer-to-peer search mechanism, basing their work on CAN [7], through a three-tier architecture.

The query mechanism proposed in [6] relies on indexes, stored and distributed across the nodes of the network: the whole system creates multiple indexes, organized hierarchically, which permit users to access data in many different ways. Indexes are distributed across the nodes of the network and contain key-to-key (or query-to-query) mappings.

As our study concerns the implementation of a web service discovery and addressing mechanism on top of a DHT, in the following we will discuss about web services and their issues.

## 1.2   Web Services

Web Services [9], which have emerged as a dominating set of recommendations and standards (e.g., W3C and OASIS), are basically interoperable software components that can be used in application integration and development: they grant loose coupling and simple integration of other software components.

Their usage is quite simple: a generic *client* (e.g., a human or another software component) discovers a service using the definitions and protocols defined in a WSDL document, querying a UDDI registry.

Various methods and procedures to discover the most suitable web service to use, depending on the desired service, are presented in [13]. Authors point out that the main obstacle affecting web service discovery mechanism is heterogeneity between services, and each solutions in the cited work try to overcome different aspects of this heterogeneity in order to match the best service available.

They suggest a higher level approach in addressing different web services in order to overwhelm this variety, that can be technological, ontological or pragmatic.

A critical factor to the overall utility of web services is a scalable, flexible and robust search and discovery mechanism. The centralized (even if replicated) UDDI registry approach lacks of scalability and introduces a single point of failure in the system. From this, many distributed approaches to web services have been proposed. To increase flexibility, the P2P system proposed in [11] supports complex queries containing partial keywords and wildcards. It guarantees also that all existing data elements matching a query will be found with bounded costs in terms of number of messages and number of involved nodes. The system is based on a Distributed Hash Table and, for preserving locality purpose, it organizes keys (mapping data elements) in a multidimensional keyword space where the keywords are the coordinates and the data elements are points in the space. The assumption is that two data elements are *local* if their keywords are lexicographically close or they have common keywords. In [10], authors address the problem of scalability in the search mechanism by imposing a deterministic shape on P2P networks, exploiting the so-named *Semantic Web Services*, a combination (based on ontologies) of *Semantic Web* and web services. They propose a graph topology, based on hypercubes, which allows efficient broadcast and search, and provide an efficient topology construction and manteinance algorithm, crucial to symmetric P2P networks. They use global ontologies to partition the network topology into concept clusters that can be queried specifically.

Ontologies (i.e., *the explicit specifications of the conceptualization of domains*) are also the core of the work in [12], where it is pointed out, once more, the fact that peers need ways to effortlessly discover, consume and provide services as they become available in a dynamic network. The *ubiquitous computing* introduced in the cited work aims to organize services in a logical manner, making peers to use an inference engine to evaluate ontologies. In the end, the work in [14] presents a distributed ontology repository based on Pastry: the system decomposes the ontologies into the corresponding triples (subject, predicate, object) and uses the DHT to store the elements (i.e., the ontologies represented in the web ontology language (OWL)).

## 2   Our Approach

Combining web services and peer-to-peer networks leads to some major problems, as underlined in [15]. For example, the bandwidth usage dramatically increases since XML documents (i.e., WSDLs) are required for exchanging information; furthermore, some security issues appear as no more central authority exists; and, finally, the maintenance of a distributed environment (with a potential high churn rate) is not as simple as a centralized one. In particular, we are studying a method that allows users to publish and retrieve services from a structured overlay network. As we told before, the key a resource is indexed with is not knowable *a priori*, and thus we built a iterative querying scheme in which every query (i.e., the lookup(key) function on the DHT) returns a list of more specific keys to be used in the next step of the discovering mechanism. More formally, in our $i^{th}$ step, we have: $k_{i+1} = lookup(k_i)$, in which $k_i$ and $k_{i+1}$ are two successive keys in the path from the most generic key $k_0$ (e.g., Yellow Pages, notice that $k_0$ is knowable *a priori*, for example by calculating the SHA1 of the string "Yellow Pages") to the most specific $k_n$ (e.g., the Yellow Pages service from Provider X, with some specific attributes) that is the key the node who maintains the specific WSDL is responsible for. It is important to underline the fact that the *navigation* in the path is up to the final user, who has to choose the appropriate key from the returned list.

## Acknowledgment

This work has been partially supported by the Italian Ministry for University and Research (MIUR), within the framework of the "PROFILES" project (PRIN).

## References

1. Stoica, I., et al.: Chord: A scalable peer-to-peer lookup service for internet applications. In: Proc. of the ACM SIGCOMM Conference. p. 149160 (2001)
2. Maymounkov, P., Mazieres, D.: Kademlia: A peer-to-peer information system based on the xor metric. In: Proc. of IPTPS02, Cambridge, USA (March 2002)
3. Zhao, B.Y., et al.: Tapestry: An Infrastructure for Fault-tolerant Wide-area Location and Routing, UC Berkeley (2001)
4. Sankararaman, S., et al.: Key Consistency in DHTs, EECS Department, University of California, Berkeley (2005)
5. Harren, M., et al.: Complex queries in dht-based peer-to-peer networks. In: Proceedings of IPTPS02, Cambridge, USA (March 2002)
6. Felber, P., et al.: Data indexing and querying in DHT peer-to-peer networks. In: Proceedings of ICDCS (2004)
7. Ratnasamy, S., et al.: A Scalable Content Addressable Network. In: Proc. of ACM SIGCOMM 2001 (2001)
8. Rowstron, A., Druschel, P.: Pastry: Scalable, distributed object location and routing for large-scale peer-to-peer systems. In: Proc. of IFIP/ACM Middleware, pp. 329–350 (2001)
9. Austin, D., et al.: Web Service Architecture Requirements, W3C Working group Notes (2004)
10. Schlosser, M., et al.: A scalable and ontology-based p2p infrastructure for semantic web services. In: Proc. of the 2nd IEEE P2P (2002)
11. Schmidt, C., Parashar, M.: A Peer-to-Peer Approach to Web Service Discovery, World Wide Web Journal, vol. 7(2) (June 2004)
12. Elenius, D., Ingmarsson, M.: Ontology-based Service Discovery in P2P Networks. In: The First International Workshop on Peer-to-Peer Knowledge Management (P2PKM) (2004)
13. Garofalakis, J., et al.: Web Service Discovery Mechanisms: Looking for a Needle in a Haystack?, International Workshop on Web Engineering (2004)
14. Babik, M., Hluchy, L.: A Scalable Distributed Ontology Repository, In: Popelínský, L., Krátký, M. (eds.) Znalosti, Proceedings, 2005, pp. 8–17 (2005)
15. Hillenbrand, M., Müller, P.: Web Services and Peer-to-Peer, In: Peer-to-Peer Systems and Applications. LNCS, vol. 3485, pp. 207–224. Springer, Heidelberg (2005)

# Peer-to-Peer Large-Scale Collaborative Storage Networks

Thomas Bocek[1] and Burkhard Stiller[1,2]

[1] Department of Informatics IFI, University of Zurich, Switzerland
[2] Computer Engineering and Networks Laboratory TIK, ETH Zurich, Switzerland
{bocek,stiller}@ifi.uzh.ch

**Abstract.** This paper presents the idea of a fully decentralized peer-to-peer collaborative network with a robust, scalable and incentive-compatible system ena-bling storage, retrieval, and manipulation of documents. Modified documents are reviewed in a voting session by other peers. Derived from a scenario, which follows the idea of a distributed encyclopedia, key research questions are concluded.

## 1 Introduction and Motivation

Peer-to-peer (P2P) mechanisms offer redundancy, scalability, fault tolerance, and load balancing [7]. P2P storage systems that are built on these mechanisms have been creat-ed for academic and private/home [2] purposes. The fundamental principle of a P2P storage system is that data from a peer is stored on multiple other peers. These peers can fail or act maliciously, and therefore, the P2P system needs to address failures as well as malicious behavior, if P2P storage shall reach a practical and reliable state.

Typically, many peers in a collaborative network try to achieve a common goal, in the sample case considered here, contributing articles to build a free encyclopedia. A peer should have always clear incentives to collaborate, since selfish peers can destabi-lize a system. Therefore, it is essential to establish an incentive scheme to encourage peers to contribute resources to achieve the common goal. It is important to count on an intrinsic motivation, because not every motivation can be accounted for.

The key idea of this work is a self-contained incentive scheme that can be applied to a P2P document storage system encouraging reviews of modified documents. The re-sulting application will be fully decentralized and scalable to many peers, enabling content control by the participating peers in a voting session. The P2P Wikipedia scenario shows how a decentralized large scale collaborative network could be used. The key concept in this scenario is to contribute non-monetary resources to a decentralized col-laborative network instead of donating money to a centralized system.

## 2 P2P Wikipedia Scenario

Wikipedia.org is a large centralized collaborative system, where anyone can store, re-trieve, and manipulate articles on any subject, with the common goal to provide a free

A.K. Bandara and M. Burgess (Eds.): AIMS 2007, LNCS 4543, pp. 225–228, 2007.

encyclopedia. The Wikipedia website is one of the top 10 sites in the world [6] and has 2 Thomas Bocek and Burkhard Stiller more than 5 million unique hits every day. The traffic and huge amount of data need a lot of disk space, CPU time, and bandwidth. Wikipedia servers are logically centralized and physically decentralized, located in Florida, Amsterdam, and Seoul. All these serv-ers need to be maintained and upgraded to keep track with the increasing popularity of this site. The total amount of support and revenue in 2006 was roughly at 1.5 M$US [8].

The largest income for Wikipedia is fundraising (about 1.3 M$US) and the last call for donations received revenues for close to 1 M$US. However, Florence Devouard, chair of the board of trustees of the Wikimedia foundation, stated that the collected money does not cover all planned projects as, *e.g.*, the planed expenditure for hardware for 2007 is 1.6 M$US. Discussions about advertisements on the Wikipedia site to in-crease revenues showed that voluntary content contributors as well as the founder of Wikipedia are opposed to displaying advertisements.

### 2.1  P2P Wikipedia

Fundraising for Wikipedia is important to pay for their required resources. The effect of a decentralization of a collaborative system can distribute resource requirements to many peers. Participating peers can donate bandwidth and storage space. Unused resources of many PCs can be used instead of the traditional fundraising to keep up with the increasing size of articles and page views. SETIghome follows a similar idea, where unused CPU time is used to search for extraterrestrial life. Fig. 1 shows on the left side the centralized approach, with the centralized Wiltimedia foundation depending on donations and where users access articles from a logically centralized site. The right side shows the decentralized approach. Participating users access articles from each other. Articles are stored in a structured overlay network, and a distributed name service [I] maps an article to a name. A peer, who wants to access an article, performs a lookup in the overlay network and receives an address of that peer who stores the article.

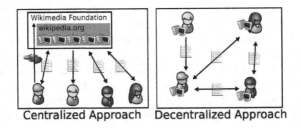

Fig. 1. Comparing the centralized and decentralized approach

## 3  Problem Statements and Approaches

Among key benefits, such as fault tolerance. load balancing. scalability, and non-monetary resource requirements. a shift from a centralized large-scale collaborative network to a decentralized network introduces drawbacks. Decentralized mechanisms are required to identify and deal with unfair and malicious Peer-to-Peer Large-scale Collaborative Storage Networks 3

## 3.1  Robust P2P Collaborative Networks

A robust system behaves, if malicious peers try to attack the system, as if no attack happens and users do not notice the attack. This means that the performance of the system shall not be influenced by these attacks. The sybil attack, where an attacker can create many peers [3], has the potential to shut down a P2P network. It is essential to implement countermeasures for these attacks. A collaborative network, which relies on contributing resources, can weaken sybil attacks, if a peer has to contribute resources in order to participate. It is essential to find a resource trading scheme to make attacks as expensive as possible, while not impairing the regular usage. In a collaborative network many resources can be traded: bandwidth, storage space, CPU time, or human resources. A resource trading scheme, where bandwidth is traded, is implemented in Bittorrent [2]. A Bittorrent peer allows to download data from another peer only, if the peer has uploaded data as well. This approach is also used by [5]. Another trading scheme, where CPU time is traded for storage is SRTCPU [1]. Both mechanisms use direct relations, where trading takes place between two peers. Some approaches [4] consider indirect relations, where trading takes place with multiple peers, which is necessary in case of asymmetric interest. However, there are still open questions to be researched on:

- How to implement scalable robust incentives with indirect, transitive relations?
- Is it possible to establish a trading scheme that fits into a collaborative network?
- How to set up a trading scheme that trades different kind of resources?

## 3.2  Decentralized Control

As a result of decentralization the control needs to be distributed to prevent arbitrary changes that may lead to editing wars and vandalism as outlined in the P2P Wikipedia scenario. The centralized Wikipedia approach allows for certain documents a modification only from registered users to deal with this problem. In a decentralized approach, this problem can be solved by voting. The voting has to be decentralized and decisions have to be made on a democratic basis. All previous editors of an article have to be asked to vote for or against a change. For new documents without previous editors, randomly picked editors can be requested to vote. Changes or newly created documents are accepted only, if a majority has been reached. Key research questions include:

- Does a decentralized robust and scalable voting mechanism exist and is the voting mechanism secure against attacks?
- How to reward users that vote as voting requires human resources and how to deal with users that never vote, should users be punished for minority voting?
- How long should a voting session wait for casting ballots and should the voting information be kept in a shared or private history?

### 3.3  Incentives

Incentives in a P2P network are non-financial compensations for a specific result and are closely related to resource trading schemes. On one hand, if a resource is only provided, when another resource has been offered beforehand, a peer might have a strong incentive to offer resources to other peers. On the other hand, there are intrinsic incentives that have to be accounted for as well. Several ideas on incentive strategies to encourage peers to participate need to be investigated, implemented, and evaluated:

- A user voting for the majority will be rewarded. The reward could be a score influencing the weight of his vote or a score that will be published, helping to establish intrinsic motivations.
- A user can only propose a modification of a document, if the user has provided resources beforehand. The user has a strong incentive to contribute resources.
- An incentive could be a public available scoreboard. A user with a high score could become a super user, who can vote, *e.g.*, on newly created documents or vote on any documents they wish.
- A user modifying an article may be accepted and he will become an editor, who can decide on the development of the document.

Centralized large scale collaborative systems have a single point of failure. If the operator cannot or is not willing to provide the service, *e.g.*, due to lack of funding, new, decentralized forms of collaborative networks will be used.

**Acknowledgment.** Many thanks go to David Hausheer, who contributed valuable input to these ideas and the paper.

## References

1. Bocek, T., Hausheer, D., Riedl, R., Stiller, B.: Introducing CPU Time as a Scarce Resource in P2P Systems to Achieve Fair Use in a Distributed DNS. In: 9th IEEE Global Internet Symposium 2006, Barcelona, Spain, pp. 1–6 (April 2006)
2. Cohen, B.: Incentives Build Robustness in BitTorrent. In: 1st Workshop on Economics of Peer-to-Peer Systems, Berkley, California, U.S.A (June 2003)
3. Douceur, J.R.: The Sybil Attack. In: 1st International Workshop on Peer-to-Peer Systems (IPTPS 02), Cambridge, Massachusetts, U.S.A (March 2002)
4. Feldman, M., Lai, K., Stoica, I., Chuang, J.: Robust Incentive Techniques for Peer-to-Peer Networks; ACM Electronic Commerce, New York, U.S.A. pp. 102–111 (May 2004)
5. Fokker, J., Pouwelse, J., Buntine, W.: Tag-Based Navigation for Peer-to-Peer Wikipedia; WWW2006. In: Proceedings of the Collaborative Web Tagging Workshop, Edinburgh, Scotland (May 2006)
6. Perez, J.C.: Wikipedia breaks into U.S. top 10 sites; InfoWorld, URL (February 2007) http://www.infoworld.com/article/07/02/16/HNwikipediatop10_1.html
7. Ratnasamy, S., Francis, P., Handley, M., Karp, R., Shenker, S.: A Scalable Content Addressable Network; ACM SIGCOMM'01, San Diego, California, U.S.A. pp.161–172 (August 2001)
8. Wikimedia Foundation, Inc. Financial Statements 2006, 2005, 2004, Florida, U.S.A (November 2006)

# Xen Virtualization and Multi-host Management Using MLN

Kyrre Begnum

Oslo University College, Norway
kyrre@iu.hio.no

**Abstract.** Xen virtualization is a powerful tool for encapsulating services and providing seamless migration of tasks on hardware failure. This tutorial shows how to set up multiple Xen instances in a network using the MLN management tool.

One of the main challenges in virtual machine administration on a large scale is the specification of complex and repeatable virtualized scenarios. Creating a singe new virtual machine, boot it and install an operating system is straight forward with many of todays tools. But what if you need to deploy 50 identical virtual machines across 25 servers and manage them as an atomic unit? How do you at a later point make consistent design adjustments such as migrating a subset of the virtual machines to a new server or adjusting memory levels? These issues are at the heart of this tutorial.

MLN is a virtual machine management tool supporting both User-Mode Linux and Xen. It has been developed at the Oslo University College in conjunction with its research on system administration and resource management. MLN and its research has previously been presented at the Norwegian Unix User Group (NUUG) and the 20th USENIX Large Installation System Administration conference LISA. This tutorial is interesting for all who want to look beyond the typical one-vm-on-my-desktop scenario. Teachers interested in virtual student labs should also attend.

We start with a short introduction to the Xen virtual machine technology and then proceed to MLN and its own configuration language. In the second part of the tutorial, we will talk about installation and configuration of MLN into a virtual infrastructure across several servers.

A.K. Bandara and M. Burgess (Eds.): AIMS 2007, LNCS 4543, p. 229, 2007.
© Springer-Verlag Berlin Heidelberg 2007

# Ponder2 - Policy-Based Self Managed Cells

Kevin Twidle and Emil Lupu

Imperial College, London, UK
kpt@doc.ic.ac.uk, e.c.lupu@doc.ic.ac.uk

**Abstract.** Pervasive systems require minimal user intervention while constantly adapting their configuration and behaviour. For example, a personal area network of sensors and computational devices monitoring the health of a patient needs to be able to reconfigure itself in response to sensor changes (failures/removals or additions), changes in the activities or context of the patient as well as changes in the health of the patient.

This tutorial will present the Self-Managed Cell architecture developed at Imperial College in collaboration with the University of Glasgow with particular emphasis on the use of policy-based techniques for implementing adaptation and reconfiguration in autonomous pervasive systems. Policies are rules governing choices in the behaviour of systems and are often en-countered as either event-condition-action rules or authorisation rules, al-though other types of policies such as negotiation, filtering and delegation can be defined. Policies can be used to define management and adaptation behaviours within autonomous cells of devices. In addition, they can govern interactions between and federation of the autonomous cells.

During this tutorial we will present aspects of the Ponder2 policy specification and implementation, structuring concepts for interactions between cells and integration of policy driven interpreters event and domain ser-vices. This tutorial will include a hands-on practical session based on the Ponder2 implementation realised at Imperial College. Ponder2 was recently designed as part of the TrustCoM project and has been used in several projects funded by the European Union and the EPSRC. More information about Ponder2 can be found at http://ponder2.net

This tutorial is aimed at those interested policy-based architectures for autonomous pervasive systems and will allow attendees to gain direct experience with the Ponder2 system. This tutorial is based on a tutorial previously given at the UKUBINET Workshop 2006. Attendees must have a laptop with Java JDK 5.0 installed (Windows, MAC or Linux platform).

A.K. Bandara and M. Burgess (Eds.): AIMS 2007, LNCS 4543, p. 230, 2007.
© Springer-Verlag Berlin Heidelberg 2007

# From Charging for QoS to Charging for QoE: Internet Economics in the Era of Next Generation Multimedia Networks

Peter Reichl

Telecommunications Research Center Vienna (ftw.)
reichl@ftw.at

**Abstract.** Over the past years, telecommunications as a research area has grown far beyond pure communications engineering and today covers the entire economic value chain up to the end customer. As a consequence, "Internet Economics" has been established as a new and promising research area of its own, aiming at a fresh perspective on familiar problems. The basic idea of this interdisciplinary approach is to understand communication networks as economical rather than technical systems, and thus to describe and solve networking issues through the use of economic concepts and techniques. This tutorial gives an introduction into basic notions, concepts and results of this highly interdisciplinary field. We start with summarizing the fundamental framework, focusing on central concepts from operations research, game theory and micro-economics, and introduce basic concepts like equilibria, efficiency, competition models and fairness. This serves as starting point for a comprehensive review of traditional charging schemes like congestion pricing, smart market and Progressive Second-Price auctions, Paris Metro Pricing, effective bandwidth pricing, Cumulus Pricing and the Contract-Balancing Mechanism. The second part of the tutorial starts with a brief overview on relevant charging protocols and architectures, with a special emphasis on the 3GPP IP Multimedia Subsystem (IMS) as a promising candidate for an All-IP Next Generation Network architecture. Finally, we discuss the imminent paradigm shift from charging for Quality-of-Service (QoS) to charging for Quality-of-User Experience (QoE) and present two recent proposals as important examples of current research trends in this stimulating area.

A.K. Bandara and M. Burgess (Eds.): AIMS 2007, LNCS 4543, p. 231, 2007.
© Springer-Verlag Berlin Heidelberg 2007

# Next Generation Semantic Business Process Management

Armin Haller[1] and Marin Dimitrov[2]

[1] National University of Ireland, Galway, Ireland
armin.haller@deri.org
[2] Ontotext Lab., Simra Group Corp., Sofia, Bulgaria
marin.dimitrov@ontotext.com

**Abstract.** This tutorial explains and demonstrates how the introduction of Semantic Web Services (SWS) to process aware software systems and to Business Process Management (BPM) in general can eliminate the deficiencies that current BPM technology exhibits. The tutorial starts with a thorough discussion of the underlying concepts, Service Oriented Architectures, ontologies, business process management systems and its relevance for today's system developers. The tutorial will further present the state of the art of current process management systems and Semantic Web Service frameworks. It will motivate the need for explicit use of Semantics to overcome the current weaknesses in BPM, and present a consolidated technical framework that integrates SWS into BPM technology.

The first session will cover the foundations and theoretical aspects, while the second session will be dedicated to a software demonstration and a hands-on session wherein the attendees actively model Business Processes and Semantic Web Services with the respective software tools. Therewith attendees will gain a comprehensive overview of the latest developments in semantically enriched BPM technology, which is one of the central trends in BPM research and development. The tutorial will be held by BPM and SWS experts that actively work on integration of both technologies.

A.K. Bandara and M. Burgess (Eds.): AIMS 2007, LNCS 4543, p. 232, 2007.
© Springer-Verlag Berlin Heidelberg 2007

# Programmability Models for Sensor Networks

Torsten Braun

University of Bern, Switzerland
braun@iam.unibe.ch

**Abstract.** Hard-coding of algorithms with tuneable parameters is not flexible in sensor networks. Also downloading executable files into each sensor node individually might be a problem when single sensor nodes are not permanently reachable or only with high costs. A user should have the possibility for programming a sensor network as a whole in a dynamic way such that the user issues instructions into the sensor network once and code is automatically distributed / executed in the whole sensor network. There are several models for (re)programming wireless sensor networks: the active sensor model based on script interpreters and virtual machines, the mobile agent model, and the database model. The tutorial focuses on the active sensor model and the database model. Reliable transport is essential for transporting management information, configuration data, and code. The tutorial discusses transport protocol design in order to perform error and congestion control.

A.K. Bandara and M. Burgess (Eds.): AIMS 2007, LNCS 4543, p. 233, 2007.
© Springer-Verlag Berlin Heidelberg 2007

# Scalable Routing for Large Self-organizing Networks

Thomas Fuhrmann

Technical University Munich, Germany
fuhrmann@net.in.tum.de

**Abstract.** Over the past years, much effort has been devoted to investigate the interplay of peer-to-peer protocols and the underlying network infrastructure. One surprising result of these studies is the insight that peer-to-peer mechanisms can be pushed down into the network layer. The probably most thoroughly researched embodiment of that idea is the Scalable Source Routing (SSR) protocol. Recently, another similar protocol has been published, the Virtual Ring Routing (VRR) protocol. This tutorial explains both protocols and discusses their potential uses in large self-organizing networks.

SSR and VRR are self-organizing routing protocols which have been inspired by structured peer-to-peer routing protocols such as Chord. Unlike Chord, SSR and VRR are genuine network layer protocols. They are especially suited for networks that do not have a well crafted structure, for example, sensor-actuator networks, ad-hoc networks and mesh networks. In particular, SSR is very memory efficient so that it can provide routing among nodes with very limited resources. This resource efficiency might also prove beneficial for large meshes of multi-homed wireline networks because it greatly reduces the size of the routers' forwarding information base.

Both, SSR and VRR work on a flat identifier space. As a consequence, they can easily support host mobility without requiring any location directory or other centralized service. Furthermore, SSR and VRR directly provide key based routing in the network layer so that they can serve as efficient basis for fully decentralized applications. Both protocols are based on a virtual ring structure which is used in a Chord-like manner. SSR builds source routes to previously unknown destinations and caches them at so-called intermediate nodes. VRR creates state along the respective paths.

This tutorial gives an in-depth introduction to SSR and VRR. It relates the protocols to previous approaches in ad-hoc networks, mesh networks and sensor networks; and it discusses the various parameters that optimize the protocols in a given scenario. The tutorial concludes with three practical examples from the presenter's research group. As a result, the participants will be well prepared to apply SSR or VRR for their own purposes.

A.K. Bandara and M. Burgess (Eds.): AIMS 2007, LNCS 4543, p. 234, 2007.
© Springer-Verlag Berlin Heidelberg 2007

# The IT Infrastructure Library (ITIL) – An Introduction for Practitioners and Researchers

Thomas Schaaf

Ludwig Maximilians Universität München, Germany
schaaf@mnm-team.org

**Abstract.** The IT Infrastructure Library (ITIL) is a today widely-used collection of best practices in IT Service Management that has, of all standardization efforts, gained the biggest popularity. Since it combines the principles of service- and process-orientation in IT Management and is easily accessible, it has become increasingly attractive for IT organizations of almost any size, branch or organizational setup. The scope of ITIL is not limited to technical issues, but also covers the human and economic dimensions (business alignment) of IT Service Management.

In this tutorial we give a survey on the ITIL framework structure and its most important concepts and contents, including an outline of five of ITIL's core reference processes. Furthermore, the tutorial discusses some important research topics related to ITIL, in particular Management Information Modelling and Tool Support. The five processes selected for presentation within the tutorial are Incident Management, Problem Management, Change Management, Configuration Management and Service Level Management. Learn how theses processes are designed and how they can be implemented.

These topics include the exemplary consideration of an IT incident being recorded, classified and investigated, triggering Problem Management and passing Problem and Error Control before creating a Request for Change for the resolution of the incident and its underlying root cause. Learn how ITIL helps the IT organization to deal with unexpected events in a highly dynamic environment on the one hand, and how it supports the continuous improvement and strategic alignment of IT management. We show how the core processes correlate to each other and point out the central role of Configuration Management and the challenge of setting up a Configuration Management Database (CMDB). Find out what makes a CMDB setup so difficult, which requirements a CMDB should fulfill and why the current commercial and scientific efforts address these challenges insufficiently.

Adequate tools are vital for a successful deployment of ITIL. But since ITIL is tool-independent and hardly formalized, sufficient and integrated tool support for ITIL is not available today. In the tutorial, we present a taxonomy for ITIL processes under tool support aspects by assessing each ITIL process as to its recurrence, lead time, organizational complexity, service level impact and structure.

Finally, we show how ITIL emerged to the ISO/IEC 20000 standard and give an overview of the innovations expected for the next official release "ITIL V.3", scheduled for this year.

A.K. Bandara and M. Burgess (Eds.): AIMS 2007, LNCS 4543, p. 235, 2007.
© Springer-Verlag Berlin Heidelberg 2007

# Peer-to-Peer Market Places: Technical Issues and Revenue Models

Giancarlo Ruffo

Università di Torino, Italy
ruffo@di.unito.it

**Abstract.** Recently, Steve Jobs, in his public "Thoughts on Music", pointed out the Digital Rights Management (DRM) systems that Apple has been imposed to adopt for protecting its music against piracy. This brings to a paradox: DRM-protected digital music is prevented from being played by devices of different producers. Conversely, DRM-free content, that uses "open" formats (e.g., MP3 for music and MPEG4 for movies), can be downloaded, distributed, copied and played on different devices. This is an implicit disincentive to legally buy copy-protected digital content, because DRM-free files are interoperable: in fact, 97% of the music filling iPods is unprotected and of obscure origins. Jobs' conclusions are quite astonishing: abolishing DRMs entirely and selling music encoded in open licensable formats. However, there is no obvious reason for believing that piracy would decrease even if the Steve Jobs' dream for a "DRM-free" world will finally occur. This implies that future legal market models have to consider serious, scalable, efficient, secure and reliable alternatives to DRM-based on-line (centralized) stores. The Peer-to-Peer paradigm provides a quite mature framework for this applicative domain, making digital content sharing applications a valid solution even for small vendors and emerging artists. In fact, small-medium parties of a market place could hardly afford production and maintenance costs that can be very high if distribution is provided by means of a resilient client-server architecture (e.g., iTunes, Yahoo!, Microsoft Media Shop). But, despite to their big potentials, Peer-to-Peer systems have became infamous through the file sharing applications that make easy for the users to access copy-protected files for free; in fact, it is very difficult to trace the peers' activity, and identification of abuses cannot be fairly performed because of the absence of a central authority. Moreover, a business model is hard to find: it is questionable if other actors than the *owner* of an object should be involved in a transaction as a *provider*. The p2p distribution framework leads to technical advantages, but its economical benefits are not clear: the *receiver* of the bought object can become the distributor later on, but why should he/she provide properly the content if the owner wants to be reimbursed? The tutorial will cover other important services that a market place must include: reputation management, implementation of different preliminary transactions (e.g., bartering, bidding an offer, auctioning), and accounting in decentralized domain. Finally, social networking and self organized communities can be exploited in order to enforce epidemic phenomena and word of mouth marketing. No need to be said, the proper interoperability of incentive strategies, reputation and trust management, accounting solutions, and efficient networking (e.g., search and peer's cooperation) techniques is critical.

A.K. Bandara and M. Burgess (Eds.): AIMS 2007, LNCS 4543, p. 236, 2007.
© Springer-Verlag Berlin Heidelberg 2007

# Author Index

# Lecture Notes in Computer Science

For information about Vols. 1–4438

please contact your bookseller or Springer